Costa Rica has won an international reputation for its primary health care programs, yet the government has not managed to involve local communities in the planning and implementation of health care. This book, written by a medical anthropologist, analyzes the obstacles to "community participation in health". Combining a rich local ethnography with an analysis of national politics and the politics of foreign aid, Lynn Morgan shows how community participation in Costa Rica fell victim to national and international political conflicts.

Community participation in health

Community participation in health

Editors

Ronald Frankenberg, Centre for Medical Social Anthropology, University of Keele

Byron Good, Department of Social Medicine, Harvard Medical School

Alan Harwood, Department of Anthropology, University of Massachusetts, Boston

Gilbert Lewis, Department of Social Anthropology, University of Cambridge

Roland Littlewood, Department of Anthropology, University College London

Margaret Lock, Department of Humanities and Social Studies in Medicine, McGill University

Nancy Scheper-Hughes, Department of Anthropology, University of California, Berkeley

Medical anthropology is the fastest growing specialist area within anthropology, both in North America and in Europe. Beginning as an applied field serving public health specialists, medical anthropology now provides a significant forum for many of the most urgent debates in anthropology and the humanities.

Medical anthropology includes the study of medical institutions and health care in a variety of rich and poor societies, the investigation of the cultural construction of illness, and the analysis of ideas about the body, birth, maturation, ageing, and death.

This new series includes theoretically innovative monographs, state-of-the-art collections of essays on current issues, and short books introducing the main themes in the subdiscipline.

Community participation in health

The politics of primary care in Costa Rica

Lynn M. Morgan

Department of Sociology and Anthropology
Mount Holyoke College

CAMBRIDGE
UNIVERSITY PRESS

Published by the Press Syndicate of the University of Cambridge
The Pitt Building, Trumpington Street, Cambridge CB2 1RP
40 West 20th Street, New York, NY 10011-4211, USA
10 Stamford Road, Oakleigh, Victoria 3166, Australia

First published 1993

Printed in Great Britain at the University Press, Cambridge

A catalogue record for this book is available from the British Library

Library of Congress cataloguing in publication data
Morgan, Lynn Marie.
Community participation in health: the politics of primary care
in Costa Rica
Lynn M. Morgan. Cambridge Studies in Medical Anthropology: 1
    p.   cm.
Includes bibliographical references.
ISBN 0 521 41898 4 (hardback)
1. Medical policy – Costa Rica.   2. Medical care – Costa Rica.
I. Title. II Series
[DNLM: 1. Consumer Participation.   2. Health Policy – Costa Rica.
3. Primary Health Care – Costa Rica.   W 84.6 M848p]
RA191.C8M67   1993
DNLM/DLC
for Library of Congress   92-9575   CIP

ISBN 0 521 41898 4 hardback

UP

For Noah and Juliana

Contents

Illustrations

Figure

Tables

x

Acknowledgments

Field research for this project was made possible through a Fulbright-Hays Doctoral Dissertation Research Abroad award, supplemented by a grant-in-aid of research from Sigma Xi, the Scientific Research Society and the Robert H. Lowie Fund of the University of California, Berkeley, Department of Anthropology. Three months of preliminary fieldwork in Costa Rica was supported by Lowie Funds and by the Center for Latin American Studies at the University of California, Berkeley, through the generosity of the Tinker Foundation. A follow-up trip to Costa Rica and additional support for preparing the manuscript for publication were provided by a faculty grant from Mount Holyoke College. I gratefully acknowledge support from each of these organizations.

Amended portions of this manuscript were previously published as "'Political will' and community participation in Costa Rican primary health care," reprinted by permission from *Medical Anthropology Quarterly* (new series) volume 3, number 3, copyright American Anthropology Association 1989; and "International politics and primary health care in Costa Rica," reprinted by permission from *Social Science and Medicine* volume 30, number 2, copyright Pergamon Press Ltd. 1990. I would like to thank Dana Hammersly for preparing the maps. I am responsible for all translations.

Nancy Scheper-Hughes has been a compassionate mentor and role model. Her quick intellect and critical eye were inspirational, as was Fred Dunn with his infinite wisdom, integrity, and willingness to share his vast experience in international health. Early stages of this project benefited from Setha Low's generous advice and assurances. From the Berkeley days I would also like to thank Stanley Brandes, Beth Ann Conklin, Mitch Feldman, Anita Garey, Judith Justice, Jane Kramer, Steve Leikin, Linda Lewin, Lois McCloskey, Lesley Sharp, Nick Townsend, and Frank Zimmerman.

I received professional assistance, hospitality, and friendship in San José, Costa Rica from Luis Antonio Meneses, Carlos Muñoz, Herman Vargas, Marlene Castro, Roberto Alvarado, Rafael Bolaños, Hilda Soto,

Patricia Salgado, Mario Cabrera, Luis Bernardo Villalobos, Jaime Sepúlveda, Marta Pardo, Jorge Arias, Juan Jaramillo, Maria Eugenia Bozzolli de Wille, and Edgar Mohs. Many other politicians, health providers and planners, community organizers, foreign aid personnel, academics, and policy analysts graciously consented to lengthy interviews. Their frank insights and analyses made this book possible, although in the interests of confidentiality I cannot thank them all by name. *Un abrazo* to Solange Muller, who shared her home and macadamia ice cream. I owe a special debt to John and Sue Trostle for always being happy to lend a sympathetic ear and to feed me good things from the "no guilt" garden. The more lucid portions of this book were composed in the serene rooms of their house in cloudy Monteverde.

In La Chira, I thank those who welcomed me into their lives and taught me to appreciate the torrential nighttime rains. Olga Araya Moreira and her family shared their home and greatly facilitated my work by introducing me to nearly everyone in the community. Edgar Aleman, Flor Delgado de Aleman, and their daughters offered companionship and a quiet place to live. To all the other Chireños who helped and befriended me, *un millón de gracias*.

Philippe Bourgois and Marc Edelman – anthropological comrades in the field – provided helpful suggestions on an earlier draft of this manuscript. Eva Paus gave me good advice (as always) at a crucial stage of the writing. I would especially like to thank Ed Royce, whose editorial genius and attention to detail helped me to clarify prose and argumentation.

Fieldwork in a foreign land makes one appreciate the folks at home. My parents, Philip and Lilly Morgan, taught me to respect and cherish human diversity. They were not always sure why I chose to live in Central America, but they always supported my decision.

My warmest, deepest gratitude is reserved for Jim Trostle, whose love (not to mention sound methodological and editorial advice) sustained me throughout.

Abbreviations

AID	United States Agency for International Development
CCSS	Caja Costarricense de Seguro Social
CSUCA	Confederación Superior Universitaria Centroamericana
DINADECO	Dirección Nacional de Desarrollo de la Comunidad
IADB	Inter-American Development Bank
INVU	Instituto Nacional de Vivienda y Urbanización
JSSS	Juntas de Salubridad y Seguridad Pública
PAHO	Pan American Health Organization
PHC	Primary Health Care
PLN	Partido Liberación Nacional
PROFOCO	Promoción y Fomentación de la Comunidad
SCISP	Servicio Cooperativo Interamericano de Salud Pública
UNICEF	United Nations Children's Fund
UNRISD	United Nations Research Institute for Social Development
UPP	Unidad de Participación Popular
WHO	World Health Organization

1 The political symbolism of health

Over the last century doctors and public health authorities have gradually asserted their control over the domain of health and medicine in most of the Western world. Since the mid-1970s and the advent of the primary health care movement, however, health planners have ostensibly been trying to reverse this trend, to give back to ordinary citizens some of the responsibility for maintaining health. Promotion of community participation in health, one component of primary health care, has been particularly important in this new strategy. Proponents of community participation envisioned self-motivated rural communities working together with the state to design their own programs to improve health and development. This grand vision has proven difficult to achieve in practice, however, particularly in countries and regions without an existing tradition of joint community–government cooperation.

Costa Rica is a small, Central American country with an international reputation for high standards of public health. In the 1970s, when the Costa Rican government began an ambitious program to extend health services to rural areas, many observers were optimistic about the prospects. They felt that if primary health care and community participation were going to succeed anywhere in Latin America, they would succeed in Costa Rica because of the state's democratic tradition and history of commitment to health care. Community participation was a key feature of the government's primary health care programs between 1973 and 1985, when four different administrations tried, in varying degrees, to promote participation in health. The program flourished, briefly, between 1978 and 1982 under the administration of President Rodrigo Carazo. But after nearly two decades of attention to rural health, Costa Rican health officials agreed in the late 1980s that active, sustained community participation had not been achieved, and some felt it was not worth pursuing any further. The 1982–6 administration of President Luis Alberto Monge cut the Ministry of Health's participation budget and moved its offices from the sunny top floor of the Ministry of Health to a windowless, cinder block room in the basement. In 1985 the program

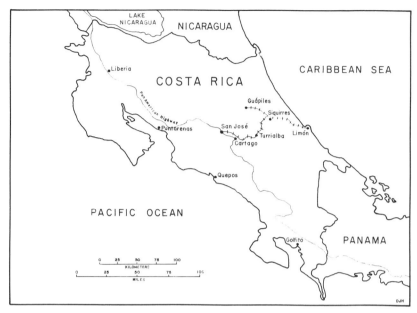

Map 1   Costa Rica

was officially dismantled. While Costa Rica enjoys a well-deserved international reputation for exemplary primary health care, by 1990 it supported only the most cursory effort to enhance community participation in health. This was a disappointment to the optimistic observers who had invested their hopes in Costa Rica. Why did the Costa Rican state try so hard to promote participation before reversing its position? Why did the concept acquire such currency in Costa Rican politics? While many details of this tale are specific to Costa Rica, the lessons are relevant to other countries where development strategies are designed and financed by foreign aid agencies.

International health policy: a dialectical perspective

This book is a political-economic ethnography of health policy. I draw on the theoretical tenets of critical medical anthropology (Baer 1982; Singer 1989) (alternatively termed the "political economy of medical anthropology" [Morsy 1990]). This perspective emphasizes the social and historical roots of disease and health care, with particular attention to the existence of stratified social relations within a world economic system. While my analysis situates Costa Rica squarely within the context of international economic dependency and global politics, I depart from the more orthodox political economists of health (e.g., Doyal 1979; Elling 1981; Turshen 1984) who imply that foreign precepts were imposed wholesale by omnipotent foreign (colonial or neocolonial) powers, accepted uncritically by national elites, and implemented with apparently no resistance from local citizens. While the political economists emphasize the expansion and global penetration of capitalism, I argue that international economic relations explain only one dimension of Costa Rica's experience with health care and community participation. We must consider, in addition, the crucial role of the state in setting the direction of social policy and the dynamic participation of subordinated peoples in resisting domination and constructing social forms even under conditions of dependency (Mintz 1977; Wolf 1982). Political economists of health have too often neglected the dynamic interplay among these different levels of analysis because they are committed to documenting the adverse health consequences resulting from the introduction of capitalist biomedicine into underdeveloped regions of the world (Ortner 1984; Morgan 1987a).

The international health literature contains numerous evaluations of community participation programs, many of which center on the administrative or cultural impediments to effective participation. Many researchers have assumed that the biggest hurdles to participation can be found at the community level, for example in the psychological characteristics or charismatic appeal of individuals, the organizational or leadership structure of specific communities, the existence or persistence of traditional beliefs regarding disease etiology, or some other intra-community variables (Parlato and Favin 1982; Martin 1983; Pan American Health Organization 1984; Paul and Demarest 1984). But such "micro," community-focused studies invariably miss the larger context which guides health policy decisions. Critical medical anthropologists have long talked about the need to incorporate "macro" levels of analysis into the study of medical systems, in part as a corrective to earlier, community-based studies in medical anthropology (Janzen 1978; De-Walt and Pelto 1985). Following in this tradition, I use the Costa Rican case to show that the interactions among international, national, and local-level forces are too interdependent to be reasonably separated from one another, even for analytic purposes. Certain social classes and interest groups at all levels will stand to benefit, both ideologically and politically, by promoting particular models of health service provision, but each group's actions are invariably influenced and constrained by competing voices. The thesis of this book, then, as demonstrated for the Costa Rican case, is that health and development initiatives must be analyzed dialectically, as consequences of the relations among international, domestic, and local groups who act in response to changing economic and political priorities.

This theoretical orientation affected my decisions about how to conduct fieldwork, as well as the organization of this book. I suspected that most of my questions about participation in health would be answered in the capital, San José, by policymakers who plotted the course of the program, so I deliberately began my fieldwork with a "micro-level" community study in the rural settlement of La Chira. Later, I moved to the capital to investigate the national and international contexts of participation in health. This book, however, proceeds in the opposite order. It starts, as might be expected from a political-economic ethnography, by describing the historic and international contexts of rural health and participation. It moves then to the national context where *participación* was highly visible as a political symbol during the 1970s and 1980s, and ends in a banana town in the tropical Costa Rican lowlands. In spite of the stepwise progression of the narrative, the local, national, and international levels of action are, in fact, inseparable, so my analysis shifts continually back and forth among them.

The concept of participation

The concept of participation is a socially constructed amalgam of ideas, defined and refined through time. Its emergence as a relatively new concept and its utilization in international development parlance thus require explanation. When international development agencies packaged and sold participation as a "one size fits all" rural development panacea in the 1970s, they did not consider the relevance of citizen–state relations in a given country or its prior history of citizen participation. The agencies pretended that history did not matter; that primary health care and participation would work as well in Guatemala, for example, with its history of military rule, as in China, with its history of popularly based revolutionary change. Yet history does matter, not just in terms of identifying the factors which make participation more or less feasible in particular countries, but as a way of analyzing changing international health fads and fashions. Because international and bilateral health programs have influenced the development of the Costa Rican health system since the turn of the century, I will trace the history of health participation both as an instrument of foreign policy and as a feature of the Costa Rican state, in the context of the political and economic conditions facing the country since the beginning of the twentieth century.

My approach differs from other evaluations of community participation which attempt to devise uniform measures of participation. International health agencies have spent millions of dollars hiring consultants to devise standardized measures of participation, identify its correlates and determine how to make it more "successful" (Agudelo 1983; Rifkin, Miller, and Bichmann 1988). Yet it is pointless to attempt to identify the extent of participation without first spelling out the political motivations and ideologies of those who design the programs and conduct the evaluations. Is there any point in measuring degrees of participation without specifying the ends it is to serve? By whose criteria will "success" be judged? Can there be an objective measure of participation, when the concept itself is so amorphous? Even contemporary evaluators who acknowledge the eminently political nature of participation fail to explain how and why it plays such a vital, ever-changing role in ongoing debates over the nature of society.

There are multiple definitions of participation, which range along a continuum. At one end, participation can be initiated at the grassroots level without professional sponsorship; at the other, it is imposed from above, with the organizational components defined by professionals and state authorities. A United Nations report on the subject (1981: 8) contains a typology typical of those developed by other researchers: "spontaneous participation" is "voluntary, base-up, without external support." This type is also referred to in the literature as informal (Sherraden 1991), bottom-up, community supportive (Werner 1976), social participation (Muller 1983), or wide participation (Rifkin, Muller, and Bichmann 1988). It is not isolated in one "sector" such as health or education, but is part of a larger process of social development intended to foster social equity. Spontaneous participation may be a deliberate effort to protest or counteract state policies. Toward the other end of the continuum, "induced participation" is "sponsored, mandated, and officially endorsed"; this type is "the most prevalent mode to be found in developing countries." At the extreme end is "coerced participation," which is "compulsory, manipulated, and contrived." Induced or coerced forms are also called formal, top-down, community oppressive (Werner 1976), direct participation (Muller 1983), or narrow participation (Rifkin, Muller, and Bichmann 1988). Induced forms are not intended to be intersectoral, nor to affect the basic character of state–citizen relations.

My use of the term follows Richard Adams, who wrote, "Participation is merely another way of looking at power" (1979: 13). Participation is first and foremost a political symbol, by nature amorphous, flexible, and adaptable. Unraveling what participation symbolizes to different people and groups at various historical periods offers insights into the relations of domination and subordination operating within and between societies. Like many international observers writing on the subject, I favor a spontaneous, bottom-up, vision of participation. Oppressed peoples have always tried, in varying degrees, to improve their standing in the social hierarchy, just as reigning elites have tried, with varying degrees of effectiveness, to stop them. Elites tend to support government-sponsored community participation when they expect the policy to reinforce (or at least not to challenge) their privileged status. According to this view, state-sponsored community participation is an oxymoron, because state sponsorship implies an inevitable degree of control and manipulation (Lipsky and Lounds 1976; see also Midgley 1986 for an outline of controversies surrounding participation). But the mere fact that a state would be willing to sponsor participatory initiatives, as the Costa Rican state did, offers a window onto the dialectics of power within that country.

When the extent of participation allowed by different countries is assessed, it is tempting to speculate that the degree of participation will depend on the nature of the regime and the strength and flexibility of the state apparatus. Some writers have asserted, for example, that spontaneous participation is more acceptable to democratic or socialistic states than to repressive regimes (see Bossert 1984; Rosenfield 1985; Baer 1989). This is to some extent true, but the Costa Rican case dispels the notion that there is a direct, linear relationship between the form of government and the form of participation. Participation is always constrained at the state level by partisanship, funding limitations, the whims of international agencies, and the resistance of local and national interest groups, including professionals and bureaucrats. And at the local level, participation waxes and wanes with the felt needs of the populace and the state's ability to respond effectively to them.

Political symbolism: participation, democracy, paternalism, and health

Costa Ricans commonly invoke four symbols when discussing government-sponsored community participation programs: participation, democracy, paternalism, and health. Each term is ambiguous, multivocal, and vaguely defined (Geertz 1973: 195); its meanings change depending on who is using it and what interests they are promoting. The symbolic complexity of the concepts is compounded when these keywords are concatenated, as in "participation in health." Looking at these terms as political symbols enables us to "unwrap" them, to reveal their ideological foundations and their function in political strategizing and agenda setting. The political underpinnings of these symbols may not always be readily obvious, however, because "many, indeed most, of the symbols that are politically significant are overtly nonpolitical" (Cohen 1974:87).

The first catchword – participation – became central to Costa Rican state politics during the 1970s. Yet many of the players refused publicly to associate participation with politics; they denied the political nature of participation. The ostensibly nonpolitical, nonpartisan character of participation obscured its use as a weapon in the struggle for power. Rival political groups tried to claim the concept as their own, hoping to monopolize and capitalize on its positive connotations. Participation was adopted as the rallying cry of political parties and interest groups who sought to influence the allocation and reallocation of public goods (Seligson and Booth 1979:4). Representatives of one party even hoped that community participation in health would eventually transform the entire political apparatus of the country. Participation was for them less a clearly defined goal than a resource and object of political struggle. Even in the late 1980s, when participatory programs were largely defunct, the concept of community participation continued to be an important political symbol as leaders used the rhetoric to convince constituents of their good intentions and their commitment to a widely valued principle. It did not matter if the goal was perennially out of reach or not being pursued, as long as Costa Ricans could continue to believe in participation as a national value. Invocation of "participation," then, could legitimize the state by reinforcing its democratic image.

Democracy is the second pivotal keyword in Costa Rican political culture. Costa Ricans openly and unabashedly prize their democratic system, which they say sets them apart from the other Central American countries. The Costa Rican state promotes its democratic self-image in part by sponsoring programs such as citizen participation. "Participation" is an important ideological element within the symbolic domain of "democracy"; participation is not possible without an involved, committed, and democratic government operating within a responsive, reformist state apparatus. On the level of popular political culture, participation is synonymous with democracy.

The presumed connection between democracy and participation is frequently discussed in the development literature. A document published by the United Nations Research Institute for Social Development (UNRISD) stated, "The issue of popular participation is basically identical with the issue of 'democracy' in its broadest sense" (Cohen 1980:21). The synchrony between effective participation and democracy is so widely accepted that development experts assumed that countries most noted for democratic governments would most assiduously promote participation. A member of the UNRISD team, for example, recommended in 1980 that a case study of participation in Costa Rica would assess the "potentials and constraints" of participation under a political system which "enjoys a high status as being the preeminent form of democracy" (Bergsma 1980: 71). Bergsma implies that gauging degrees of participation in development projects will reflect the degree of democracy present in a given country. But participation is not an objective, quantifiable "thing." It is a symbol used by competing factions in the continual process of making, remaking, and restructuring Costa Rica's democracy.

The third symbolically laden term – *paternalismo* – has negative connotations, but its practical effects keep Costa Rican politicians in office. Paternalism is frequently invoked in Costa Rica as a ubiquitous but lamentable feature of the national character and a major barrier to participatory democracy. Academics have analyzed paternalism as a vestige of Latin American social relations during the colonial period, when local political bosses (*caciques* or *caudillos*) controlled all political favors in small communities. Community residents were forced to develop strong patron–client relations with the *caciques* to acquire political concessions. The notion of paternalism is different in Costa Rica today, where the state has largely replaced the traditional *cacique* as the major power broker. *Paternalismo* now refers to relations between the state and local citizens, whereby complacent citizens rely on state largesse instead of their own initiative to acquire goods and services. The Costa Rican welfare state fosters paternalism and dependence on the state; in fact, paternalism could be cited as one of the reasons for the regime's continuing popularity. Nonetheless, politicians often blame paternalism for impeding greater participation in the democratic process. A similar refrain is heard in rural communities, where I listened to citizens assail paternalism and the laziness and apathy of their neighbors even as they awaited the arrival of a government truck bringing them free powdered milk. Politicians try to escape the contradictions between paternalism and participation by insisting that they abhor the former and actively support the latter. Because participation is supposedly a reflection of commitment to democratic principles, they insist, a government that promotes participation *ipso facto* promotes democracy.

The fourth slogan – good health – is similarly related, on a political-ideological level, to the benevolence of the Costa Rican state. The state has proclaimed itself the legal guarantor of the public health, and set up one of the most comprehensive public health and social security systems in Latin America. Politicians take every opportunity to identify themselves with health issues, which may explain why they so eagerly adopt

international slogans such as "Health for all by the year 2000." Health
becomes a symbol of the politician's altruism in what otherwise might be
perceived as a selfish struggle for political power.

People on all sides of the political spectrum publicly corroborate the
assertion that health is of a higher moral order than politics. Health is
imbued with the highest moral connotations – altruism, purity, self-
control, charity, goodness – while politics is regarded as a necessary evil
characterized by deceit, corruption, avarice, and a lust for power. Costa
Ricans who openly use health issues to serve political ends will stress
that they are motivated by the desire to eradicate disease, not the desire
to maximize power. A well-known Costa Rican doctor who worked in
community health programs for 30 years told me, on one blustery
afternoon in 1985, that "Health is above politics." Half an hour later he
invited me to a political rally, where he said he would use his name and
reputation to lobby on behalf of a presidential candidate who had
promised to restore funding that had been cut from his clinic budget.
The doctor admitted he had a reputation for switching from one political
party to another but this was necessary, he said, to safeguard the health
of people in his district. He built his political clout on the battles he
fought in the name of public health.

Maintaining the moral imbalance between politics and health is useful
to politicians, who can inflate their own moral standing by professing
their concern for health. By reinforcing and reproducing the notion that
health is above (that is, both superior to and immune from) politics,
political interest groups can and do manipulate the myriad meanings of
health to their own perceived advantage. Alford makes a similar argument
in his study of health care politics in New York City, where he
demonstrates that health issues are often used to satisfy politicians' goals
rather than community ends. He shows how health-related issues can
serve "simultaneously to provide tangible benefits to various elites and
symbolic benefits to mass publics, quieting potential unrest, deflecting
potential demands, and blurring the true allocation of rewards" (Alford
1975: x). Politicians create, or fabricate, health crises by calling urgent
attention to previously unproblematic features of health care systems.
This creates an opportunity for them to garner votes by "solving" each
crisis. People judge the politician's success by looking at what programs
were initiated and what efforts were intended, rather than whether their
programs actually changed anything (Alford 1975: 12).

Similarly, a government which deliberately promotes health places
itself, by symbolic association, above the dirty business of politics. What
better combination of symbols than a government which stands for
participation in health? And what more effective way to criticize such a

government than by asserting that it has politicized health? Allegations of politicization are particularly stinging in the Costa Rican context, where many politicians *are* sincerely motivated to improve the public health; Costa Rica's demonstrated ability to improve health standards is testament to the positive results of governmental action. Yet politicians may simultaneously use their concern for health to political advantage. These issues will frame the debate over Costa Rica's efforts to promote community participation in health and help to explain why the program became so important in Costa Rican political ideology.

The influence of international agencies

Costa Rica is known for its stable parliamentary democracy and exemplary health programs, unique to Central America in the 1980s. Yet the state's commitment to health care, and the form that commitment takes, are not determined solely by autonomous decisions made at the national level. Developing countries are obliged to follow the public health agendas set by international donors (Quimby 1971; Justice 1986; Foster 1987). The international health mandates are received by and filtered through the state, where domestic priorities and competing political interests strongly affect implementation. This highly politicized process of state mediation and negotiation results in national health programs which may bear only a perfunctory resemblance to original international formulations. National programs are interpreted and refined yet again in the process of being implemented at the local level, where another set of political considerations inevitably enters in. The local manifestations of international health programs must therefore be regarded as a consequence of the interactions among global, national, and local forces.

International health agencies are composed of government representatives, usually ruling elites from the upper strata of society throughout the developed and less-developed world. Policy edicts emanating from what Navarro (1984) calls the "development establishment" tend to reflect an international political-ideological consensus about the proper relations of government to governed: "Like any other international apparatus, WHO is the synthesis of power relations (each with its own ideology, discourse, and practice) in which one set of relations is dominant" (Navarro 1984: 470). The WHO ideology presumes that democratic governments will be able to withstand participation, indeed will encourage and welcome it as a way to improve rural health indicators without challenging basic political-economic structures. For the international agencies, community participation was the quintessential symbol of an elusive ideal: a democratic rural development process which would be controlled by the state but built by local people using their own resources.

The international arena is critical to the future of debt-ridden Latin American nations like Costa Rica, which in the 1980s had the second highest per-capita foreign debt in the world (Edelman 1983). Developing countries compete in the international arena for grants, loans, and favorable terms governing debt repayment. It is important, therefore, for each country to comply with international mandates, to convey a good impression to donors and multilateral lending agencies.

International agencies have influenced the development of Costa Rican health care by providing scholarships to train doctors, sending technical advisors to set up intervention programs, underwriting disease control campaigns and sanitation projects, and determining health priorities. Perhaps their most influential impact, though, has been the least tangible: international agencies have paved the way for Western biomedicine and public health models (which have dominated public health thought and practice in the United States and Europe since the late nineteenth century) to penetrate Costa Rican medicine and public health, thus limiting Costa Ricans' ability to forge their own responses to public health problems. Consequently, Costa Rica is extremely dependent on the United States and Western Europe for its health models as well as medical materiel.

International health agencies and national health planners share a tendency to minimize the agencies' effect on national health policy. National planners and politicians would prefer to claim personal credit for health improvements, and donors themselves are reluctant to admit the extent of their own power and authority, insisting instead that successful public health programs result from the "political will" of national governments. Few would deny that Costa Rica manifests a high degree of "political will" concerning public health, yet other factors account for the rise and demise of community participation in health in Costa Rica (Morgan 1989). Most notably, analysts must consider the state's preoccupation with acquiring international prestige and financial assistance. Debt, dependency, and the availability of international assistance always form part of the tableau of national health policy, even when most of the players deny this simple fact.

Community participation became a part of international health jargon when the primary health care strategy began to generate enthusiasm, in the mid-1970s. International agencies such as the World Health Organization (WHO), UNICEF, the United States Agency for International Development (AID), and the World Bank focused their attention on rural health at that time, acknowledging that existing hospital-based, curative models of health care were not reducing morbidity or mortality among the needy rural populations of less-developed countries (Djukanovic and Mach 1975; Newell 1975). Their proposal to reform health care was synthesized in the now-famous WHO/UNICEF Alma Ata Declaration of 1978. The Declaration's central organizing principle, primary health care (PHC), was a low-cost strategy utilizing paraprofessional health workers (modeled after China's barefoot doctors) to administer preventive and simple curative measures in the countryside. This approach was intended to extend inexpensive health coverage to rural areas, to promote community participation in health, and to achieve no less ambitious a goal than "health for all by the year 2000." The Alma Ata Declaration differed from previous international efforts in two ways: it emphasized intersectoral involvement (that is, the integration of health with other development targets such as agriculture and education); and it focused on community participation in health (Taylor 1979: 1). In a report on PHC issued jointly by WHO and UNICEF, community participation was defined as a process whereby individuals and families come to view health not only as a right, but as a responsibility. The report encouraged active participation rather than passive acceptance of community development programs, emphasizing that participation should accompany every stage of the primary health care process from needs assessment to implementation. Furthermore, individuals were to assume "a high degree of responsibility for their own health care – for example, by adopting a healthy life style, by applying principles of good nutrition and hygiene, or by making use of immunization services" (WHO and UNICEF 1978: 21). The report specified that national governments should coordinate and implement participation programs, providing material, human, technical, and financial resources. It viewed the community as an untapped reservoir of vast potential, whose active cooperation could assist the government in its efforts to improve rural standards of living. The Alma Ata Declaration and accompanying documents presented community participation as a technical, apolitical strategy for implementing primary health care programs.

The phrases found in the Alma Ata Declaration continue to reverberate across Latin America. Primary health care, community participation, and "Health for all by the year 2000" (abbreviated in English as "HFA 2000," in Spanish as "SPT 2000") are slogans that synthesize and reinforce values publicly championed by the government of nearly every country. Politicians use the phrases in their campaign platforms to capitalize on their symbolic associations: inclusion in the international endeavor to improve health, membership in the prestigious international development community, and commitment to equality, social justice, and participatory democracy. The phrases spelled out in the Alma Ata Declaration have been incorporated into political discourse about health in virtually every Latin American country regardless of political orientation. Social democratic governments, military dictatorships, and authoritarian regimes alike espouse commitment to the Alma Ata principles. Beyond the uniform rhetoric, however, lie national differences in how community participation programs were implemented and in the symbols used to debate the value of participation.

In response to the WHO/UNICEF mandate, many countries set up PHC programs (including community participation components) primarily through their Ministries of Health. The programs looked remarkably similar on paper, although the details of implementation varied considerably from one country to another (see UNICEF 1988). Several governments were initially enthusiastic about participation, but became disillusioned as they realized that participation could not be easily controlled or confined to the realm of health. Costa Rica's experience with community participation in health followed this general pattern, although the program's ultimate demise there was more significant than in other, less democratic countries. International health and development experts had been watching Costa Rica as a paradigmatic example of whether community participation could transform or hasten the pace of rural development. That it did not succeed (an opinion now widely shared within Costa Rica) raises questions not only about the viability of participation as a development strategy, but about the nature of Costa Rica's democracy.

A specific political vision was implicit in the WHO/UNICEF mandate. The mandate presumed that central government knows what is best for its citizens and that communities should acquiesce in government plans. It assumed that "successful" participation would indicate a certain degree of democracy, and that democracy would foster good health. Participation was to be defined, labeled, and managed by states, in accordance with guidelines set by international agencies. This circumscribed vision of participation ruled out a range of autonomous or informal community actions not condoned by government, including everything from indigenous healing to confrontations and protests against state policies.

Another view of participation holds that states promoted participation as a smokescreen, using it to legitimize their own policies while simultaneously pursuing other policies detrimental to the poor. Ugalde (1985), for example, contends that community participation has been used as a mask, a façade, to hide the exploitative motivations of national elites. His analysis tends to overemphasize the conspiratorial aspects of health service provision, but he does make a persuasive case showing the political-ideological agenda implicit in the development establishment's promotion of community participation in health. His assertions are strengthened by Foster's report that WHO, for example, never offered any empirical evidence to buttress its claim that increased community participation would improve health indices (Foster 1987). The World Health Organization, motivated by a political commitment to democracy as the path to social equity, had decided *a priori* that community participation would be a component of primary health care.

Participation, *Tico*-style

Costa Rica is the wealthiest, and not coincidentally the healthiest, country in Central America. Its land mass (51,000 square kilometers) supports close to 3 million inhabitants. After the Spanish Conquest in the early sixteenth century, Costa Rica never developed the same degree of social stratification as Guatemala or El Salvador, mainly because there were few commodities for the Spaniards to exploit and virtually no indigenous labor force to work the land (MacLeod 1973; Gudmundson 1986). Since the late 1940s Costa Rica has remained a stable parliamentary democracy where the presidency has consistently changed hands through peaceful elections.

The Costa Rican state has a long-standing commitment to social welfare programs, spending one of the highest percentages of its GNP on health in all of Latin America. *Ticos* (as the Costa Ricans affectionately refer to themselves) have come to expect ever-greater state involvement in the provision of health care. The trend started in 1941, when a social security program began to provide health and disability coverage for all salaried workers (Rosenberg 1981, 1983). This nationalized health program grew gradually through a series of legislative reforms, to the point where it covered approximately 85 percent of the population by the late 1980s. The Caja Costarricense de Seguro Social (CCSS), as the social security program is known, provides curative care based in hospitals and clinics. In addition, the government began an ambitious rural health program in the early 1970s (Villegas 1977), utilizing the principles of PHC: building rural health posts in underserved areas of the country and using village health workers to extend basic health services to rural populations at low cost. Between 1980 and around 1985, Costa Rica suffered a severe economic crisis which inevitably affected the health system (Mesa-Lago 1985; Morgan 1987b). The social unrest and political upheaval surrounding the economic crisis, in turn, affected the state's commitment to community participation programs.

The demise of government-sponsored ("induced") community participation in Costa Rica is traced, in the final analysis, to several intersecting factors. First, there was little historical precedent for citizen involvement in rural health projects prior to the 1950s. Earlier attempts to improve rural health were paternalistic endeavors designed to elicit compliance. Health planners and providers disregarded local health practices, nor were they concerned with public reactions to their programs. In the Atlantic lowlands, rural health programs were sponsored not by the state, but by foreign agencies like the United Fruit Company or the Institute for Inter-American Affairs (see Chapters 2 and 3). Second, rivalries between political parties in the 1970s and 1980s resulted in the politicization of community participation in health (see Chapter 5). Many Costa Ricans blame the demise of the program on partisanship, but larger forces also militated against participation. The third factor, the economic crisis of 1980, had immediate adverse effects on the provision of rural health services but a longer-lasting impact on the meaning of participation. Whereas participation had once been conceived by some factions (in Costa Rica and in the international agencies) as a mechanism for empowering rural communities, in the wake of recession participation became more often viewed as a method for getting rural communities to underwrite the costs of providing health services. By convincing community residents that they must take greater responsibility for their own health, as Sherraden notes in the rural Mexican case, "many participation activities are aimed at minimizing the need for costly public health infrastructure" (1991: 261). Fourth, participation was the victim of changing fashions in international health. The international agencies began to shift away from primary health care and community participation in the early 1980s, in response to factors such as the international debt crisis (which called into question the economic sustainability of government-sponsored programs), the decline of military dictatorships in Latin America, and the laissez-faire economic philosophy dominating U.S. foreign policy. In addition, health planners from several different countries told the representatives of international agencies that state-sponsored participation programs were having a destabilizing political impact by raising the expectations of citizens and placing excessive demands on the state (United Nations Research Institute for Social Development 1983: 36–7; United Nations 1987: 19–20). International health experts responded to these trends by shifting the focus quietly away from community participation; by 1990 international health agendas were dominated by other concerns.

Community participation in health was (and still remains) a vital symbol in Costa Rican political ideology. It carries near-universal appeal because it represents the unity of state and citizenry and perpetuates the image of the state as guardian of a precious democracy. But community participation in Costa Rica cannot be viewed solely as an instrument of the state (although there are social control elements evident in the structure of participation programs). Rather, disagreements over participation should be seen as manifestations of conflicting agendas concerning the creation and re-creation of Costa Rica's democracy. Debates over participation are thus elements in the struggle over access to political decision-making processes.

2   Banana medicine: the United Fruit Company in Costa Rica

> Behind every bunch of bananas stands a man, and that man cannot be a sick man.
>
> *Wilson* 1942: 274

Long before foreign organizations or the national state got involved in doctoring, Costa Rica's inhabitants managed their own health care. Prior to the introduction of biomedicine, people relied on various sociocultural adaptations, including personal hygiene and settlement patterns, to prevent sickness. Indigenous and traditional healers practiced their craft (Richardson and Bode 1971; Low 1985), while a rich herbal pharmacopoeia provided the first line of attack against disease. Popular classifications even today include a number of illnesses not recognized by biomedically trained doctors (Simpson 1983). In these ways, community involvement in health care is far from new. Communities have always been active in safeguarding and attending to their own health and, in any case, until very recently could not afford to wait for outside assistance.

The circumstances surrounding the settlement of Costa Rica's Atlantic coast in the late 1800s undermined community self-sufficiency. The province of Limón, as the region along the Atlantic littoral was known, had been sparsely inhabited until the rise of the banana industry in the late nineteenth century created a demand for vast numbers of male workers. The men who came to clear the land and plant bananas were mainly transient laborers, uprooted from their families and in many cases from their countries of origin. The new settlements that sprang up along the coast were thus "artificial" communities. Because they lacked the healing traditions of home, alternative strategies had to be devised for protecting health and combating disease.

This chapter traces the history of international health assistance to Costa Rica, focusing on the United Fruit Company and its negotiations with the Costa Rican government over the provision of health care to the residents of Limón province. United Fruit's health programs were not explicitly concerned with community participation, but a history of health participation in Costa Rica must begin with United Fruit. The

17

Company's health programs created the context into which participatory initiatives were later introduced, and in retrospect it is clear that governmental conceptions of participation were influenced by United Fruit's health-related goals and methods. The antecedents of the contemporary community participation in health can be found, then, in banana medicine.

The United Fruit Company, incorporated in 1899 and with its headquarters in Boston, had a direct interest in health and sanitation in the regions of Central America conducive to the production of bananas. The prime banana-growing land was located in inhospitable tropical swamps, infested with mosquitoes which carried the dreaded "tropical fevers." This land needed to be cleaned up, "sanitized," and made habitable before the business of exporting bananas could begin. United Fruit's Medical Department, created in 1905, undertook this formidable task.

The Costa Rican government, which at that time virtually ignored the entire Atlantic coast region, welcomed United Fruit's medical efforts. The state was glad to give the foreigners free reign over health programs in Limón, in part because there was no central Costa Rican authority to coordinate or oversee health. Matters of "public hygiene" were the responsibility of the Secretariat of Interior and Police (Secretaría de Gobernación y Policía) until 1922, when the Sub-Secretariat of Hygiene and Public Health was established (Ministerio de Salud, Memoria 1939: 33). But because Limón was considered peripheral to the rest of the nation, the state was concerned primarily with the "public hygiene" of citizens living in the central plateau. The state's lack of attention to Limón enabled United Fruit to operate as the quintessential enclave economy, with one major corporation, assisted by government concessions, producing a single export crop. Workers in this enclave were dependent on the Company for virtually everything, including schools, churches, grocery stores, bakeries, cemeteries, and ambulances, dispensaries, and hospitals.

The operations of another international agency involved in Costa Rican health in the early years of the twentieth century were of greater interest to the government. The Rockefeller Foundation – a private, philanthropic organization with health programs in many foreign countries – sponsored disease-specific control programs designed primarily to eliminate hookworm in the coffee-growing regions of the central plateau (Brown 1979). The efficient production of coffee was vital to the livelihoods of Costa Rican politicians, who cooperated with Rockefeller's efforts to build a healthy labor force. Thus these two wealthy and powerful U.S. organizations – the United Fruit Company and the Rockefeller Foundation – poured money, equipment, people, and technical know-how into Costa Rica. In the process, they gradually transformed the health infrastructure and dominant models of medical care along the lines of the germ-theory model of disease etiology, using disease-eradication techniques perfected during the Spanish–American War.

While the Rockefeller Foundation was formulating a global vision of improved health concomitant with the expansion of capitalism, United Fruit was expressly motivated by the desire to maximize profits. Its supporters made no secret of the fact that United Fruit considered medical service sound business investment more than humanitarian charity:

> Good health is good business anywhere, but in the tropics good health has to be bought. This investment in health is prerequisite to all other investments... The United Fruit Company does not conduct its medical department as a charity. On the contrary, being the world's largest banana company, it is interested in profits. (Wilson 1942: 279)

United Fruit's Medical Department always acted in the interests of the Company's bottom line. Their strategies for improving health between 1900 and 1940 were autocratic, indeed almost militaristic, based as they were on the stringent measures used successfully by Colonel William Gorgas to control tropical disease in Cuba during the Spanish–American War of 1898. The rural populace in the tropics was cajoled and coerced into complying with mandatory health-related edicts passed down by Company officials and municipal authorities. Popular cooperation was elicited by threats of fines and jail sentences; not until much later did the authorities use the more subtle means of education to encourage voluntary compliance with public health measures.

Labor scarcity had been a perennial problem in Costa Rica since the colonial era, and was severe in the late nineteenth century as well. The productivity of workers in the lowlands was hampered by endemic disease. If malaria and yellow fever could be controlled, reasoned United Fruit managers, then workers would be cheaper and more productive, and business more profitable. The Company wanted to control disease to improve economic opportunity, and their reports are filled with images of "conquering the tropics" (Adams 1914; Black 1988) and making the sparsely inhabited jungles fit for economic exploitation. Dr. William Deeks, General Manager of the Medical Department, said:

> Agricultural development and commercial activity on a large scale are impossible until medical science brings tropical disease under control, and sanitation transforms pestilential areas into health localities... The commercial success of

the company is largely due to its accomplishments in reducing the prevalence of these diseases formerly responsible for an appalling morbidity and death rate. (Quoted in Kepner and Soothill 1935: 111)

When the United Fruit Company began its operations, the coastal regions of Central America were so unhealthy that few Central Americans would contemplate living there. The United Fruit Company addressed the problem by importing black laborers from the West Indies, Chinese, Italians, unemployed adventurers from the United States, and, later, the laid-off workers who had built the Panama Canal. It also instructed its Medical Department to improve sanitation and hygiene and construct a network of hospitals and dispensaries. Improving health indices was United Fruit's best hope for building a successful business enterprise. Without dramatic reductions in malaria, the Company would not have been able to sustain a large enough work force to produce and export bananas. By 1912 the Company was operating five "hospitals" in Costa Rica – the United Fruit Company Hospital (in Puerto Limón), the Northern Railway Company, Charity, Guápiles, and Cartago (United Fruit Company 1912) – although some of these were little more than rustic dispensaries without doctors. By 1942 the Company managed a total of fourteen hospitals and medical centers in Central America and Cuba, including by then just three in Costa Rica (in Limón, Quepos, and Golfito) (Wilson 1942: 280). The staff included physicians and nurses from the United States and from Central America, as well as orderlies, dispensers, and sanitary inspectors.

Community participation – in the sense of local support and assistance for health care – never entered the minds of most North American physicians and sanitary engineers sent to Central America to battle against sprue and blackwater fever. Part of the reason was that United Fruit's health programs were targeted less to the concerns of local residents than to the needs of United States citizens living in the zone. United Fruit's anti-malarial precautions are a good example. From 1914 to 1922, long after the vector of malaria had been identified as the *Anopheles* mosquito, malaria remained the number one killer in banana territories, responsible for 14 percent of deaths on plantations and 40 percent of hospitalizations (United Fruit Company 1922: 77–8). In 1921, a United Fruit Company Medical Department Annual Report stated:

In order to protect further our employees, we have provided wire-screened houses, particularly for the better class of employees…Among the more intelligent employees, who realize the importance of the protective measures instituted, we usually get loyal support; but among the uneducated unintelligent laborers, which class constitutes the great majority of our employees, close cooperation is almost impossible. (United Fruit Company 1921: 6)

The "better class of employees" were often North American citizens, who were judged "more intelligent" than local or imported laborers and thus, presumably, more worthy of being protected against malaria. The Medical Department Annual Reports contain endless derogatory comments about the native character. Banana laborers, in particular, were portrayed as crude and unintelligent by nature:

Approximately 90 to 95 per cent of our employees in the tropical divisions are laborers whose numbers include negroes, native Indians and mixtures of different races absolutely unfamiliar with even the rudiments of sanitary regulations ... If it were possible to obtain that cooperation which can rightly be expected in an educated community, and if each householder could be held responsible for the sanitary conditions in the immediate vicinity of his dwelling, the problem of disease-prevention would be greatly simplified. (United Fruit Company 1923: 47)

Even as late as 1958, analysts warned that health and sanitation improvements could be wasted unless the Company educated its laborers on the proper use of indoor plumbing (May and Plaza 1958: 198). The medical Department reasoned that it was not worth spending money to meet unappreciative workers' health needs. Although United Fruit deducted 2–3 percent from workers' salaries for health coverage, its policy was that medical services should primarily benefit the "better class of employees," who were best able to appreciate them. The Company took every opportunity to remind the public of its largesse, as when a pro-United Fruit newspaper announced the appointment of Dr. Segreda as surgeon in charge of the "Old Line" division west of Siquirres: "His appointment by the Company will undoubtedly mean that laborers working in that section will receive the benefit of immediate medical attendance in case of sickness without the necessity for coming to Limón. This action on the part of the Company is one more proof of the care they evince on behalf of their employees" (*Times of Limón*, August 12, 1905, p. 5).

The same workers judged "ignorant" and "unappreciative" on one hand were regarded as shrewd and conniving on the other, eager to take advantage of United Fruit's unique medical resources. Company doctors constructed a vision of the medical opportunist to justify their efforts to screen out the sickest employees. Workers imported from the West Indies (primarily from Jamaica) to work on the plantations were given physical examinations upon arrival and sent home if they were judged too ill to work. In addition, workers who became chronically or terminally ill while working on the plantations were repatriated to their home countries without pension rather than be treated in United Fruit hospitals. One United Fruit official explained:

We operate in many locations where there are no hospitals except those under our own administration, and a certain amount of charity work is therefore compulsory. We believe, on the other hand, that there are many instances of abuse. Chronic diseases that have developed in men before they entered our service have been treated for long periods of time at the Company's expense. Many suffering from such troubles get themselves placed on our pay-roll, simply to gain free hospital privileges, and with no intention of working for the Company. (United Fruit Company 1926: 23)

When not blaming workers for their ignorance or abuse of the system, United Fruit could blame their diseases and deaths on an insalubrious environment. One year, a Medical Department official explained the high rates of morbidity and mortality by noting that the Company had that year planted 40,878 acres of virgin lands. "Such a program requires a great many laborers working under conditions where necessarily no preventive measures can be undertaken except by quinine prophylaxis" (United Fruit Company 1923: 47). In his view, the environmental conditions presented obstacles beyond the capacity of United Fruit's medical personnel to overcome. Similar rationalizations must have been common during the early, land-clearing days of United Fruit's operations: whereas the Company "owned or leased" 325,000 acres in 1899, by 1922 it owned over 1·5 million acres (United Fruit Company 1922: 71–2). While some of the land was used to grow bananas, some was held as security against competitors, and in 1922 the Company cultivated just 24 percent of the land it owned (United Fruit Company 1922: 72). Rather than admitting the Company's obligation to keep its workers alive as they cleared and improved these lands, however, Medical Department officials chose to portray their deaths as a regrettable but inevitable fact of nature.

Their characterizations sound shocking today, but at the time educated doctors commonly blamed banana workers for their pitiful living conditions. In one of the more egregious examples published in United Fruit's Medical Department reports, a United Fruit doctor in Honduras wrote about his Indian and mestizo patients:

There is an air of dreaminess about them that verges on apathy, as they lounge in front of their camps ... Their sense of responsibility is nil; but we must remember that their minds are as virgin as the primeval jungles which surround the plantations. The future is something intangible and non-existent. Their "mañana" is only a convenient waste basket to which can be relegated all the tasks that should be accomplished in the present – especially so if, in any way, they would interfere with rest of soul and body. Their mental age is that of a moron. (López 1930: 164)

When workers got sick, they were hospitalized at United Fruit expense in racially segregated wings of the hospital. White workers were hospitalized at disproportionately high rates, although there is no indication that they were sicker than the so-called "colored" employees. In 1917, for example, 24 percent of United Fruit employees in the Costa Rica Division were white, yet 46 percent of employees treated in Company hospitals were white (United Fruit Company 1917: 16).

The racist attitudes and employment strategies used by United Fruit (see Bourgois 1989), combined with the sincere conviction that medical personnel alone possessed the secrets to good health, reduced the possibility that Medical Department employees would have considered the potential the community had for becoming actively or constructively involved in sanitation programs. Laborers had to be treated, and disciplined, like children: "They are not bad; they are only children who have never grown up mentally, and their helplessness should always stimulate us to give them our very best assistance" (López 1930: 107). This was an era when mandatory compliance, not voluntary cooperation, was judged to be the most efficient way to bring health to illiterate populations. Unlike contemporary visions of community participation which render rural residents as partners in a unified governmental-local effort to improve health, United Fruit managers saw the banana workers of the early twentieth century as the very antithesis of healthful living.

Consequently, Company health programs emphasized strict compliance with Company mandates and a preoccupation with profit rather than humanitarian attention to the needs of the local populace. For example, when laborers got sick their salaries were suspended, although officials and clerical employees continued to be paid when ill (Wilson 1942: 146). This policy might help to explain the comments of Dr. Deeks, United Fruit's Medical Director, when he boasted in 1922 that United Fruit's absenteeism rate due to illness and injury was 1·1 percent on the plantations, compared to 2·5 per cent in U.S. factories (United Fruit Company 1922: 80).

United Fruit policy sometimes coerced people into complying with sanitation measures: in 1912 fines were levied against boarding-house managers (the majority of laborers lived in the less-expensive boarding houses rather than in Company housing) for failing to report to the Company any illness among the lodgers (United Fruit Company 1912: 27); in 1929 a United Fruit anti-malarial expert noted that "malaria control methods have to almost be forced upon [the workers]" (United Fruit Company 1929: 94). Kepner and Soothill noted that in at least one of the Company's divisions pressure to comply with hygienic measures "is brought to bear upon uncooperative workers by the withholding of wages, and reproof is administered or fines are imposed upon careless non-employees by local magistrates" (1935: 113). On the other hand, recognized sanitary benefits were sometimes withheld from the workers because the Company anticipated non-compliance: "The transient character of the labor procurable makes it impossible to enforce rigid regulations that would permit of the satisfactory maintenance of screened quarters" (United Fruit Company 1925: 309).

Yet another example of the Company's self-interest is evident in its treatment of non-employees (including dependents), who were charged for use of the United Fruit hospital in Limón when it opened to the public in 1913:

[Private patients] are now admitted to the privileges of the U.F. Co's Hospital attention by paying two colones and fifty cents daily. By putting down two weeks attendance in advance patients can obtain the attendance of these famous doctors Lynn and Fest, one a first-class physician and the other an eminent surgeon. Mr. Mullins must be congratulated for this sympathetic consideration to the public; if he continues in these lines he will secure the goodwill of the community. (*Times of Limón*, June 14, 1913, p. 1; see also Kepner and Soothill 1936: 122)

Apart from the deliberately self-serving dimensions of United Fruit's medical policies, the existence of the banana industry also had indirect negative effects on health status. For example, the plantations created an opportunity for short-term work for men only, which resulted ultimately in the spread of disease when transient laborers contracted malaria and sexually transmitted diseases on the plantations and then transported them to other regions of Costa Rica or the Caribbean (see Kepner and Soothill 1936: 123). The migration back and forth to the coast also resulted in social dislocation because the majority of laborers were men traveling without their families. For those who did bring their families, living conditions were difficult at best. Malnutrition was a widespread consequence of the poverty and uniformity of diet, exacerbated by the synergistic effects of parasite loads and other diseases.

But the United Fruit Company also had positive effects on health. While certain political economists have documented the deleterious health effects of capitalist expansion (e.g., Doyal 1979), a more complete account of United Fruit's presence in Limón must also mention the beneficial results of "banana medicine." Despite their customary severity and rigidity, United Fruit's health programs were remarkably successful in controlling disease in the plantation regions. The Company's record of health improvement is acknowledged even by United Fruit's harshest early critics, who noted significant declines in the death rates of Limón province from 1906 to 1929 (Kepner and Soothill 1935: 119). Kepner and Soothill make the important point that United Fruit employed healthy, young men, whose rates of death and disease were low compared to those in the population at large. Comparisons of death rates between various provinces must take these underlying demographic differences into account. Nonetheless, the Company did effect tremendous health improvements as measured by changes occurring over time within Limón province. Much of their success can be attributed to an ambitious program of malaria surveillance and control, which reduced the prevalence of malaria along the Atlantic coast from 29 percent in 1926 to 12 percent in 1929 (United Fruit Company 1929: 95). (Judging by the following quotation, it is tempting to speculate that the high incidence of malaria may have been superseded by a high incidence of alcoholism: "To induce our laborers to take quinine, a liquid preparation with half an ounce of rum to the dose is administered" [United Fruit Company 1922: 88].)

The Company's sanitary programs also had beneficial consequences by making possible the economic viability of Costa Rica's only Atlantic port, Puerto Limón. The Company literally made the region habitable for the first time since the Spanish colonizers introduced vector-borne disease in the 1500s. As a result, the population of Limón province rose from 1,858 in 1883 to 7,484 in 1892 (three years after United Fruit was incorporated), to 32,278 in 1927 (Casey 1979: 215). The Company also provided the only biomedical services in the entire region, first in a wooden hospital constructed in 1906, replaced in 1921 by a concrete hospital which was, by United Fruit's own estimation, "one of the finest buildings in Costa Rica" (United Fruit Company 1921: 13).

From banana medicine to state medicine

While United Fruit launched many beneficial health programs, the company gradually managed to get the Costa Rican government to underwrite many of its medical costs. For example, Company hospitalization policy called for sick workers to be briefly hospitalized in Limón and then sent, as soon as possible, to hospitals in San José where they would be treated at public expense (Fournier Facio 1974). In addition, the government financed half the construction costs for the 150-bed hospital United Fruit built in Limón in 1921, even though the Company did not treat private, non-employee patients there (Kepner and Soothill 1936: 122). Not until the early 1930s did the Costa Rican Legislative Assembly begin to become involved in monitoring or questioning Company health practices.

Why did Costa Rican officials wait so long before pressuring the Company to assume greater responsibility for medical care? In Seligson's opinion:

A conflict with the "Frutera" meant a confrontation with the economic, political, and ultimately the military power of the United States – a confrontation which Costa Rica was guaranteed to lose. It should be remembered that at this time the United States was very actively pursuing its Big Stick policy in the Caribbean, and Costa Rica had received more than one taste of it. (Seligson 1980: 58, citing examples from Monge Alfarao 1966: 277)

After 1933, however, U.S. President Roosevelt instituted the "Good Neighbor" foreign policy toward Central America and the Caribbean. The change tempered the blatant imperialism of U.S. military and economic policies and opened the way for strengthening the state apparatus. Furthermore, prior to the 1930s not many influential Costa Ricans ever made their way to the coast to experience plantation living. Most workers were English-speaking blacks from the West Indies, and other foreigners; the few Costa Rican banana workers came from the lowest economic echelons of society and were not likely to be heard by policymakers. Several Costa Rican doctors were employed at various points in their careers by the United Fruit Medical Department, but they were not inclined to denounce the medical practices of their employer, at least not in public. One doctor reportedly quit working for the Company in Turrialba because he was given only two medicines to dispense: quinine for those with malaria symptoms, and bicarbonate of soda for those with stomach aches. Workers knew that if they had an accident or got seriously ill they would be unable to get to a hospital, especially because their salaries would not cover transportation costs and their families would be left alone without a source of income (Fournier Facio 1974: 67).

The first public denunciations of Company health practices came in 1931, when a sanitary engineer from the Secretariat of Public Health filed a report condemning the Company's poor compliance with a government agreement. The accord had specified that the Company would build an emergency hospital in the banana zone of Siquirres and operate medical dispensaries out of specially equipped railroad cars. The engineer's report appears in the archives of the Costa Rican Legislative Assembly:

We visited what they call the Siquirres Hospital, and saw that it was nothing of the sort. It consists of an examining room without any hygienic precautions, with three army cots; and in one dark room there are some medicines and a few surgical instruments under the care of an untrained practitioner [*empírico*]. The representative of the Company affirmed in writing on the 21st of February, 1931, that this hospital was by then established in Siquirres, with a pharmacy staffed by a pharmacist, an office with an operating table, complete with instruments, gases, and medicines for first aid; but there is no pharmacist there. The existence of an operating table, and of surgical instruments and medicines is worth nothing without the presence of a doctor in charge of this dispensary or hospital. When we questioned the person in charge whom we found there, he informed us that he acted as doctor, surgeon, and pharmacist; in other words, the Siquirres hospital is a comic imitation of what it should have been. We did not succeed in finding a *single dispensary*, even though we covered vast expanses of land within the United plantations, yet they informed us that they did exist. We did visit the Company camps in a section of Guácimo, and sorrowfully observed the miserable state in which those poor peons live. Crowded into forty poorly-built huts, worse than those the indigenous people lived in and with deplorable hygiene; there is not one dispensary there, even though the area is malarious. Naturally, the Company should be obligated to construct simple quarters surrounded by all the hygienic precautions necessary to avoid the propagation of malaria. (Archivo Nacional, Congreso 1932: 9561; emphasis in original)

With this report, national authorities were alerted to the abysmal living conditions on the plantations.

Although the Legislative Assembly became aware of conditions on the plantations in the early 1930s, an urgent impetus for change came when the banana workers in Limón went on strike in 1934 (see Fallas 1978 [1941]). Banana production had fallen since 1925 due to two intractable diseases, sigatoka and Panama disease (Seligson 1980: 67), and living conditions on the plantations had been deteriorating steadily since the Depression. As a result, many Atlantic coast laborers had lost their jobs. The workers, organized by Carlos Luis Fallas of the recently formed Costa Rican Communist Party, presented a list of demands to Congress in an attempt to draw national attention to their plight. Improved health was one of their top priorities: they wanted the Company to provide quinine and snake antivenin and to pay them in cash rather than in scrip (Seligson 1980: 71). In addition, they petitioned to have the Company install medical dispensaries on every plantation with more than ten employees, and to guarantee that sick workers would be transferred to and treated in hospitals (Acuña Ortega 1984: 33). When their proposal was rejected, the workers walked out. The strike lasted 19 days, until the government interceded on the workers' behalf: "the Company agreed to increase the salary to 4.20 colones (20 centimos over the old wage), eliminate scrip, make available free hospitalization, improve hygiene and housing, provide some work tools, and recognize the union" (Seligson 1980: 72). When United Fruit refused to honor the state-mediated accord, a second strike was called, but the Company never did grant any concessions to the workers.

The strike did not bring the workers any personal or collective benefit, yet it did show how potentially powerful they could be, and it also "demonstrated the Company's capacity for deceit" (Seligson 1980: 73). The strikers' plight evoked sympathy on the part of politicians, who became less tolerant in the future of the Company's attempts to shirk its medical responsibilities. In 1935, the Company refused to hospitalize workers who became sick on the job. This was a violation of the law, since the Company was deducting one U.S. cent per stem of bananas to cover costs of hospitalization. The Company insisted it could not comply with the law because the Executive branch of government had not yet supplied the necessary protocol to govern hospitalization procedures, but the government interpreted this as another abdication of responsibility by the Company (*Voz del Atlántico*, February 2, 1935, February 16, 1935).

In fact, United Fruit had little incentive to settle with the strikers in 1934, because the Company was then making plans to abandon its Atlantic coast operations. Company officials knew that the striking laborers would be superfluous as soon as new banana plantations could be established on Costa Rica's Pacific coast, then still free from sigatoka and Panama disease. It was in the Company's interest, nonetheless, to support a smear campaign against the Communist Party, because a confrontative union would, in their view, eventually threaten the stability of Pacific coast operations. When the Company finally did transfer its operations to the Pacific coast in the late 1930s, it pulled out virtually all the infrastructure it had built on the Atlantic coast: railroad lines, schools, and clinics and dispensaries (Kepner and Soothill 1936: 90). Only the central Limón hospital continued to function under United Fruit direction. The entire province of Limón (with the exception of downtown Puerto Limón) was left without medical services for nearly 30 years, since the national government did not have the resources or motivation to provide medical services there.

The devastation left in the wake of United Fruit's withdrawal from the Atlantic coast points out how dependent the region was on the Company's largesse. In lowland areas all over Central America, United Fruit was the only existing source of medical services, yet the Company showed little regard for the well-being of local inhabitants. The Company's attitude toward community involvement has to be viewed from an entrepreneur's perspective. The Company needed a labor supply large enough to work its vast Central American plantations. Faced with rampant malaria and no coordinated state-run medical programs, their own disease control efforts were the only guarantee that the United States would have bananas and the stockholders would have dividends. Their idea of community participation combined severity with paternalism and entailed strict social control: health would be subordinated to profits; people did not have a "right" to health, so those who were judged too sick were either not given employment or were repatriated to their homelands at Company expense; all laborers contributed an obligatory 2–3 percent of their wages to cover medical costs; all illness would be reported immediately to Company officials and treated by Company doctors in Company hospitals. The imperialist mentality is clear. Community members were expected to comply with Company regulations and at the same time to thank the Company for its munificence. Although United Fruit health efforts earned praise from many corners, Company headquarters in Boston was interested in health as a business investment. Profiting from concessionary business contracts, from a healthy labor force, and from the good press that its health programs earned, the United Fruit Company experience in Central America gives new meaning to the expression "for-profit health care."

The overt tension between United Fruit and the Costa Rican government in the 1930s was the beginning of a trend toward reduced corporate – and greater state – involvement in the provision of health services. A number of factors made this change possible. By the 1950s, international development agencies such as the Institute of Inter-American Affairs and the Pan American Health Organization had begun to provide significant health assistance to rural areas, relieving private corporations of the necessity to doctor the agricultural proletariat on the plantations. Malaria infection rates were dropping and yellow fever had been eliminated even before the widespread use of DDT after the war. In addition, the Costa Rican state was gradually forcing United Fruit to pay higher taxes. President Rafael Angel Calderón Guardia (1940–4) set up a national social security system, only one of several of his programs which required "increased state expenditure, particularly on social infrastructure" (Bulmer-Thomas 1987: 122). Leaders recognized that the country's tax and tariff structure would have to be changed to obtain the revenues necessary to finance the program. After the Costa Rican civil war of 1948, José Figueres Ferrer, the emergent leader of the Social Democratic movement, urged the Legislative Assembly to increase United Fruit's tax burden. By 1949 Costa Rica had imposed a 15 percent profits tax on the Company. By 1954, "the tax had been raised to 30 % with UFCO also agreeing to hand over most of its schools, hospitals, etc. in Costa Rica to the government" (Bulmer-Thomas 1987: 109).

In light of these changes, United Fruit was ready to get out of the medical business by the early 1940s, but the Second World War and the Costa Rican civil war of 1948 made change difficult. By the 1950s, U.S. business analysts agreed that it was time for the Costa Rican state to assume responsibility for providing social services to banana workers. May and Plaza said that when social security systems "become effective, and are extended to workers on its installations, the United Fruit Company will be relieved of the necessity of maintaining its own [health] program" (1958: 189). They added:

There can be little doubt about the direction in which it is desirable to move to free the company from the weight of paternalistic responsibilities. The evolution will necessarily be gradual, but a clear policy leading to the transfer of more and more of these nonbusiness activities to governments and communities will serve the long-term interests of everyone. (1958: 199)

Finally in 1954, United Fruit signed a contract turning over its medical responsibilities to the Costa Rican state (*La Gaceta*, December 28, 1954). This was part of a larger Central American trend: in the wake of the 1954 U.S.-sponsored coup in Guatemala – prompted by the Arbenz government's threats to expropriate unproductive United Fruit lands (Schlesinger and Kinzer 1983) – and a devastating strike the same year in Honduras, the Company gradually lowered its political profile and began to pay higher taxes to all Central American governments (Bulmer-Thomas 1985: 109). Even after the 1954 contract was signed, however, the hospitals were not actually turned over to the state until the 1960s (Roemer 1963: 173). State-run health services continued to focus on the central plateau and strategic rural areas (like the agricultural basin of Turrialba) rather than on the banana plantations. The state's neglect of medical care in banana regions changed in the mid-1960s, when Standard Fruit Company set up extensive plantations in areas of the Atlantic coast previously abandoned by United Fruit. In order to make Standard's business investment more attractive, the state set up social security dispensaries and hospitals in the banana-growing regions to care for the influx of workers. The era of the enclave economy had ended.

United Fruit and its Costa Rican subsidiaries still do business in Costa Rica, but the Company no longer offers medical services. It provides potable water, drainage, housing, and garbage disposal services for laborers who live on Company plantations, and the Company contributes to Costa Rica's nationalized health and social security fund by paying a percentage of its payroll in mandatory taxes. In contrast to its great power and autonomy in the first half of this century, however, the Company is now integrated into the national economy.

Community participation revisited

The relative success of United Fruit's disease control efforts raises a question which will surface repeatedly as we trace the development of health and participation in Costa Rica. Is community participation essential to the improvement of health indices in rural areas of the country? In the first decades of the twentieth century, the dominant model of public health practice emphasized subordination of individual interests to public authority. Individual citizens could no longer construct houses, businesses, or drainage ditches to their own specifications without the approval of sanitary engineers. Public health was given priority over individual concerns. Costa Rica's first Minister of Health, Dr. Solon Nuñez (who had studied at Johns Hopkins University under a grant from the Rockefeller Foundation), remarked in 1929 that in times past

the attention of the State revolved around the individual and not the collectivity. To go in search of the impoverished ill was yesterday's principal preoccupation. Today's medicine is social medicine, is protection of the public health, is prophylaxis, is hygiene. (Ministerio de Salud, Memoria 1929: xx)

Public health experts operating within this philosophical framework were not likely to solicit the opinions of individual citizens about the direction of public health policy. They had acquired their own specialized knowledge at great expense and personal sacrifice, which made them disinclined to share their decision-making prerogatives with uneducated laborers or peasants. The newly consolidated Costa Rican medical profession, encouraged by the Rockefeller Foundation and the successes of tropical disease heroes like Walter Reed, William Gorgas, Carlos Finlay, and the United Fruit Company, was determined to improve the public health by enforcing sanitary legislation. Health professionals were convinced that the benefits of their policies would soon become apparent to people who adhered strictly to the law.

Community tactics for affecting health care have remained relatively consistent over the years. Fifty years ago, banana workers and community members sometimes organized to obtain better health, hygiene, and hospitalization benefits. Then, as now, they evaluated their alternatives and used the only means they had available. On occasion this meant they would strike, if the Company was intransigent and the government apathetic toward their plight. Styles of participation are conditioned by the options available to community members, and when health committees do not function or professionals do not listen, participation can take the form of strikes, protests, and open conflicts with authorities. Yet when residents break the law or threaten established policy, few officials will concede that they might be "participating" in health. (One 1975 editorial in the Costa Rican press was titled, "Popular participation or illegal pressures?" [*La República*, October 16, 1975].) The line between "participation" and "subversion" is sometimes quite fine. The United Fruit Company, for its part, offered its laborers virtually no voice in setting health policy. This left workers with three options: acquiesce, organize, or die. The workers, by all accounts, did all three in great numbers.

3 The international imperative: foreign aid for health in Costa Rica

Costa Rica's health system has long been influenced by foreign models of health care. Thus it is essential to analyze the international as well as national context of health service provision. In keeping with the macro-analytic focus begun in the last chapter, I here explore the role of other foreign agencies that influenced the direction of Costa Rican rural health care after the Second World War: the Institute of Inter-American Affairs, the United Nations community development movement, the Inter-American Development Bank, and the United States Agency for International Development's Title IX program. Beginning in the 1940s, these agencies presided over a change in the meaning of health in Latin America, whereby health came to be used in campaigns to support a specifically pro-United States political ideology. It also served as a way of introducing U.S. personnel, technology, and values into the Latin American countryside.

In defense of U.S. strategic interests: the Institute of Inter-American Affairs

International development agencies began to expand their Latin American operations during and after the Second World War, in part to promote hemispheric solidarity in the face of perceived German, Italian, and Japanese threats. It was then that the Office of Inter-American Affairs was established (later the Institute of Inter-American Affairs, which subsequently became the model for the U.S. Agency for International Development) to improve Latin American health and nutrition standards as part of its overall strategy to consolidate ranks against possible military threats. War thus became another reason to justify health work in less-developed countries. Defense of U.S. strategic interests was, in this case, the primary argument for investing U.S. dollars in health and sanitation in Latin America.

The U.S. Congress favored establishing the Office of Inter-American Affairs because of their concern for the military security of the western hemisphere. American business interests saw an opportunity in Latin America to increase their share of the market in medical equipment, supplies, and services. Recipient governments, on the other hand, were motivated by the potential for increased productivity and grassroots political support outside their major cities. They, in turn, could tell their constituents that health and sanitation programs were a priority of a concerned and altruistic leadership. International health programs are multifaceted, and the Institute of Inter-American Affairs was particularly adept at presenting the face which would most appeal to audience tastes.

The Office of Inter-American Affairs comprised five offices during World War II, all designed to promote "hemispheric solidarity." Three of the highly specialized offices (called "Corporations") were eliminated immediately following the war: the Navigation Corporation, the Radio Corporation, and the Transportation Corporation. Two others, founded in 1942, continued to function. These were the Institute of Inter-American Affairs, which dealt with health and sanitation, and the Inter-American Educational Foundation, which trained teachers and ran literacy programs throughout Latin America (United States Congress 1949: 15).

The goals of the Office were military, political, and economic. They included: securing U.S. national military interests in Latin America during the war; removing fascist elements from the hemisphere and promoting regimes friendly to the U.S.; setting the stage for the incipient Cold War; and taking advantage of the naval blockade to lessen Latin America's dependency on Europe and increase its dependency on the U.S. as a market for raw materials and a source of imported goods. Nelson A. Rockefeller, as first Director of the Office, designed cooperative U.S.–Latin American programs to meet these goals. Given the family connections of its Director, it should be no surprise that the Office's health programs were "borrowed from observation of the health work of the Rockefeller Foundation in Brazil and elsewhere" (Glick 1957: 19).

The Institute of Inter-American Affairs was billed as a cooperative U.S.–Latin American program to achieve medical preparedness, which Rockefeller saw as an essential part of U.S. defense strategy. He established a "hemispheric plan for health" in 1942, designed to "promote the health and defense of the Western Hemisphere." The health programs, Rockefeller said, would "concentrate on those areas which are considered vital in carrying out the defense of the hemisphere. They will, for example, work in areas holding potentialities for the development of rubber and other supplies necessary to our war effort" (*New York Times*, March 6, 1942). Planned projects included improving water supplies and waste disposal systems, building hospitals in defense areas, and training Latin American health and sanitation specialists. Dillon S. Myer, who later became President of the Institute of Inter-American Affairs, explained that the programs

were to assist people in Latin America to feed themselves better during the war, to be sure to provide food for our own Army and other people who were down there, in view of the navigation situation that existed at that time. The health program was set up...to eliminate such diseases as malaria and other similar diseases in areas around the mines and other defense activities in particular. (United States Congress 1949: 15)

This health and sanitation division of the Office of Inter-American Affairs was known in Latin America as the Servicio Cooperativo Interamericano de Salud Pública (SCISP), or Inter-American Public Health Service Cooperative. Costa Rica participated in the U.S. defense strategy from the earliest stages of the war, in part because of the country's proximity to the Panama Canal and because of the presence of German submarines in the Caribbean Sea. Costa Rica's participation in the SCISP program dovetailed nicely with Costa Rican President Rafael Angel Calderón Guardia's reformist plans. When Calderón Guardia came into office in 1940, Costa Ricans were already feeling the deleterious effects of war: "The nation was cut off from normal sources of imports; its domestic production was taxed by the greater demands of a growing population and by pressure to increase exports to Panama and the Canal Zone – its contribution to the allied cause" (Bell 1971: 26). To ease growing social unrest, Calderón Guardia implemented a series of reforms, including establishment of a social security system (see Rosenberg 1981, 1983). When the United States offered health assistance to the Costa Rican countryside, Calderón Guardia undoubtedly recognized that the program could be used to enhance his administration's image.

Costa Rica was a staunch U.S. ally during World War II. It was the first Latin American country to declare war on Japan (on December 7, 1941). Five days later, Costa Rica also declared war on Germany and Italy (Rojas Suárez 1943). Costa Rica had a sizable population of German citizens at the time, many of whom were deported or interned, their property confiscated by the government (Bell 1971: 109–10). From January 1942 through March 1945, U.S. soldiers and a squadron of U.S. planes were stationed just outside the San José airport (Rojas Suárez 1943: 74–5). The only bellicose activity Costa Rica reportedly witnessed, however, was when a United Fruit Company steamer ship, the *San Pablo*, was torpedoed while docked in Puerto Limón on July 2, 1942 (Rojas Suárez 1943; 65). Understanding the close relationship between the United States and Costa Rica during this period helps to place the SCISP health programs in context.

The SCISP was formed by cooperative agreement between the governments of the United States and Costa Rica in 1942, for a duration of five years. The agreement resulted in the construction of ten health centers and seven health posts, water and drainage systems for several communities, financial assistance for the Children's Hospital in Tres Ríos, design of a 200-bed tuberculosis treatment facility, and technical assistance on assorted other projects (Ministerio de Salud, Memoria 1977: 30–2). The Costa Rican government's legal documents establishing the SCISP program contain only one reference to the strategic or war-related nature of the program, in a clause which states that the Institute is not committed to offer accessory equipment or material to Costa Rica in the event of any "bellicose force." Clearly the interests of the Costa Rican government at this time were distinct from (albeit compatible with) those of the U.S. government, and the way the SCISP program was presented to the public in each country reflected those differences. The SCISP was presented in the United States as part of the national defense effort and a good-willed humanitarian effort to raise the standards of living in a democratic neighbor to the south. It was presented to Costa Rican citizens as a benevolent act of charity fostered by their own President, who used U.S. money and technical expertise to bolster his own image as champion of public health and sanitation.

The political and tactical uses of health are evident in this example. Rockefeller wisely wrapped his military interests in a humanitarian veneer, thereby legitimizing the U.S. presence in Costa Rica. He appealed to the war-mobilized U.S. public, however, by emphasizing the strategic nature of the program, since it was unlikely that the U.S. Congress would have condoned spending money on humanitarian foreign aid programs when the domestic population was suffering the deprivations of war. In addition, U.S. supporters of the program attempted to convince Congressional appropriation committees that the programs would promote trade among the American republics. One representative from the U.S. Department of State said:

It means better markets for our products and more effective suppliers for our needs. Incidentally, these programs have a direct effect in increasing the demand for particular United States products by introducing and demonstrating on a large scale the use of our agricultural machinery, our pharmaceuticals, hospital equipment, medical supplies, and so forth. (United States Congress 1949: 3)

The Institute of Inter-American Affairs was the wartime guardian angel of U.S. entrepreneurs in Latin America, insuring not only that their economic investments would be safe, but hinting that its policies would likely result in higher profits after the war. Some critics argued that the Institute's alliance with U.S. business interests contradicted the humanitarian principles espoused in the cooperative Inter-American programs, citing as evidence the membership rosters of the Institute coordinating committees. In each country, the coordinating committees were composed of representatives of the largest U.S. corporations operating in Latin America – United Fruit Company, Standard Oil, and General Electric (Collier and Horowitz 1976: 233). The contradictions between humanitarianism and business interests were evident in certain of the Institute's recommendations. For example, it advocated arms shipments to Latin American dictators, thus calling into question its declared support for democratic reforms, and causing some Latin American and North American intellectuals to question whether the humanitarian goals espoused by the Institute would ever materialize.

Institute health programs were further accused of catering to business interests by the New York Physicians Forum for the Study of Medical Care. This group, composed of several hundred members of the Medical Society of the County of New York, sent a letter to the participants (including Nelson Rockefeller) in a National Conference of Planning for War and Post-War Medical Services. They charged "that the conference was an 'unholy alliance' between organized medicine and the manufacturers of drugs and surgical supplies and that rather than being national in scope and aiming to improve the health of the people, the conference really was designed to promote profits for special groups" (*New York Times*, March 16, 1943).

The Institute managed its Costa Rican public relations more carefully. All programs initiated through the Office of Inter-American Affairs were deliberately and widely publicized to show Costa Rican citizens just how good a neighbor the United States was. Nelson Rockefeller himself appeared at the March 18, 1944 inauguration of the Solon Nuñez Health Center in Turrialba. After his speech, "the Military Band played the national anthems of the United States and Costa Rica" (*Revista Salud* 1944: 21–2). An Institute memorandum submitted to Congress mentioned that United States contributions to the program were well publicized through public ribbon-cutting ceremonies, personal appearances by U.S. diplomats, speeches, newspaper and magazine articles, and the distribution of 15 movies (United States Congress 1949: 79). In this respect, the SCISP and other development programs functioned as publicity campaigns, showing Costa Ricans that continued alliance between their government and that of the United States could be advantageous. Nonetheless, the purportedly humanitarian character of the SCISP was belied by sudden neglect as soon as the war was over. The Turrialba health center, inaugurated with such a fanfare by Nelson Rockefeller, was abandoned by the SCISP after 1944 and the Costa Rican government did not pick up the slack during the turbulent years surrounding Costa Rica's civil war of 1948. Investigators assessing the Turrialba health situation in 1953 said that services had deteriorated there since 1944 (Morales, Scrimshaw, and Arce 1953: 153). Abandonment of the Turrialba center, reminiscent of United Fruit's abandonment of Limón province in the late 1930s, provided evidence of the relative unimportance of rural inhabitants.

Some of the U.S. policies implemented in Costa Rica during the war were not favorably received there. Negative reactions accompanied President Calderón Guardia's willingness to allow U.S. troops to be stationed on Costa Rican soil and his compliance with the U.S. demand to penalize German nationals in Costa Rica (Bell 1971: 109–10). The dissent was muted, however, by the social reforms Calderón Guardia enacted. Even 40 years later, Calderón Guardia is revered in the countryside for the labor and social security guarantees he legislated. His name is still associated in the public's eye with medical care and a major San José hospital is named after him. During his administration, his image was enhanced by the SCISP programs which improved water, drainage, and sewage systems, and constructed rural and suburban health centers. These health-related efforts were congruent with Calderón Guardia's image as a benevolent, humanistic physician and President, concerned about the health and living standards of the poor and the working class.

Costa Ricans may not have heard much about the military or strategic justifications for the SCISP program, but Rockefeller's motivations cannot be mistaken. In 1943 he addressed a conference of U.S. physicians concerned about the medical effects of war. He explained the SCISP program to them, saying, "The projects ... provide sanitation for areas around defense bases. They provide health services for millions of workers on the production fronts of the Amazon and Central America, in the mining regions of the Andes and Brazil, on fiber-growing projects in Haiti" (*New York Times*, March 16, 1943). Rockefeller chose as the United States Director of the SCISP program a Dr. George C. Dunham, who, in the 1944 SCISP agreement between the Costa Rican and United States governments, listed his affiliation as Major General, U.S. Army, and Executive Vice President of the Institute of Inter-American Affairs (Colección de Leyes y Decretos 1944: 250–5). On loan to the SCISP from the Army Medical Corps (Glick 1957: 16), Dunham's appointment underscores the connection, in this program, between health and defense.

After the war, the fate of the Office of Inter-American Affairs remained unclear. Rockefeller resigned to pursue his career in politics, and the future of the Office was uncertain for about two years. Some argued that, as a wartime contingency, the Office should now be disbanded, especially since they had never been fully convinced of the wisdom of using technical assistance to conduct American foreign policy (Glick 1957: 26). Others argued that with the United States financing European reconstruction through the Marshall Plan, Latin America should not be abandoned. The need for hemispheric solidarity was as great as ever before, they argued, notwithstanding the relative peace in the wake of war. In 1947, Congress approved the merger of the Office's agencies responsible for agricultural, educational, and health development in Latin America. This new entity, named the Institute of Inter-American Affairs, operated in 14 Latin American countries between 1945 and 1947. Costa Rica was not included, because U.S. officials decided that the scarce resources of the Institute needed to be spread as effectively as possible and Costa Rica's health indices were already better than in most other Latin American countries (United States Congress 1949: 31).

During wartime, the health programs had been geared specifically toward buttressing U.S. military interests. In the postwar period, however, health programs were redefined for U.S. audiences as a means of propping up democratic regimes sympathetic to the United States. Health programs were justified, as the Cold War intensified in the early 1950s, as a means to thwart communist expansion. U.S. politicians repeatedly stressed that the Institute of Inter-American Affairs was the key to stable U.S. foreign policy toward Latin America. Democracy would be strengthened, they said, by helping friendly governments to improve the health and living conditions of their citizens. When the cooperative health and sanitation program between the United States and Costa Rica was reactivated in 1951, its first objective was "To promote and strengthen understanding and good will between the peoples of the United States of America and Costa Rica *and to further secure growth of democratic ways of life"* (United States Treaties 1951: 1017; emphasis added). As the United States entered the Cold War era, U.S. politicians stressed that improved health standards were a shield against communism. Willard L. Thorp, Assistant Secretary of State, testified,

The activities of the institute are based on technical and scientific cooperation with other free nations of the world to strengthen the foundations of their freedom and ours. This activity is not unassociated with self-interest. It is based on a realistic appraisal of what the threat to our own freedom would be if those who seek to regiment and enslave mankind should triumph in the rest of the world.

He continued:

The programs are recognized by the Latin American statesmen and the American diplomatic corps as an effective instrument for strengthening democratic ideas and institutions and counteracting the spread of communism among the masses. They do this by demonstrating the practical capacity of democratic governments, aided by their form of cooperation, to improve basic conditions of human life and successfully meet the challenge of totalitarian propaganda. (United States Congress 1949: 1–2)

Dillon Myer, President of the Institute in 1949, argued:

Consequently a more stable type of government, of the type that we would like to see continued within the Western Hemisphere, would be provided, if we can provide the basis for people to keep full bellies, to eliminate some of the more drastic diseases which cause people to suffer and which affect their work patterns. (United States Congress 1949:13)

The relationship between international assistance and U.S. national security interests became particularly pronounced in the 1950s, after the Mutual Security Act of 1951 explicitly made aid eligibility contingent on each country's willingness to uphold U.S. foreign policy goals. Under the Eisenhower administration, "All forms of foreign aid, including technical co-operation, came increasingly to be regarded as instruments to advance the military strategic interests of the United States" (Glick 1957: 48). In this sense, the World War II era set the precedent for future relations between the United States and Costa Rica, because the United States continues to pursue its foreign policy interests in Central America in part through its bilateral health and nutrition programs.

Popular participation institutionalized: the United Nations community development movement, 1955–70

The United Nations, formed in 1945, was the first multilateral organization to take an active interest in community participation, during what became known as the community development movement of the early 1950s. In fact, the community development movement was one of the "conventional" antecedents of community participation in health as elaborated in the 1970s. Twenty years earlier, the United Nations began to publicize the importance of popular participation in development and helped to spread the idea around the world, alerting all member nations to the purported wisdom of involving communities in their development plans.

The community development movement first focused on constructing buildings – community centers – in which to conduct the important business of community development. The United Nations adopted a resolution to support the "use of community development centres as effective instruments to promote economic and social progress throughout the world" (United Nations 1955: 1). Within a very short time, U.N. advisors realized that the physical entities were not as crucial to development as the concept of "social progress through local action," which they came to call community development (United Nations 1955: 2).

Even though the U.N. membership realized that community organization and participation in decision-making for development were more important than buildings, the early focus on community welfare centers provides an indication of the model of development U.N. members had in mind. Prototypes for the centers were drawn from the developed countries of western Europe and the United States, and a 1955 U.N. document cites successful case studies in France, New Zealand, the United Kingdom, Australia, Italy, and Switzerland. Antecedents to the community development movement were also found in the settlements and neighborhood houses started in London in the 1880s, and in the community councils set up in the northeastern United States and Canada (United Nations 1955: 20–1). Although the U.N. report noted that the usefulness of these models was limited in underdeveloped countries, it seemed clear that the community development movement was stimulated by U.N. desires to have Third World countries emulate the development trajectories of developed Western democracies.

Community development was defined as "a process designed to create conditions of economic and social progress for the whole community with its active participation and the fullest possible reliance upon the community's initiative" (United States 1955: 6). This statement notwithstanding, participation was never made the centerpiece of the community development movement, in the way it later became the cornerstone of the primary health care movement. Community development was perceived as being intersectoral, involving all governmental agencies and institutions working together with local people and multilateral agencies for the benefit of rural communities. Ideally, U.N. specialists hoped, the communities themselves would take the initiative for particular development projects, but in the absence of community motivation outside influence would be preferable to inaction. Community development proponents stressed that projects would be more likely to succeed with than without the involvement of community members, but they also suggested that development efforts should not be made contingent upon the participation of community members. In other words, participation was preferable, but not essential.

The U.N. report suggested that where communities were not involved a "vertical-style" program – designed to provide quick, observable results over a short period of time – might convince skeptical community members of the benefits of working together under government auspices. The report mentions malaria control several times as an excellent way to demonstrate that government programs could be beneficial to the communities. With good planning, they suggested, a malaria program would be quickly followed by a vaccination or other public health campaign to keep community members interested and active in governmental public health programs (United Nations 1955: 29).

These early efforts to induce community participation were rather clumsy. Costa Rican health workers interviewed about the U.N. malaria control programs often mentioned them as the first systematic attempts at enlisting the principles of community participation in health on a national scale. The malaria control program began in the early 1950s. It entailed house-to-house spraying of DDT (well before the adverse health and environmental effects of DDT became known). The spraying was unpopular among rural homeowners, who objected to the unsightly residue left on their walls. Program coordinators recruited *colaboradores voluntarios* (volunteer collaborators; the prototype for later village health workers) in rural areas where spraying was scheduled (mainly lowland regions where the *Anopheles* mosquito thrived). The *colaboradores* were to explain the importance of spraying to community members, to instruct them not to clean the walls of their homes after they had been sprayed with DDT, and to convince them to consume the anti-malarial treatments dispensed by health workers.

In La Chira, the lowland community in Limón province where I worked, an elderly woman told me about the malaria control campaign. At first the spraying took place every two weeks, then every three weeks, then every month, then every two or three months, then once a year until finally the sprayers never returned. People had to remove all the furniture and dishes from their houses each time they were sprayed. The spray left dust over everything, and ruined walls and floors. If people refused the spraying, they would be fined: "Many people put their feet down and refused to give permission, said they didn't want anyone dirtying their houses. The sprayers said 'Fine' and went to Guápiles and filed a report. Right away they were sent back with an order that they must open their houses to the sprayers, or else." Other community members grudgingly allowed the sprayers to do their jobs, but treated them badly. "Oh, how those poor people suffered," she said of the anti-malaria workers.

The community collaborators employed in the malaria control program illustrate what community participation meant in the 1950s: collaborators were recruited by officials of the central government to convince community members to do voluntarily what they were required to do by law. Initiative for the program did not originate within the communities; in fact, community members often had little desire to comply with the program. These antecedents to contemporary community participation programs demonstrate that: (1) the initiative for development programs could come from outside the community, justified by the conviction that the program was for the community's own benefit; (2) governments and international agencies gave themselves the prerogative to define what constituted "participation" without input from the communities themselves; (3) communities had no choice about whether to participate in government-inspired programs; and (4) compliance with the government program was defined as "participating," while refusing to cooperate was a crime.

The United Nations community development movement was also designed (although perhaps not intentionally) to promote the political model which existed in the developed Western democracies. United Nations representatives wanted rural peoples to participate more actively in electoral politics, reasoning that their involvement in governmental decision-making processes would turn rural peasants, tribal peoples, and other marginal residents into "effective" citizens. The point of view expressed in the United Nations report implied that rural peoples who do not vote in national elections or vie for elected office are not participating in political processes. Yet contrary to the report's supposition that citizen participation was lacking, rural Central Americans have a long history of trying to influence the power structure. Twenty years before the 1950s community development era, many participated actively in labor organizations, especially on United Fruit Company's banana plantations where they agitated for better living conditions. The prototypical Central American land dispute, cases of which date back to the colonial period, could be considered another instance of citizen participation; the long history of land battles shows continuous tension between peasants and landholding (and office-holding) elites.

The differences between the kind of participation envisioned in the United Nations report and these other forms of participation have been distinguished into "conventional" and "unconventional" forms of political participation (Seligson and Booth 1976: 101). In essence, participation condoned by the state is conventional, whereas participation opposed by the state (for example, "strikes, protests, riots, and rural and urban land invasions") is unconventional. This distinction raises questions about how participation is defined and which interest groups are served by the definition. If political participation is defined broadly, as "behavior...intended to influence the political system, be it at the national, regional, or communal level" (Seligson and Booth 1976: 96), then the outlook expressed in the United Nations report seems too narrow, because political participation can obviously take non-electoral forms. Seligson and Booth, writing about political participation in Latin America, say, "Recent studies on rural participation have dispelled the commonly held notion that peasants are politically inert in all but revolutionary circumstances" (1976: 97). In fact, the very existence of a distinction between "conventional" and "unconventional" forms of participation both derives from and demonstrates the state's hegemony over the concept of participation: if the state did not define some forms of participation as "legitimate," political scientists would not need to form a separate analytic category for "unconventional" forms of participation. The United Nations, perhaps unwittingly, contributed to the process of increasing state control over the concept of community participation.

The underlying premise of the United Nations community development movement was that unconventional forms of participation were undemocratic, and that social activism outside the electoral framework was an unacceptable means of working toward community development. Because the United Nations is composed of government-appointed representatives, U.N. resolutions represent the interests of formally organized governments over unincorporated social movements. The community development movement was no exception. Its adherents assumed that governments had both the power and the right to define what would constitute community participation, and to exclude popular social groups from the process.

The community development movement was not intended to affect the power structure within individual countries; like many participation programs which would follow, its impact was mainly symbolic. Groups "working collectively to solve problems not handled by government" (Seligson and Booth 1976: 96), like labor organizations and *ad hoc* social movements, did not secure any better influence over politicians than before the community development movement began. The major difference was that now individual states could count on multilateral agencies like the United Nations to support their control over the process of rural development.

United Nations agencies are prohibited from becoming involved in the internal political processes of member countries, although members of course realize that politics affects the implementation of U.N.

resolutions. Statements made with respect to community development reflect this awareness. For example, one report acknowledges that most governments will want to schedule community development programs so as "to achieve results within a brief period (say three to five years) which will create in people confidence that they can obtain higher levels of living" (United Nations 1955: 12). In other words, governments want quick results to show that the office-holding administration is capable of benefiting its constituents. The immediate political payoffs of community development projects were undoubtedly very important to governments and certainly influenced the timing and implementation of projects in many countries. The potential of development programs to generate political capital is an important consideration, which will surface again when we discuss the primary health care movement of the 1970s.

The United Nations community development program was designed to promote local-level political and social development, but now, 30 years later, it cannot be judged a success. The program "had little eye for the different socio-economic and political contexts" of different countries and communities (DeKadt 1982: 574). It viewed communities as homogeneous collections of individuals, forgetting that individual community members had different degrees of control over productive resources and hence disparate (often opposing) interests, and that they would not necessarily share the same ideas of what constituted development. The community development movement sought to revitalize what was presumed to be the villagers' "natural qualities and capabilities for decision making and cooperative action," even when there was no evidence that such a condition had ever existed (Foster 1982: 190). Rural life was romanticized and its political dimensions left unexplored. As DeKadt says, the program "failed to understand the fundamental social – and political – dynamics of communities in many parts of the world" (1982: 574).

The community development movement marked the first time a multilateral organization mentioned the importance of involving community members in the process of development. The vision of community participation which emerged, however, was paternalistic, opportunist, and unsophisticated when compared with today's myriad renditions of what community participation is and can be. In the 1950s, community participation was viewed as a desirable – yet dispensable – component of government-inspired development programs. Governments were seen as the ultimate arbiters of what would and would not constitute active, acceptable community participation, much as they decided which development programs would be implemented and how. Communities were expected to cooperate with government efforts, but, barring active cooperation, they were expected at least to appreciate governmental efforts. In addition, community members were expected to "progress" politically through increased participation in the local, regional, and national electoral processes. All of these factors contributed to a particular vision of community participation in development as a process defined and controlled by governments, to enlist local support for government plans and projects, to obtain cheap labor for building rural infrastructure, and to extend the dynamics of national politics into rural areas. Only later did community participation programs begin to emphasize the role of local communities in diagnosing community needs and planning development projects. In the 1950s, the dominant philosophy was that government knows best.

In the mid-1970s, the United Nations made another explicit attempt to capture the concept of popular participation, to claim it and place it squarely within the purview of United Nations activities. Their lengthy, carefully documented study "attempts to define the concept of popular participation through examination of its application in present-day development efforts, linking theory to practice by deriving theory from observed experience" (United Nations 1975: 3). The definition they offered centers around "active involvement in decision making" and is supposedly value free (United Nations 1975: 7–8). This declaration notwithstanding, the document contains a number of implicit directives about appropriate and advisable forms of government. It is an ideological treatise that reveals something about the definitions of "participation" being constructed during those years.

To give just one example, the document assumes that participation should be institutionalized through government, and that governments will be concerned with maintaining the status quo. Therefore it offers assurances designed to make popular participation appeal to national leaders:

The most visible benefit of increased popular participation is the elimination of popular resistance to decisions. Should the leaders' actions not be accepted and provoke massive popular resistance, the fabric of political order could be threatened. (United Nations 1975: 11)

"Resistance" is thus counterposed to "participation"; the former is unacceptable while the latter is desirable. This characterization, of course, represents the views of political rulers and elite classes, not of those doing the resisting. It offers "participation" as a reformist strategy, an antidote to anti-government activity.

The United Nations stated very explicitly that its goal was to define firmly the concept of participation. In doing so the agency took a political stance, eliminating alternative definitions which would allow "resistance" as a form of participation, and promoting forms of participation which were institutionalized through governmental channels and supported the political status quo. During the late 1970s many development agencies acted similarly, articulating circumscribed definitions of participation and proclaiming themselves the most appropriate avenues for implementing strategies of "participatory development."

Financing Latin American development: the Inter-American Development Bank

Until the 1960s, the Rockefeller Foundation, the Institute of Inter-American Affairs, and United Fruit Company were the primary U.S. organizations active in health in Central America. United States involvement in Latin American development reached new levels with President Kennedy's Alliance for Progress, adopted by the countries of the Inter-American system at a Special Meeting of the Inter-American Economic and Social Council held in Punta del Este, Uruguay, in August, 1961. The Alliance for Progress was motivated, in large part, by U.S. fears that the 1959 Cuban revolution would be exported to other Latin American countries. Part of the Alliance for Progress strategy involved increased external financing for Latin American development projects, including a program of social development which was to be coordinated by the Social Progress Trust Fund of the Inter-American Development Bank. The amount of money suddenly available to Latin American governments was impressive: "Measured in terms of net disbursements, [this financing] rose from US$155 million in 1960 and an average of US$374 million a year in 1956–60 to US$1,139 million in 1961 and an average of US$980 million in 1961–64" (Inter-American Development Bank [IADB] 1969:79). The money came from an assortment of public and private, multilateral and bilateral, organizations, with the United States providing the major share of funding to Latin American countries. For a few years, a large percentage of these funds went to social projects including health and sanitation.

The Inter-American Development Bank (established in 1960) had a Social Progress Trust Fund which loaned money for projects like land settlement and improved land use, low-income housing, community water supplies and sanitation, and facilities for advanced education and training related to economic and social development. Fully 58 percent of the Bank's loans went into such areas in 1962, while the remainder financed projects in agriculture and industry (DeWitt 1977: 16). DeWitt points out that loans to the social sector were eventually limited by restrictions specifying that aid money must be spent either purchasing goods produced by donor nations or producing goods which would be consumed in donor nations (1977: 20). Such clauses encouraged the Bank to fund export-oriented rather than social projects. This shift is obvious when the Bank's lending record from 1961 to the mid-1980s is reviewed.

By 1965 the Bank's lending policy had shifted from social projects to industrial and infrastructural development loans to the transportation, communications, mining and industrial sectors (DeWitt 1977: 16). After those first few years, the Bank would never again offer large loans to the social sector. By the mid-1970s the individual country summaries contained in the Bank's annual reports ceased to mention the country's standing on social indicators such as health, education, or agriculture. And by 1983 the Bank's reports focused exclusively on each country's standing within the international economy, on economic growth, employment, trade, exports, economic policy, debt servicing and balance of payments.

Costa Rica was able to take advantage of the Bank's 1960s lending policies to underwrite some of its well-known social welfare programs in the areas of housing and health. The Instituto Nacional de Vivienda y Urbanización (INVU) obtained a $3·5 million loan in 1961 to erect an estimated 38,500 low-income housing units over the next two decades. In 1964 the Bank lent another $1·3 million to the agency for construction of housing in rural and urban areas. INVU was then and continues to be an important symbol of the state's commitment to social welfare.

In accordance with its capitalist credo, the Bank proposed fee-for-service solutions to basic problems of service accessibility. A case in point is how the Bank proposed to extend potable water supplies. The Inter-American Development Bank, the U.S. Agency for International Development (AID), and the Export-Import Bank worked together in Latin America in the early 1960s to construct and expand potable water supplies and sewage systems, continuing the priorities set by the Institute of Inter-American Affairs twenty years earlier. U.S. bilateral agencies had provided most of the external aid for environmental sanitation programs until this time; in the early 1960s, however, the United States turned over its programs to the multilateral health and lending agencies such as the Pan American Health Organization and the Inter-American Development Bank (McCamant 1969: 153). The Bank justified this emphasis by noting in 1965 that diseases caused by lack of an adequate water supply were the primary or secondary causes of death in nine Latin American countries, and one of the top three causes of infant mortality in 14 Latin American countries.

The Inter-American Development Bank saw inadequate financing as the root of the water supply problem in Latin America. Policymakers at the Bank reasoned that the Latin American governments were having trouble maintaining and expanding water supply systems because "it was not the prevailing view that these services should be operated on a self-liquidating basis, [therefore] the problem of direct compensation for services rendered was usually not considered to be of fundamental importance" (IADB 1969: 133). In other words, the Bank preferred that beneficiaries, not states, should pay for water. Eventually the Bank convinced many of the governments receiving loans that people should buy water. It later credited its policies with "the now widespread acceptance of the view that water supply and sewage services must be operated on a self-liquidating basis and with adequate provision for amortization, depreciation, maintenance and expansion, whenever possible" (IADB 1969: 134). The Bank, together with AID and the Export-Import Bank, changed the attitude toward water all over Latin America. Previously considered a government-sponsored service (at least in the more affluent areas of urban Latin America), these agencies turned water into a commodity for which people were expected to pay.

Costa Rica, one of the smallest countries in Latin America and one with a relatively good water system, received just a fraction of the $458 million which the Bank loaned to Latin America for water and sewage systems between 1961 and 1969. The Bank estimated in 1962 that 98 percent of urban residents and 50 percent of rural residents in Costa Rica had access to potable water, though only 44 percent of urban residents and less than 5 percent of rural residents had access to sewage service (IADB 1962: 237). Costa Rica therefore received a lower priority than other, more needy recipients of Bank loans. Nonetheless, in 1961 Costa Rica established a semi-autonomous governmental agency called the Servicio Nacional de Acueductos y Alcantarillados (SNAA) which was "charged with gradually taking over the technical, administrative and financial phases, including the establishment of rates" (IADB 1962: 245). SNAA was the type of agency the Inter-American Development Bank was promoting throughout Latin America. SNAA's development was underwritten by $5·9 million in loans from AID between 1962 and 1965 to expand the potable water system of the capital city of San José. At the same time, the Social Progress Trust Fund lent SNAA $240,000 to prepare "preinvestment" studies of water and sewage project needs in the provincial capitals of Limón, Liberia, and Puntarenas. The Export-Import Bank extended a $4·5 million credit for the improvement of water supplies in metropolitan San José (IADB 1965: 267). Between the housing, water supply, transportation, and communications programs, the Inter-American Development Bank lent Costa Rica $12·6 million for infrastructural development between 1961 and 1964.

Between 1961 and 1974, the primary objective of the Bank was to promote Latin American economic integration, a policy which would increase the investment and export opportunities for U.S. businesses (DeWitt 1977: 58). Only 8·5 percent of the loans provided to Costa Rica by the Inter-American Development Bank were directed to public health projects during this period. Nonetheless, the Bank's role in Costa Rican health care was significant for several reasons. First, the Bank probably did contribute to economic growth and improved labor productivity when it provided money for the construction of Costa Rica's nationwide potable water system, unparalleled in Latin America. Clean drinking water has enabled Costa Rica to reduce the incidence of water-borne and diarrheal diseases, reducing general and infant morbidity and mortality. Second, the Bank helped turn water into a commodity in Costa Rica, thus creating a forum for tensions which continue to the present day between SNAA and its often-dissatisfied customers. As Costa Rica's population and demand for water has grown, SNAA has never been able to keep pace. Water supplies have been chronically insufficient in many regions of the country, especially during the dry season. Costa Ricans are vociferously critical of these inadequacies, often protesting loudly that the water fees they pay should entitle them to ample and adequate service. Third, even though public health loans were a small proportion of the Bank's overall lending packages, other Bank loans allowed the state to reallocate money for health improvements. For example, when the Alliance for Progress was getting underway in 1961, the Costa Rican Legislative Assembly approved a plan to extend social security coverage to the entire population, thereby widening the circle of Costa Rican citizens covered by state health and disability services. Also, virtually all of Costa Rica's rural health programs throughout the years have been financed by international agencies. The Bank may not have given a lot of money to health, but along with the loans, grants, and technical assistance provided by other international agencies, such aid was instrumental in providing low-cost health and sanitation facilities to rural regions.

In 1965 the Bank's Annual Report expressed a twofold rationale for providing loans to improve environmental sanitation and health: the first motive was humanitarian, to improve the health status of the impoverished majority; the second motive was utilitarian, to stave off social unrest among the masses of Latin American citizens who have lived without basic sanitary services: "These vital but unattended [health] needs lead to social discontent and tensions, which in turn discourage efforts to accelerate economic development, improve labor productivity and enable the population to participate more effectively in the advantages of modern life" (IADB 1965: 77).

By 1969 the Bank shed its altruistic and humanitarian rationale for funding health improvements. Its reports stressed instead that an investment in health was an investment in "human capital formation" (IADB 1969: 113). "Human capital formation" was a phrase used by economists who proposed that investments in workers' health, nutritional, and educational status could be justified by an expected increase in their labor participation and productivity. Thus, the Bank reasoned, controlling debilitating diseases would contribute to higher economic yields. The Bank's blunt materialism sounds callous to those who believe that health should be a strictly humanitarian issue. The "human capital" philosophy treats human beings as commodities, valued mainly for their contribution to production as measured in the marketplace. But for the development agencies operating in Latin America in the 1960s, health was a means to economic growth, and the agencies were influenced by modernization theories that assumed economic growth would enable further social development (see Rostow 1960). As the Inter-American Development Bank became more interested in economic indicators and less in social development, it played down the humanitarian veneer and began to phrase traditionally social concerns – like health – in economic terms.

The view of community participation in health held by the Inter-American Development Bank during this period can only be inferred. The Bank makes no explicit reference to participation in health, but its philosophy toward water financing makes clear that the populace should expect to pay for adequate water supply and sewage disposal systems. Documents published by the Bank also imply that people could expect to participate in the benefits of improved health and sanitation by living longer, healthier lives and eventually by enjoying the higher standard of living which Bank policymakers presumed would result from their lending policies.

The modernization theory of development, associated with Walt Rostow (1960), provided the theoretical justification for many international development policies enacted in the early 1960s. The theory stressed economic growth, insisting that social equity would follow naturally from increases in the gross national product. Modernization theory disapproved of government-subsidized health programs, preferring instead to substitute fee-for-service programs where possible. The theory could justify significant investments in health only in areas where high labor productivity was critical to economic growth, and where health status was poor. The health programs enacted by U.S.

agencies in Latin America in the early 1960s show how the political and economic priorities of U.S. academicians and commercial interests came to dominate the ideology of health care. In the 1940s, foreign assistance programs were rationalized to U.S. audiences using the argument of military preparedness and to Latin American audiences on the basis of humanitarian neighborliness. In the Cold War context of the 1950s, sociopolitical justifications were given center stage as stated U.S. foreign policy strove to promote democratic regimes throughout Latin America. And in the late 1960s and early 1970s, a changing political climate in the United States led policymakers to articulate yet other justifications for international health programs.

Meanwhile, as U.S. interests came to dominate the direction of rural health policy in Costa Rica and throughout Latin America, the chronically poor states of the region were pleased to accept foreign financing for what were, in their eyes, low-priority social programs. Accepting U.S. generosity allowed them to reap public relations benefits and consolidate their political bases.

The United States Agency for International Development (AID)

The Agency for International Development (formerly the International Cooperation Administration) has been the principal U.S. bilateral agency responsible for international health programs since the mid-1960s. Although the United States government contributes substantially to multilateral agencies involved in health (such as the World Health Organization), the U.S. government has complete budgetary and policy control over AID. One of the agency's goals in the early 1960s was to administer Alliance for Progress development efforts in Latin America. Because those programs emphasized economic growth rather than social infrastructure, health was not then a major priority of AID. This changed in the 1970s, however, with the introduction and popularity of concepts such as primary health care, basic needs, and community participation. In the mid-1970s, primary health care became AID's highest health priority.

In the early 1960s when our overall AID strategy stressed attempts to raise GNP, direct health sector assistance decreased. During this period much of AID's large professional health and sanitation staff left the Agency or moved into other fields... In the 1970s, with the shift in emphasis away from GNP growth to a "basic human needs" approach to development, interest in the social sectors revived, with a particular concern to find ways to adapt the developed world's expensive high technology health system so as to be relevant to health problems of poor countries. (Joseph 1980: 72–3)

Whereas in 1971 AID was funding only one low-cost health care delivery program, by 1975 it was assisting 25 such programs (AID 1975: 17), and community participation had become an indispensable component of its development strategy. Agency documents asserted, "Programs most likely to succeed, and which receive highest priority emphasis under the congressional mandate and AID policy, are those involving the active and effective participation of the poor in all facets of the development process" (AID 1975: 7).

The idea of community participation surfaced at this time with the passage of Title IX of the U.S. Foreign Assistance Act, enacted by Congress during the Vietnam war.

Popular participation in development: Title IX of the U.S. Foreign Assistance Act

By the mid-1960s, U.S. policymakers were beginning to question the assumption that economic growth alone would lead to social justice in the Third World. The Alliance for Progress, still in force then, had been inspired by the conviction that "(1) sustained economic growth would set in motion social and political development, (2) most underdeveloped countries were anxious to realize economic growth and, therefore, (3) it would be appropriate to employ academic theories of economics as the bases for the criteria for giving aid" (Hapgood 1969: 59). All too often in the 1960s, however, U.S. policymakers saw their foreign assistance dollars help consolidate the power of the rich, while the vast majority of Third World citizens continued to live in poverty. Some concerned legislators speculated that the situation could be alleviated by involving the poor more directly in policy deliberations. In Latin America, they reasoned, oligarchies and military governments could be made more accountable to the poor by making U.S. foreign aid contingent on the participation of the poor in decision-making for development. The idea of popular participation was born anew with these trends.

Bilateral U.S. foreign aid efforts began to support popular participation in development in the late 1960s, when Congress passed the Title IX amendment to the Foreign Assistance Act of 1961. By examining the rhetoric and underlying ideology of Title IX, rather than its actual effects, we can begin to understand policymakers' competing notions of "democracy," "participation," and the functions of U.S. foreign aid. Prior to Title IX, U.S. foreign aid had been directed almost exclusively at economic growth. Title IX, in contrast, specified that the U.S. bilateral aid programs, especially the programs administered by AID, should concern themselves with political development as well; that is, with building democratic institutions and training future democratic leaders. Most importantly, Title IX stated that "emphasis shall be placed on assuring maximum participation in the task of economic development on the part of the people of the developing countries, through the encouragement of democratic private and local governmental institutions" (Hapgood 1969: xiii). Earlier aid programs had occasionally mentioned the importance of building democracy in the Third World, but the Title IX amendment was the first time that U.S. foreign aid programs explicitly endorsed popular participation as a means to achieve democratic political institutions. There are several explanations for why this particular policy was enacted when it was, in the late 1960s.

U.S. involvement in the Vietnam war had escalated dramatically under the Johnson administration. The war was increasingly unpopular at home, and strong dissent was voiced from many sectors of U.S. society. Criticism was directed at U.S. foreign policy, which some perceived as overemphasizing military and economic exploitation of Third World countries while not sharing the benefits of U.S. wealth and technological superiority. Heightened political awareness in the United States pressured lawmakers to respond to domestic social unrest, in part by making U.S. foreign policy more responsive to popular concerns. By promoting popular participation abroad, Congress could convey a coded message to U.S. constituents that it would be equally responsive to domestic opinions about civil rights, the Vietnam War, and other pressing national issues. Congressman Donald Fraser, the House Democrat from Minnesota who introduced the Title IX legislation, testified before Congress:

In America today, there is deep apprehension among the people over the nature of our present involvement overseas and anguished uncertainty about the shape of involvements in the future. A positive goal consistent with American ideals and shared by most of the people of the world must be found. Surely sound health of the human body is such a goal. It is above and beyond politics, it is universally beneficial, and has been proven to be attainable. (United States Congress 1971: 2)

Fraser obviously thought that increasing social unrest at home (an "unconventional" form of participation in political decision-making) could be alleviated by putting greater emphasis on popular participation abroad. A report assessing the impact of Title IX said, "It is no coincidence that Title IX was written into the Foreign Assistance Act at a time when Americans were trying to increase popular participation within the United States itself" (Hapgood 1969: 19).

In 1968, two years after Title IX was signed into law, some Congresspeople were concerned that the legislation had had little impact abroad. Money was made available to hold a six-week conference at the Massachusetts Institute of Technology (MIT), attended by AID representatives and university scholars, to assess the impact of Title IX and to analyze ways to expedite implementation. The resulting document (Hapgood 1969) offers a frank and explicit discussion of the political motivations guiding formulation of U.S. foreign policy. It outlines the competing interest groups potentially affected by Title IX legislation, illustrating how arguments in support of the amendment were carefully "packaged" to address the concerns of these various groups. The conferees' recommendations for how to juggle these various interests reveal a great deal about U.S. foreign policy priorities, leading to the conclusion that Title IX was a piece of legislation flexible enough to serve the distinct ends of several opposing interest groups. Title IX was designed to project the image – both abroad and at home – that the U.S. Congress was eager to promote democratic values through its foreign assistance programs. However, U.S. lawmakers knew they would have to exempt many countries from Title IX conditions when U.S. commercial or military interests would potentially be affected. As the central feature of Title IX, popular participation was a kaleidoscopic concept, distorting certain U.S. objectives abroad while creating a beautifully refracted image at home.

Domestic popular and Congressional support for foreign aid had been wavering in the late 1960s, and Congressman Fraser apparently thought that his legislation would help reverse that trend. Title IX could do this in three ways: (1) by creating a bilateral aid program completely under the budgetary discretion of the U.S. Congress, rather than relying on multilateral aid agencies like the United Nations to disperse U.S. funds; (2) by adding a humanitarian component to U.S. foreign aid, thereby diverting public attention from the imperial or exploitative aspects of other foreign assistance programs and giving Congressmen the moral grounds to support continued U.S. foreign aid, as well as giving them something to feel proud of when speaking to their constituents; (3) by reinforcing the rhetoric of American commitment to democratic ideals, thus perhaps reducing public uneasiness over U.S. involvement in Vietnam. In the late 1960s a budget-conscious Congress was inclined to reduce its contributions to international organizations as well as to individual countries (with the exception of strategically important countries like Vietnam) (Quimby 1971:32). Congress was uncomfortable about its large contributions to multilateral organizations like the United Nations, where it had relatively little control over programs and budget allocations. Supporters argued that Title IX would be an inexpensive way to foster good will toward the U.S. around the globe while keeping

NEW A.I.D. DANCE:
"THE TITLE NINE CRUNCH"

"SWING YOUR PARTNER, SWING YOUR MATE
EVERYONE PARTICIPATE"

Figure 1   Cartoon from Hapgood 1969: 105

the funds strictly under Congressional control. Within a short time, Title IX became a key focus of U.S. foreign policy debate.

Despite all the attention given Title IX, everyone agreed that the amendment had little impact abroad during its first two years as part of the Foreign Assistance Act. Nonetheless, the MIT conferees agreed that Title IX should remain a bilateral program and should not be transferred to multilateral agencies. They said, rather vaguely, that multilateral agencies were "not well equipped to handle Title IX concepts" (Hapgood 1969: 14). Intervening years have proven that the conferees were mistaken, for various United Nations agencies, UNICEF, and the World Bank have adopted popular participation as a development strategy. At that time, however, the conferees obviously thought that the United States needed to keep control over the participation initiative in order to promote a particular image:

We believe it would be a serious error if all U.S. programs with Title IX implications were turned over to multilateral administration ... Such a transfer might ... be damaging to the U.S. image abroad, for it would put the humanitarian programs into the hands of others, leaving the U.S. with the *Realpolitik* programs that cannot be placed in multilateral agencies. (Hapgood 1969: 14)

In other words, the programs initiated under Title IX could act as a counterweight, or even a smokescreen, to divert attention from less popular programs financed by the United States Congress. With Title IX, politicians could point to the "good things" that U.S. foreign aid dollars promoted: public health nurses vaccinating children, Peace Corps volunteers building schools, and agricultural extension officers training farmers to increase crop yields. Such public relations propaganda could be used to hide the actual distribution of U.S. aid programs. For example, Quimby (1971: 48–9) notes that of the 501 health and sanitation technicians employed by AID in 1967, 197 were in Vietnam and only 34 were working in the whole of Latin America.

The humanitarian component of Title IX arose from an increasing awareness that the earlier U.S. foreign policy emphasis on economic growth could not, in itself, bring about development (Packenham 1973: 99). Title IX was preceded in Latin America by the Alliance for Progress, which channeled large amounts of U.S. money into Latin America. Unfortunately for liberal-minded legislators, many dictators used the Alliance for Progress to pad their pockets at the expense of U.S. taxpayers. In Latin America, a number of right-wing coups in the mid-1960s, combined with the knowledge that little Alliance for Progress money was reaching the neediest citizens, made it difficult for U.S. legislators to justify providing more aid to the region. Some U.S. liberals argued that foreign aid could be used as a tool to redress social imbalances. Rather than accepting the status quo, they said, U.S. foreign aid could create mechanisms to benefit those most in need. This argument appealed to those who sided with the Third World poor against dictatorial rulers. The MIT report said that because the American dream has always been more populist than elitist, traditional American sympathies could be tapped for support of Title IX (Hapgood 1969: 19). Latin America was one important target of the Title IX legislation, since U.S. legislators thought it would be relatively easy to bring about greater degrees of participation in the relatively stable Latin American countries which have been "closely associated with us for many decades and [are] generally within the American economic ambit" (Hapgood 1969: 50). Supporters of Title IX argued that one concrete mechanism for achieving more populist forms of government without disrupting the sovereign power structure in Latin America would be to use U.S. technological advances and technical expertise, together with popular involvement, to build democratic institutions.

Hardliners and Cold War ideologues skeptical of Title IX had to be approached with a different argument. They were told that the principles of Title IX were already accepted by Third World governments, even by those governments not known for their willingness to allow popular participation in democratic decision-making. The MIT document said, "While Title IX goals are not pursued throughout the Third World, it is also true that popular participation is a stated value among most of the region's regimes" (Hapgood 1969:4–5). This line of reasoning contained three implicit arguments which appealed to Title IX skeptics: first, that the United States should not have too much trouble selling Title IX to governments which already embraced such policies in principle (if not in practice); second, that the rhetoric of participation could be valuable on its own merits, and that the policy would not necessarily affect the status quo; third, that Third World governments might appreciate the benefits of giving center stage to a concept which made themselves, as well as the U.S., look more responsive to the needs of their citizens.

The U.S.-based multinational business community had to be assured that passage of Title IX would support, not undermine, the economic growth goals of U.S. foreign aid (Hapgood 1969:1). Supporters of Title IX tried to convince U.S. commercial interests that money spent to enhance participation would not threaten their Third World investments, even when those investments were tied to undemocratic regimes. The MIT conferees argued that economic growth and popular participation were compatible goals, which together would "form the twin pillars of the foreign assistance program" (Hapgood 1969; 1). The MIT report encouraged the business community not to jump to conclusions about the effects of implementing Title IX. Title IX could, they suggested, have a positive impact on U.S. business interests by diffusing political unrest in oligarchic countries from which U.S. raw materials are obtained (Hapgood 1969:56–7). Furthermore:

Title IX may have utility, even where short and middle run U.S. security interests are engaged, (a) if timely reforms will help preserve our access to bases and communications; (b) if a regime, hard pressed by externally supported insurgency, needs to gain more popular support and is likely to obtain it by extending participation; or (c) if a change in regime is the only way of obtaining enough popular support to deal with the nation. (Hapgood 1969: 66)

Where economic growth and the vitality of U.S. investments abroad might be threatened by Title IX mandates, the pragmatic MIT conferees were willing to consider certain exceptions. Examples of cases which might qualify for exemptions from Title IX were: countries with U.S. military bases or of strategic importance (such as those bordering communist states; this policy was called "perimeter containment"), countries whose governmental structure was threatened by a communist insurgency, or countries in which U.S. business has strong economic interests. In cases where increased public participation might result in calls for the nationalization of U.S. business enterprises, the conferees agreed that it would be better to sacrifice Title IX (Hapgood 1969: 56–7).

This was realistic political forecasting in action: the conferees conceded that U.S. business interests, together with national elites in Third World countries, could argue successfully that Title IX should not be pursued in particular countries when it might pose a threat to their investments. Essentially, they promised that U.S. leaders of multinational corporations could simply inform the Department of State or AID if they thought Title IX would adversely affect their economic affairs in Third World nations; in such cases, Title IX mandates would not be pursued.

The Title IX amendment was subtitled "Utilization of democratic institutions in development." Architects of the legislation reasoned that Title IX could promote political development by supporting "democratic institutions," such as cooperatives, labor unions, community development organizations, and training facilities for potential leaders. The net effect of such action would be to fight communism by using constructive examples of what "democratic" governments could offer. The Cold War was still underway, but the social consciousness of the 1960s called for more accommodating, less divisive, approaches to building democracy in the Third World. According to the MIT conference participants:

The Congress and AID explicitly reject any insistence upon the establishment of carbon copies of American or Western institutions. However, programs and activities aimed at fostering democratic public and private institutions, at the local, provincial and national levels, should work toward results along these lines ... Institutions should be established and strengthened which are open to the citizens they service, receptive to influence from below, sensitive to requirements and aspirations, and which, in sum, lead to a broadened base of decision-making and reflect a democratic organization of popular efforts. (Hapgood 1969: 29–30)

Other analysts disagree with the assertion that Title IX was not designed to re-create Third World countries in the image of the United States. For example, anthropologist Richard Adams argued that the definition of political development offered by some supporters of Title IX was ethnocentric. Their definition suggests, he said, "that political systems should be stable, that they should involve popular participation, and be 'responsive to the wishes of the people'." He lambasted U.S. political scientists who implied "that political development occurs when other governments become more like ours so that they act more like we do" (Adams 1968: 205).

The idea of "participation" gained prominence as U.S. foreign policy came increasingly to emphasize the need for building democratic political institutions around the world. Policymakers seemed intuitively to feel that increased participation (especially political – i.e., electoral – participation) would result in the strengthening of democratic regimes. Title IX contained the first explicit U.S. foreign policy attempt to equate democracy with participation. Congress hoped that they could mold Third World countries to the U.S. image by promoting political institutions and mechanisms common in the United States. The correlation was drawn so closely that Packenham said "the distinctions which Title IX supporters attempted to draw between 'popular participation' and democracy sometimes were...little more than verbal sleights of hand" (1973: 106). But this fundamental aspect of Title IX contained an inherent contradiction: while it claimed to respect the differences between political structures in various countries, it also "instructed that AID encourage democratic institutions and support democratic trends" (Packenham 1973: 105).

There are at least two obvious problems with the contention that participation is synonymous with U.S.-styled representative democracy. First, elections are not the *sine qua non* of true democracy: a choice among non-democratic candidates is not necessarily much better than no choice at all, and elected leaders do not necessarily respond to the popular will any more readily than leaders installed through less democratic means (El Salvador in the 1980s was a case in point). Second, when participation is defined "conventionally," by involvement in government-sanctioned projects and programs, it is, *de facto*, a form of cooptation; it does not allow people to choose or legitimize their own forms of political participation.

The MIT conferees were aware of some of these contradictions, although they did not explore the possibility that the fundamental contradiction was not in the wording of Title IX, but in the goals of U.S. foreign policy. Their statement on this topic, written in the passive voice and using benign euphemisms for social unrest, is uncharacteristically noncommittal:

> To broaden participation indiscriminately without regard for improving the apparatus which already exists or without being able to increase resource availabilities to respond to the pressures of increased participation may very well bring to the system more instability than it can support. This risk is said to exist in those highly-politicized, low-income countries whose economies and socio-political structure would be unable to meet the demands which broadened participation could generate. (Hapgood 1969: 31)

By supporting popular participation in countries where it had not existed before, Congress and AID were implicitly endorsing a strategy that potentially endangered political stability. By promoting popular participation, they were adopting (or providing) the rhetoric used to mobilize anti-government forces in some countries. In fact, the term "popular participation" was not utilized by Central American governments, because in Spanish *participación popular* is a phrase associated with leftist organizers; it implies that states are not otherwise responsive to the popular sectors of society. Some critics of participation would later argue that Congress and AID had, unintentionally, supported anti-democratic tendencies by supporting popular participation.

MIT conferees and Title IX proponents did not explicitly acknowledge that by creating exemptions for U.S. military and business interests in the Third World, they were in some cases actually impeding the creation of more democratic forms of government. Examples from Central America provide numerous instances of such contradictions: the United Fruit Company was behind a U.S.-sponsored coup to oust the Arbenz government in Guatemala in 1954; since then the United States has supported several anti-participatory military dictators there (Schlesinger and Kinzer 1982); U.S. military occupation of Nicaragua in the 1920s and 1930s led to the installation of the elitist and anti-participatory Somoza dynasty, and U.S. policy toward the Sandinistas in the 1980s sought the overthrow of a government which had made popular participation a cornerstone of its social policy (see Donahue 1986; Braveman and Mora 1987). While certain U.S. lawmakers undoubtedly believed that Title IX would lead to the creation of more democratic forms of government, in practice it was obvious that popular participation would not take precedence over other U.S. interests.

Title IX was important for at least two reasons. First, it established the symbolic equation between democracy and participation as a stated goal of U.S. foreign policy. The correspondence between these two concepts continues to surface, both implicitly and explicitly, in development literature and national development plans written from the late 1960s to the present. The second lesson of Title IX is that Congress used the rhetoric of participation as part of a public-relations campaign to enhance the U.S. image at home and to draw attention away from the other, less popular tasks then facing the foreign assistance committees of the U.S. Congress. Congressional proponents of Title IX did not necessarily try consciously to delude their constituents; they sincerely sought to humanize U.S. foreign policy, but without disrupting the essential socioeconomic or political structures of affected countries.

AID and Title IX were not solely responsible for inventing the strategy which catapulted community participation to center stage in the 1970s. Independent but analogous developments were, no doubt, occurring simultaneously in other agencies (such as the World Bank, the

International Monetary Fund, and the World Health Organization). There are indications, however, that AID was taking a greater role behind the scenes in shaping multilateral policy initiatives in the late 1970s and early 1980s, and coordination among donor agencies was becoming more common. For example, one analyst said, in a report prepared for the President's Task Force on International Private Enterprise:

AID's greatest prospects for effective policy impact [in promoting the private sector] appear to be when the policy framework is defined by the IMF/World Bank and the LDC [less developed country] Government. Then AID can select particular policy areas for dialogue, financing, and other forms of assistance. (Muscat 1984: 246)

In spite of the Agency's professed commitment to respect national sovereignty and promote self-sufficiency, the U.S. government used its clout to reinforce and strengthen policies compatible with U.S. business and political interests. The dynamic dialogue among donor agencies contributed, then as now, to the formulation and maintenance of a hegemonic international political ideology of health, discussed in greater detail in the following chapter.

4   The primary health care movement and the political ideology of participation in health

Every so often an innovative new health strategy promises to revolutionize the world's health profile. So it was with the primary health care (PHC) movement of the 1970s. PHC became famous following the Alma Ata Conference sponsored by the World Health Organization and UNICEF in the Soviet Union in 1977, where conferees coined the now-famous slogan, "Health for all by the year 2000." The PHC strategy was based on the realization that health problems exacting the highest toll on Third World peoples could be alleviated with relatively simple health and sanitary measures, assuming that dispersed rural populations could be given access to such services. (The U.S. Agency for International Development estimated that less than 20 percent of people in developing countries had access to basic health services in 1980 [AID 1980: 10].) Two components of the PHC strategy were designed to meet these needs: (1) extending basic health services (such as immunization, sanitation, family planning, and nutritional surveillance) to underserved areas of less-developed countries; and (2) using community participation to improve health.

The primary health care strategy was indeed an improvement over medical models then prevailing in the developing world. Earlier initiatives emphasized costly, urban, hospital-based, curative services while PHC emphasized rural, community-based, low-cost, preventative services to be provided by village health workers, paraprofessional health assistants, or nursing auxiliaries. Primary health programs provided the impetus for many Third World governments to expand their health infrastructures, building rural health posts and secondary care clinics throughout the countryside. In the first few years after PHC became popular, many countries built hundreds of small rural health centers, making modern medical attention available to rural residents for the first time. The construction was financed, in many Latin American cases, with loans and grants from donor agencies including WHO, AID, and UNICEF.

Primary health care initiatives also necessitated a revamping of health personnel and training. In Latin America, as in all other parts of the world, doctors are reluctant or unwilling to practice in rural areas. This, combined with the awareness that doctors are overqualified for the simple tasks of PHC, led WHO and UNICEF to promote community health workers as the front-line providers of primary health services in rural areas. These paraprofessionals received anything from a few months to a year of instruction before being posted to underserved regions of their countries, where they immunized children, promoted environmental sanitation and personal hygiene through community education, monitored child development and nutritional status, taught oral rehydration therapy, followed up on people under treatment for chronic diseases such as tuberculosis and diabetes, treated simple afflictions, and referred people to doctors for more specialized care.

While PHC had certain obvious advantages over earlier models of providing medical care, nowhere has the implementation of PHC proceeded smoothly. The advantages and disadvantages of PHC initiatives are constantly being revised and negotiated as program plans unfold and problems emerge. This process of negotiation can be interpreted as a reflection of underlying ideological and political struggles over the very organization of society. The ideological differences which underlay disagreements over the subject of community participation in health are the focus of this chapter.

The Alma Ata Conference marked the beginning of a virtual explosion of interest in the subject of participation in health. All the major international agencies issued documents analyzing community participation in primary health care: the Pan American Health Organization (1978a, 1984), UNICEF (1982), the United Nations Research Institute for Social Development (1983), and AID (Parlato and Favin 1982; Martin 1983), not to mention countless articles appearing in the Bulletin of the Pan American Health Organization and other WHO publications. Governments were encouraged to establish special units to deal specifically with community participation. Latin American countries anticipated the trend, and some countries had already set up special participation programs before Alma Ata. For example, "statutory participation bodies were set up in the early 1970s in Peru and Chile [under Allende], and somewhat later in Colombia" (DeKadt 1982: 577). Panama's community health program began in 1969 (La Forgia 1985: 56). These units functioned to coordinate domestic participation programs and to foster the impression that countries shared the international agencies' commitment to the PHC strategy.

With such a sweeping reorganization of national health systems, one might have expected that some historical research would be commissioned to assess the strengths and weaknesses of previous governmental attempts to involve rural communities in development projects. However, the international health literature is marred by a conspicuous absence of historical insight. Perfunctory historical sections found in some of the literature trace the concept of participation back only as far as other multilateral development efforts initiated since World War II. Some accounts trace the roots of PHC and community participation only to the mid-1970s and the publication of Newell's *Health by the People* (1975) and Djukanovic and Mach's *Alternative Approaches to Meeting Basic Health Needs* (1975). In other words, the vision of history contained in the literature includes only the ideas and programs emanating from other United Nations agencies. Foster wrote that the short-sightedness resulted from the conviction that "the medical profession [had] developed an innovative approach to development" (1982: 189).

The near-total exclusion of history from the PHC literature reveals more than naive enthusiasm on the part of medical professionals. It also suggests that PHC framers did not think (or could not say) that improvements in health status might be contingent on changes in political organization. For example, the success of China's barefoot doctor program prompted international experts to think about how a similar model might be applied globally, yet few experts analyzed China's health successes in the context of other political developments occurring simultaneously in China (Navarro 1984: 470). By looking only at the history of multilaterally sponsored health and participation programs independent of local political context, the international agencies overlooked the relationship between politics and health. Being ahistorical, then, PHC framers were also apolitical and consequently uncritical. Their style of analysis is consistent with most WHO discourse, which routinely depoliticizes the political dimensions of health, preferring instead to focus on technological health interventions such as immunization or oral rehydration therapies (Navarro 1984: 470).

PHC planners, lacking an historical and political-economic analysis, did not view social struggles as relevant to their attempts to promote community participation in health. They thus excluded from their examples cases where labor unions became involved in health advocacy, where health issues became central issues in political campaigns, where communities organized to protest inadequate public sanitation, and where health workers were assassinated because they were perceived as representatives of a contested political authority. All such examples are relevant to community participation in health, but only if one accepts the premise that communities have the right to initiate efforts to improve health, whether or not such efforts are condoned by national governments or international agencies. The PHC strategy, as outlined in the Alma Ata charter, did not subscribe to this vision of community involvement. The impression left by the Alma Ata charter was that health could be improved without touching the realm of politics.

There are at least four reasons, then, why the PHC literature lacks a historical or political-economic perspective: (1) health planners thought the PHC strategy was new and revolutionary and therefore without historical antecedent; (2) health planners were concerned with maintaining their own jobs as well as with improving world health, thus it benefitted their profession to reinvent the concept of community participation by hiring consultants and commissioning new studies; (3) health planners did not see how various political factors – state organization, government policy, and political partisanship – influenced the organization of health services; (4) health planners ignored how the nature and extent of community participation in health was shaped by social struggles occurring outside the government arena.

Despite the lack of history in the literature, community participation was a new idea in the 1970s only in the sense that the international health agencies then began to promote and finance it on an international scale. As noted earlier, the concept has at least two sets of "conventional" ancestors: the community development movement spearheaded by the United Nations in the 1950s (see Foster [1982] for an analysis of similarities between community development and primary health care); and expansion of the U.S. bilateral Title IX concepts (see Chapter 3) as the participatory strategy got picked up by multilateral aid agencies and applied to various sectors such as agriculture, political organization, education, and health. Incidentally, the concept of participation was also adopted by U.S. academics in the 1970s, especially in political science, where a veritable avalanche of literature was produced (see Booth and Seligson 1978; Seligson and Booth 1979).

A third ancestor to community participation, in the opinion of at least one observer, was the *conscientización* movement popular in Latin American grassroots rural development schemes (DeKadt 1982). *Conscientización* is a concept associated with Paulo Freire's book, *Pedagogy of the Oppressed* (1970), first published in 1968. Freire suggested that adult education and literacy techniques could utilize the life experiences of oppressed peoples to awaken a "critical consciousness" about the roots of oppression. Many organizers used Freire's techniques to promote social awareness. It is difficult, however, to document DeKadt's assertion that *conscientización* was a direct forerunner of community participation in health. What seems more likely is that "community participation" was both a label and a strategy for community mobilization used not only by national and international development planners, but also by non-governmental personnel, including social reformers and activists who aspired to change existing political structures. Several groups working with poor peoples – including religious "base communities," revolutionary peasant movements, urban guerrilla groups, and private voluntary organizations – had established grassroots development projects in areas where poor people had little (if any) access to government social welfare programs. Their motivations varied dramatically. Some wished to win support of the masses for their political agendas while others sought to win souls, yet all shared an awareness that community support and involvement would be critical to their success. Several groups used health as a "point of entry" into rural communities, but while some highlighted the relationship between socioeconomic organization and health status, others provided curative services without encouraging community members to examine the social causes of illness. All the extremes were found in Latin America; some of the best known began as private, grassroots health centers but rapidly evolved into broader foci of social change, such as Project Piaxtla in Mexico (Werner n.d.), the Behrhorst clinic in Guatemala (Behrhorst 1975), and the Hospital Without Walls in San Ramón, Costa Rica (Serra and Brenes 1983).

Grassroots programs may have provided the models and impetus for participation in health in some areas, but in the mid-1970s multilateral and governmental institutions moved quickly to set up their own network of programs. AID, WHO, UNICEF, the Pan American Health Organization (PAHO), and the World Bank began to coordinate their support for primary health care, including community participation. An AID document reported "AID supports collaboration among donor organizations in health planning activities. A significant degree of compatibility in the health planning methodologies of AID and WHO has been established" (1980: 47); and, on another page, "AID is interested in increasing its participation in multilateral projects and in cooperating with other donor agencies such as UNICEF and the World Bank in supporting health activities" (1980: 55). Despite the coordination among bilateral and multilateral agencies, however, their definitions of community participation (if not always the effects of their policies) varied considerably, reflecting each agency's priorities and political philosophies. Comparing the definitions of "community participation" contained in official policy documents of the Ministers of Health of the Americas, the Alma Ata Conference, and the World Bank will give an indication of each agency's political ideologies and allegiances, and will help to define the arena of struggle within which debates over participation were carried out.

Community participation according to the Pan American Health Organization

The Pan American Health Organization, one of six regional divisions of the World Health Organization, is responsible for developing health policies and priorities for the western hemisphere. In 1972, the Ministers of Health of the Americas agreed on a Ten-Year Health Plan for the region. The plan's major strategy was to extend health service coverage to all previously unserved or underserved populations using the methods of PHC and community participation. Those who drafted the report did not devote much space to defining or elaborating what they meant by community participation, except to emphasize the need for community organization, voluntary collaboration with health workers, cooperation, motivation, and education (PAHO 1973). The community was treated as an untapped resource of vast potential, whose active cooperation could assist governments in their efforts to improve living conditions in the countryside.

The concept of community participation was further elaborated in PAHO's 1978 report on the IV Special Meeting of Ministers of Health. Community participation was more aggressively defined there as a conscious process of change. The report introduced the concept of "capacitating participation," defined as an effort to identify and promote:

(a) The structural changes in the social and institutional systems and subsystems that are necessary if a society is to develop; (b) The transformations that individuals and the community and its institutions must undergo if the ends of individual and social development are to be attained. (PAHO 1978b: 21)

This conceptualization evinced respect and vowed support for indigenous (community-based) knowledge, human dignity, and decision-making capabilities. It assigned equal responsibility for health care decision-making and priority-setting to community residents and health personnel. Recognizing the need to resolve differences and develop common goals through continuing education and dialogue between communities and health personnel, it acknowledged, in a radical departure from most international rhetoric, that "the meaning, content, and scope of community participation...are governed by the socio-political setting" (PAHO 1978b: 27). It defined genuine participation as much more than a contribution of labor and material resources.

Participation is perfected as it is practiced. In the course of its development, participation becomes: active, when the people take part in its various stages; conscious, when they fully understand the problems, translate them into felt needs, and work to solve them; responsible, when they commit themselves and decide to move ahead in full awareness of the consequences and their obligations; deliberate, when they express their voluntary resolve; organized, when they perceive the need to pool their efforts to attain the common objective; and sustained, when they band together permanently to solve the various problems of their community. (PAHO 1978b: 27–8)

This definition relegates to the government a subsidiary role, allowing greater autonomy and self-determination on the part of Latin American communities. It is a much more empowering, progressive definition than that which emerged in the Alma Ata Declaration, where government was given a pivotal role in channeling community participation in health. Efforts to implement this policy were not always as enlightened as the definitions would imply, but our concern here is with the rhetoric of participation and its ability to motivate social action.

Community participation according to the Alma Ata Declaration

As defined by the World Health Organization and UNICEF representatives in 1978, community participation in health was the process whereby individuals and families would come to view health not only as a right, but as a responsibility. The strategy would discourage passive acceptance of government-sponsored programs, substituting active participation (or "cooperation") at every stage:

[The community] must first be involved in the assessment of the situation, the definition of problems and the setting of priorities. Then, it helps to plan primary health care activities and subsequently it cooperates fully when these activities are carried out. Such cooperation includes the acceptance by individuals of a high degree of responsibility for their own health care – for example, by adopting a healthy life style, by applying principles of good nutrition and hygiene, or by making use of immunization services. In addition, members of the community can contribute labour as well as financial and other resources to primary health care. (WHO and UNICEF 1978: 21)

The utilitarian aspects of participation in this report are inescapable. Governments are assigned principal decision-making responsibility, based on the assumption that they will decide in the best interests of rural communities, and communities are expected to cooperate with their plans. Reading between the lines, this report does not include the principle – fundamental to constitutional rule in many developing countries – that the right to health is guaranteed by the state. Instead, it places greater responsibility on individuals for their own health, on what is called "self-care" (or *autocuidado* in Spanish; one contemporary definition of community participation offered by a Costa Rican graduate student of public health was, "The process by which the community gradually assumes responsibility for its own health"). Community participation is thus defined as a tool of government: communities are to cooperate with government initiatives, and will be urged to "practice health," thereby minimizing the need for governmental health interventions. "Participation" can, in this way, be consistent with proposals to privatize health services, to remove them from government control and turn them over to private entrepreneurs. In this – as in other rightist interpretations of the role of government – consumers are "empowered" when given the widest possible choice among health providers. The paradox of this position was not lost on critics who saw some government actions (such as price supports for tobacco) as among the major impediments to "practicing health" (Muller 1979; Hatch and Eng 1984; see also Stebbins 1987, 1990).

Community participation according to the World Bank

The World Bank has not been one of the principal actors in the primary health care movement, but the agency's policy toward community participation is important because the lending agency wields great influence over economic and social policy in less-developed countries. In 1975, the Bank issued its first Health Sector Policy paper, which established the Bank's concern with health issues. The second edition, issued in 1980, indicated that community participation in health may assume various forms,

including self-help for the construction of facilities, community contributions of construction materials, development of local cooperative mechanisms to finance drug purchases, unpaid volunteer workers, and community selection of health workers. Community participation requires that villagers be both willing and able to cooperate. (World Bank 1980: 61)

Even more so than with Alma Ata, the Bank's definition is notable for its utilitarian, unidirectional bias: communities are subordinate to governments, and should cooperate by relieving governments of financial burdens. There is no mention of community involvement in planning or decision-making except to allow community members to select village health workers, yet the Bank's vision requires communities to commit significant resources. The optimal goal of community participation, the Bank report states, is "to obtain successively larger and broader acts of participation from the community over an indefinite period; *those villages that fail to maintain the momentum are dropped from the program"* (World Bank 1980: 61–2; emphasis added).

One of the Bank's later dissertations on community participation continues in the same vein:

[W]e propose to define community participation as an active process by which beneficiary/client groups *influence the direction and execution of a development project* with a view to enhancing their well being in terms of income, personal growth, self reliance or other values they cherish. (Paul 1987: 2; emphasis added)

Paul goes on to detail five potential objectives of participatory initiatives: "(a) empowerment, (b) building beneficiary capacity, (c) increasing project effectiveness, (d) improving project efficiency, and (e) project cost sharing," but acknowledges that "[w]hile references to effectiveness, efficiency and cost-sharing as objectives of CP are made in Bank's policy documents, *empowerment and capacity building have received much less attention"* (Paul 1987: v; emphasis added). In other words, utilitarian considerations have dominated the Bank's interest in community participation.

While Paul criticizes the Bank for not being sufficiently concerned with empowerment, his own document contains another set of flaws. It is written in jargon-laden "development-ese," complete with a complex and nearly useless chart detailing the "mix of instruments" and "mix of intensity" that might, theoretically, characterize different types of participation programs (1987: 9). However, his major failing is his Bank-centeredness, as though the decisions over whether, when, and how to promote participation can, should, and will be made by Bank employees rather than by "beneficiaries." It could be argued, however, that the quiescent, compliant community Paul envisions does not exist, so in the end his abstractions are moot.

Paul's study suggests that one function of the "participation fad" has been to generate income for agency staff and consultants. The final words of Paul's study cite the need for yet more studies: "In view of the paucity of training materials, it would be useful to prepare case studies of projects with CP as the focus. Detailed accounts of how a public agency organizes CP in its projects are not available; if written up, they could form a valuable part of the project management literature" (1987: 31). Yet another document, issued by the World Bank's Economic Development Institute the following year, contains yet another proposal for lining the consultants' pockets: "regional seminars" should be held to "strengthen contacts with regional training and research institutes and to develop regional training material and training activities; develop and test community participation training materials; and coordinate with other international and national organizations involved in this field" (Bamberger 1988: x). Participation had become big business.

The contrasting definitions presented above show the variation that existed within the international development establishment concerning the meaning and function of community participation in health. But a common feature characterized these diverse definitions: in the process of developing them, the international health establishment hammered out a concept of participation which left little room for active citizen involvement. The agencies redefined the idea of participation as a specific, bounded feature of state–citizen interaction rather than as the continuation of a timeless process that had always been practiced by self-reliant rural communities and grassroots social movements. Under the auspices of the international development establishment, the idea of community participation no longer required – indeed, precluded – the initiative of local populations. Citizens were to participate only by obeying the directives handed down by health authorities. This evolving concept of participation, which excluded citizen involvement, set the parameters for subsequent debate over community participation in health.

When the ideology of participation had been articulated in agency publications, the new policies began to be translated into practice. This process entailed having national governments and international health agencies wrest control over participation from the very communities they intended to serve. Central governmental and foreign advisers decided what would constitute participation and what would not. Rather than involving communities in health development using their own means on their own terms, the idea of community participation in health became another way to deny rural communities the power of self-determination.

The changing nature of primary health care

The effectiveness of the primary health care strategy is still being debated, although many analysts agree that, when diligently pursued, universally accessible primary health services have been responsible for lowering disease and mortality rates, especially in rural areas. In Costa Rica, the rural health program undertaken in 1973 has been credited with impressive achievements: between 1970 and 1983 infective and parasitic diseases went from the first to the seventh leading cause of death, and the infant mortality rate went from 61/1,000 to 18/1,000 live births (Ministerio de Salud 1981; Rosero-Bixby 1986). In countries with more repressive governments or severe economic or political constraints, however, primary health care had a less discernible impact on health status (Heggenhougen 1984). Consequently, debates over the utility of a comprehensive PHC strategy began within a few years of Alma Ata (Walsh and Warren 1980; Rifkin and Walt 1986; Wisner 1988). International health agencies have since backpedaled from the emphasis on comprehensive PHC and have fashioned new, less expensive health strategies – such as child survival, oral rehydration therapy, and local health systems (rendered in Spanish as Sistemas Locales de Salud, or SILOS) – for the less-developed world.

There are clear reasons why primary health care began to lose some of its shine after 1978. A world recession and skyrocketing foreign debts caused many Third World governments to adopt conservative fiscal and social policies. The International Monetary Fund (IMF) forced debt-ridden governments to reduce social programs in exchange for renegotiating their loan agreements. In the United States, the election of Ronald Reagan to the presidency in 1980 ushered in a new era of free-market economic policies which favored turning government-run social programs over to the private sector, in the U.S. as well as abroad (see Muscat 1984; Bandow 1985; Pilon 1986). Reagan's advisers used their influence over the IMF and the Inter-American Development Bank to urge that foreign public sector spending be cut, in part by reducing or eliminating government subsidies for education, nutrition, and health programs. Conservative policy analysts proposed that the Reagan administration should reduce its contributions to the World Health Organization unless that agency adopted positions more amenable to their conservative agenda. In fact, the United States was in arrears on its WHO membership dues throughout the late 1980s. A dues payment of $78·4 million, payable on January 1, 1990, had not been paid as of April of that year, and $32·9 million was still outstanding from previous years (World Health Organization 1990: personal communication; see also Fruchtbaum 1988). A document issued in 1986 by the Heritage Foundation, a conservative think tank, argued that WHO had gotten too politicized: "politics seems to be replacing medicine and health on the WHO agenda" (Pilon 1986: 1). Pilon documented a number of WHO initiatives which supposedly showed the political nature of international health policy, including national planning for health care, regulation of infant feeding formulas, and anti-smoking campaigns directed against the tobacco industry. Pilon said she wanted to "oppose the politicization of WHO." She suggested that the U.S. should

[o]ppose the provisions of the "Global Strategy for Health for All by the Year 2000" that involve national, state-controlled, rather than private sector approaches to health care. The U.S. should disseminate information regarding

the pitfalls of socialized medicine and explain the success of the private sector. (Pilon 1986: 10)

The right-wing frustration expressed in this document is, of course, political in the extreme, yet it is interesting that the author describes only the positions incompatible with her own as "politicized." She implies that health can and should be above politics, when "politics" can be defined as any divergent point of view.

The implications of this conservative agenda for AID-funded health programs are clear when one compares the AID Health Sector Policy papers published in 1980 under the Carter administration and in 1982 under the Reagan administration. AID's 1980 Health Sector Policy paper assigned the highest priority to low-cost, government-assisted primary health care services, particularly to maternal and child health care in rural areas. Following the PHC strategy articulated in the Alma Ata documents, AID instructed its employees to promote intersectoral health programs, based on the understanding that health status depends not only on health services but also on agricultural, nutritional, educational, and economic development (AID 1980). In the 1982 AID Health Sector Policy Paper, as well as in a revised version issued in late 1986, government-subsidized health programs are criticized as a form of socialized medicine. The document encourages government austerity and argues that fee-for-service medicine and "cost recovery" should be sought whenever possible (AID 1982). Community participation in health is not mentioned. A similar philosophy was expressed by a former special assistant to President Ronald Reagan:

[Foreign assistance should be funneled through the] indigenous private sector – firms, cooperatives, and individuals – instead of the central government. Low-cost health care could be provided through private clinics, contraceptives distributed by private vendors, etc. In this way, aid will help meet the demands of consumers rather than enrich the local elites that control state institutions. (Bandow 1986)

Thus began the decline of comprehensive PHC and community participation in health. The UN agencies were not as quick to drop primary health care and community participation from their list of priorities, but as we saw with the Title IX program, the agencies tend to follow each other's leads. It was not long before UNICEF started emphasizing "GOBI" (the acronym for growth monitoring, oral rehydration therapy, breast feeding, and immunization) as an "interim strategy" toward comprehensive primary health care. Critics saw this as a retrenchment from the principles of comprehensive PHC and a return to a highly technological, vertical approach to disease (Newell 1988;

Wisner 1988). The World Bank – never an advocate of nationalized health care – began to investigate strategies for getting consumers to assume some of the costs of primary health care (Akin, Birdsall, and de Feranti 1988; Birdsall 1989). By 1990 it appeared that community participation would henceforth be relegated to the periphery of international development policy, although the rhetoric would live on for a while. A document published by the United Nations Research Institute for Social Development concedes as much, stating:

> In 1979 there was a general feeling and consensus among developmentalists, planners and policy-makers in international organizations and national administrations that popular participation had to be promoted as an essential ingredient of future development strategies in order to assure a better distribution of benefits. Today, in 1983, this feeling seems to have changed somewhat: participation is regarded with increasing scepticism and proponents of a growth strategy are again gaining strength. (United Nations Research Institute for Social Development 1983: 36–7)

Concomitant with this statement, donor agencies were beginning to soft-pedal community participation.

Other macroanalytic factors should be considered in explaining the gradual decline of primary health care and community participation in health. The world economic crisis of the early 1980s made it hard for debt-ridden governments to finance the recurrent costs of rural health centers, and foreign seed money for project development had been spent. Yet the ideology of participation necessitated social expenditures in the interests of intersectoral community development. The international agencies were unable, as a matter of policy, to address the increasingly acute contradictions between their stated policies and changing economic and political realities.

Comparative perspectives on participation

Community participation in health presents an apparent puzzle in analyzing the relationship between health policy and the political organization of the state: effective, "bottom-up" community participation seems to decrease in proportion to increasing state involvement in health care. Socialist-oriented countries, such as Cuba and Tanzania, have made primary health care a top priority, with impressive results (Elling 1981; Cereseto and Waitzkin 1986), but analysts agree that both countries have minimal community participation. On the other hand, participation thrives among the more disadvantaged and oppressed peoples of shantytown Peru, for example, or the guerrilla-controlled zones of El Salvador. Is effective participation then inconsistent with state-sponsored health care? Does socialism stifle popular participation in health?

Cuba, for example, has been a socialist state since 1959, and health indicators have improved dramatically since then. Cuba now has among the longest life expectancy and lowest infant mortality rates in all of Latin America. Yet Werner argues that the Cuban health system is both a "model service and a means of social control," especially with respect to popular participation in health:

If health care is the full responsibility of the State, does this not entail restricting or depriving the responsibility of individuals and communities for their own health?... If the State takes over full responsibility for people's health, yet insists that the people must participate in health matters, then in what irresponsible, subservient way are the people obliged to participate? (Werner 1983: 34)

Similarly in Tanzania, health policy has been explicitly guided by socialist ideologies of social equity and self-reliance. Yet while rural health has received explicit emphasis, and community health workers have been a top priority of the state, formal community participation in health has been persistently absent (Klouda 1983: 54; Heggenhougen et al. 1987: 163–5; Muhondwa 1989: 188). The contradiction is obvious: if socialist states are presumably more responsive to citizen concerns than are other forms of government, then why do they lack participation?

Full answers to this question will await a more exhaustive comparison of the political-economic aspects of health participation in Latin America, but indications from Peru and Panama suggest that "successful" participation arises precisely where the state refuses to act. In Peru, for example, a history of collective struggle or political activism was, in Muller's view, a fairly accurate predictor of greater community participation in health (Muller 1983: 204). Davidson and Stein (1988: 56) note, in their study of 32 urban and rural Peruvian health projects in the mid-1980s, that Peruvians responded to economic hardship by forming hundreds of base community organizations to provide basic services such as the distribution of milk and water. For these people, participation was a survival mechanism, necessary and appropriate given the non-responsive nature of a bankrupt state. Government-sponsored, or "top-down" participation was, according to Davidson and Stein, a contradiction in terms (1988: 68). Similarly, in Panama, "successful" participation was often predicated on conflictive relations with the state:

Officers representing successful health committees often speak of the need for rural dwellers to "unite and organize" for the "future of the community." They reject paternalistic partnerships and assert their "right" to demand government services stipulated in the constitution. (La Forgia 1985: 60)

In Panama, as in Costa Rica, the state's attitude toward community participation was initially enthusiastic. But by the time of La Forgia's fieldwork in 1983, Ministry of Health officials were inclined to let local health committees disappear, in part because it would have been impossible for the Ministry to respond to the institutional and social changes demanded by the communities. The Panamanian case, then, corroborates Davidson and Stein's assertion for Peru that "successful" participation is, by their definition, not sponsored by government.

This conclusion, however, suggests a problem with the language of "successful" versus "unsuccessful" participation. Who decides the criteria to be used in determining "success" or "failure"? If formal participation is defined as "a supplement to the health system – a means to enlist additional cooperation and resources to support the system's programs, on its terms and under its control" (PAHO 1984: 30), then the programs described for Peru and Panama could certainly be interpreted as "successful." An assessment of "success" or "failure" does not tell as much about the particular program being evaluated as it does about the political convictions of the evaluators. A more useful approach, then, is not to judge whether or under what conditions participation "succeeds" or "fails," but to analyze the negotiations and debates among groups competing for ideological, political, and economic control over the concept, including political parties, state and local representatives, professional elites, labor organizations, and the collection of individuals who comprise heterogeneous local communities. Struggles about – for or against – "participation" are struggles about social stratification and the distribution of and control over political and economic resources within a society. Using this framework, people are more likely to want to participate where the established order offers them fewer formal opportunities to participate; in other words, participation will be greater where (and when) there is a more urgent and immediate need for social change. "Bottom-up" participation is therefore more likely in situations where "top-down" programs do not exist or are not operative because of higher-priority exigencies such as economic crisis. Conversely, participation is less *apparent* in socialist contexts where the government provides more basic services and development is more intersectoral, but this should not be interpreted as a sign of "failure" (Escalona 1980; Elling 1989: 134; Tesh 1986). Greater participation is simply unnecessary and unwarranted where relations between state and citizen are more cooperative and mutually respectful, or, to put it more succinctly, where the citizens are the state.

The meanings of community participation can and do change over time. For example, participation took on another meaning in Central

America during the 1980s, when the region was torn by civil and international strife. United States' foreign policy toward Central America was reminiscent of the 1960s, when Kennedy's Alliance for Progress aimed to prevent "another Cuba." This time, health and community participation were used to ward off "subversion." In every Central American country with the exception of Nicaragua (which was denied U.S. foreign aid funds as long as the Sandinistas were in power), the U.S. paid for health programs designed to enhance support for U.S.-backed governments and ideologies. The U.S. singularity of purpose is evident in the breakdown of the AID health budget. El Salvador, with less than one percent of the total population of Latin America and the Caribbean, received 53 percent of AID's health budget for the region in 1988 and 48 percent in 1989 (U.S. Congress 1987, 1988). Meanwhile, the coalition of Contadora nations working to achieve a negotiated settlement to the regional conflict backed its own plan to solicit health aid from foreign donors (Ministers of Health of the Americas 1984).

Yet the realpolitik of Central America was such that tolerance for community participation seemed to decrease as social unrest increased. The Nicaraguan revolution of 1979, escalating civil wars in El Salvador and Guatemala, and social instability exacerbated by the 1980 world economic crisis were perceived as threats to so-called "democratic" governments. Under these conditions, community participation easily disrupted the status quo because it provided avenues for focusing and channeling dissent, for creating instability on a national scale. This, then, was the ultimate paradox: "democracy" became more important than ever, but participation became redefined as a threat to the democratic process.

The ideology of community participation reflected in the health policies of international agencies

The social history of community participation outlined in this and earlier chapters shows that the concept underwent a series of transformations as it was shaped by corporate, governmental, and multilateral entities. These groups – the so-called "development establishment" (Navarro 1984) – made community participation a central feature of international political ideology. Community participation came to represent unspoken assumptions about why development assistance is necessary, what its goals are, who should control the process, and who should benefit from it. Many in the development establishment spoke openly about participation as a means toward building and reinforcing Western-style democratic political processes. Donors claimed community participation would create more effective citizens, inspire confidence and good will toward Western democracies, and teach Third World citizens that existing governments were worthy of their support. In this sense, the agencies envisioned that governments would use participation as a way of legitimizing their own existence and activities.

In the relatively peaceful and prosperous Central America of the 1970s, community participation in health was a particularly effective way to legitimize government activity because the rhetoric appealed to so many audiences. Its early success as political ideology lay precisely in the fact that the concept was endorsed enthusiastically by the heterogeneous membership of international agencies, by socialist governments and military dictators alike, and by competing interest groups within each national context. At least at the level of rhetoric, community participation succeeded in forging the illusion of consensus among all groups and social classes (see Green 1989). While parties from all sides of the political spectrum had agreed that community participation was a desirable, even essential, component of their social and political development philosophy, they had radically different ideas about the political ends participation should serve.

Problems, inconsistencies, and tensions arose when it came time to discuss the details of implementation. This should not have come as a surprise, although apparently it did. Cohen and Uphoff wrote:

After undertaking many hours of discussion and a thorough review of relevant literature in economics, sociology and political science over the past ten years, we are properly impressed with the complexity of "participation" as a concept and we can understand better why so much confusion surrounds the use of the term. It is no wonder that practitioners find it difficult to promote or even report on "participation" when there is so much disagreement on the scope and substance of the term. (Cohen and Uphoff 1977: 1)

The participation literature is filled with the laments of frustrated analysts who wish for a more precise definition of the term (Forman 1979; Paul 1987; Villalobos 1989). If we look on participation from a political-economic and historical perspective, however, the lack of definitional specificity seems not only predictable, but positively inevitable. Even before the phrase became common in development circles, the extent and nature of citizen participation was a contentious feature of political ideology. People sharing the same political stripes will tend to agree about the necessity, direction, and goals of community participation in health. And people who hold differing political points of view will hold conflicting ideas about who should participate in health and how and under what circumstances. Community participation is a metaphor for discussing the power structure of society, and whether, how, and by whom it should be adjusted.

While the ideological vision promoted by the development establishment was not uniform, as we saw in the contrasting definitions offered above, the collective ideology expressed in the definitions had much in common when contrasted with more radical visions. Two other schools of thought on community participation in health operate on the fringes of the development establishment or outside it altogether. The first approach is reformist: it is critical in tone, but not revolutionary in scope. Reformers are often hired by international agencies to evaluate programs thoughtfully and critically, but to stay within the confines of the assignment. Reformers must offer recommendations which support the basic premise that community participation in health is a desirable, attainable goal. Many have written critically of the top-down, obligatory, opportunist nature of many community participation programs. They insist repeatedly (although apparently to deaf ears) that community members must be involved in planning, decision-making, and evaluation of programs as well as in implementation and in making use of government-provided services (UNICEF 1981; White 1982; Hollnsteiner 1982; PAHO 1984: 28; Rifkin 1985). Reformers generally acknowledge the political implications of community participation by making statements to the effect that "there are risks involved in community participation. Because of its implications for changing basic political and social relationships, CP [community participation] is not to be undertaken lightly" (PAHO 1984: 29). Beyond such ominous-sounding warnings, however, reformers rarely recommend ways to circumvent or face such risks; reformers do not say enough about risks to change the overall direction of policy. Consequently, their admonitions might cause a cautious planner to resist community participation altogether. Some of the questions left unanswered by the reformist approach include the following: Are some political systems more conducive to participation than others? If so, which ones? What is the precise relationship between "basic political and social relationships" and the prospects for achieving active, ongoing community participation in health? What role should international agencies play in resolving the political conflicts generated under the guise of promoting participation? Reformers generally downplay the underlying sociopolitical conditions that perpetuate the status quo.

Radical critics of primary health care and community participation, in contrast, insist that social inequalities are the primary causes of disease and poverty, and that improved health is a product of greater social equity. They talk about health and community participation within a social, political, and economic context, and do not believe that apolitical or strictly technological health interventions exist. Segall, for instance, says that all international health aid is "an instrument of Western foreign policy; it is part of the means by which these countries establish their presence in the developing world – and keep it dependent" (1972: 48). The Latin American literature on community participation in health shows the radical perspective in the work of David Werner, Fredrick Muller, and the Confederación Superior Universitaria Centroamericana (CSUCA) Health Sciences Program, which sponsored a Central American conference on community participation in 1980. In addition, social scientists such as DeKadt (1982), Ugalde (1985), Midgley (1986), Green (1989), Stone (1989), and Morgan (1989, 1990) are taking a more critical, political-economic approach to Latin America community participation. They take for granted that community participation in health is a political issue, because it inevitably challenges existing relations of power and the prevailing distribution of resources. It also challenges biomedical assumptions about what constitutes health and threats to health. For example, in the United States, community participation has been used by radical critics of the health system to support an alternative political ideology and a broader definition of health:

It is imperative to continue this creativity and momentum in community-oriented health programming for poorer and less well served citizens of this country. It is important for health planners and providers working with these communities to broaden the definition of health so that it goes beyond the reduction in morbidity and mortality and includes such social characteristics as underemployment, poor schools, oppression, poor housing, and self-reliance. (Hatch and Eng 1984: 244)

An example of a similar attitude about community participation is found in the proceedings of CSUCA's 1980 Health Sciences Program conference on participation. The symposium's unwritten agenda was to contemplate new participatory strategies for providing health services in revolutionary Nicaragua and in the guerrilla-controlled zones of war-torn El Salvador. The final report of the symposium was highly critical of the forms of popular participation conceived within Ministries of Health, which were interpreted as cynical efforts to manipulate the population in a blatant, desperate attempt to legitimize corrupt governments (CSUCA 1980: 16). Organizers rejected the development establishment's assertions that health was above politics, and went on to place health squarely within the arena of issues to be contested in civil war or class struggle. Their approach can be characterized as "vulgar Marxist," with attendant rhetoric, but their comments serve to demonstrate what participation means at this end of the ideological spectrum:

The ideologues of the capitalist state have traditionally tried to portray the health sector as neutral from the point of view of politics. However, this regimen of the State promotes community participation to exercise control over the masses. It is here where the workers must appropriate the health arena as an area of struggle [and] participate to confront the political control of the State. All health workers and academics should participate for control and dominion over health as a political project to defend the interests of the working class... Any form of popular participation in a capitalist state is controlled by the political power of the governing classes; however, when the class contradictions become acute (state of war), the health area is a battlefront to dispute, and it is there where popular participation, as the germ of popular power, becomes the embryo of the new society... For the working class, participation in health represents a political option, to the extent that it is the people who take the health project and integrate it into their general political agenda. (CSUCA 1980: 17)

In other words, "health" is so inextricably entangled with politics that its definition should be expanded to encompass oppression and social inequality. The political ramifications of such a redefinition, of course, would be serious indeed. The radicals have, nonetheless, had an impact on mainstream discourse. Statements by UNICEF, WHO, the World Bank, and AID all downplay the importance of politics, but today almost all the literature on the subject now acknowledges (if only in a footnote) that community participation in health is at least potentially, if not profoundly, political (Martin 1983: 15; PAHO 1984: 29; United Nations 1987).

This raises another contentious issue. Exactly how is community participation manipulated to advance one political perspective while simultaneously denigrating another? One consequence of this largely covert struggle for power has been the appearance of rhetoric designed to invoke territoriality and ownership over the concept of participation. Multilateral and bilateral organizations try to claim it for themselves, in part by reciting a history which includes only their own attempts to enhance participation. Radicals likewise try to claim it for themselves, in part by citing a litany of revolutionary examples of communities successfully engaged in struggle. All players in this game – whether representing corporations, embassies, private voluntary organizations, political parties, religious sects, or multilateral agencies – attempt to manipulate participation to suit their own needs. The struggle for control is not necessarily conscious or deliberate. Rather, it emanates from sincere and legitimate disagreements about the determinants of health and causes of disease, the reasons for and solutions to endemic poverty, and the role of the state versus the private sector in solving social inequities.

Community participation in health initially appealed to everyone who heard about it, from international diplomats to physicians to banana workers. Yet when definitions and program plans began to emerge, it became obvious that "participation" was a multivocal symbol. At one extreme, popular participation could be a means to wrest power from ruling elites, while at the other extreme it was a means to get poor people to underwrite the costs of building a health infrastructure and to assume responsibility for their own ill health. The next chapter examines how these ideologies were played out in Costa Rica.

5 Participation in Costa Rica: dissent within the state

A select history of state-sponsored health care in Costa Rica

State sponsorship of health and medical care programs was not a feature of Costa Rican society until the 1920s. Before then, health services for most of the population were provided by a few doctors and many traditional healers. The only organized health care available in the country was associated with the two major export crops: bananas and coffee. In the banana-growing enclaves on the coasts, the United Fruit Company offered medical services under an early "tropical occupational health" program designed to keep bananas supplied to foreign markets. In the coffee-growing highlands, disease control and curative efforts assisted by the Rockefeller Foundation kept coffee pickers healthy. Health care was thus offered through Costa Rica's major landowners and their foreign allies, who considered medical services a necessary economic investment. The state did not assume responsibility for health care, nor was health considered a right.

In 1850 Costa Rica was a poor and sparsely populated country beginning to find its niche in the world economic market. Coffee exports had begun around 1830, and European demand for coffee was leading to higher production. Land concentration began during this time as a coffee-growing landed elite took increasing control over commercial and political life, while subsistence farmers lost their lands and were forced to become coffee pickers (Seligson 1980). Before the 1830s there had been considerable social differentiation which led, with the growth of coffee exports, to social conflict between "on the one hand, the processor-exporter-financier elite and its commercial capital, and, on the other, the smallholding cultivators beginning the long historical process of capital differentiation in agriculture" (Gudmundson 1986: 54).

The conversion of land to coffee production meant that fewer food crops were planted; thus the late 1800s saw a national decline in food production (Monge Alfaro 1966: 204, cited in Seligson 1980: 22–3).

Contemporary evidence shows that landlessness and undiversified export crop production – in the absence of an equitable distribution of income – are associated with poor nutritional status (Whiteford 1985). We can assume, in the absence of detailed epidemiological evidence, that the disease profile must have worsened under these conditions. Disease, combined with the chronic paucity of workers to harvest coffee, posed a serious problem for coffee growers in the early 1900s, who took it upon themselves to organize medical services in the coffee-producing regions of the country.

Between 1860 and 1890, coffee growers spent some of their new-found wealth and political power to organize medical services for inhabitants of the central plateau. In 1860 they organized the first functioning Junta de Caridad, or Charity Group, to lobby for construction of the first Costa Rican hospital, the Hospital San Juan de Dios. Charity figured in the dominant social ideology of the day, and the Junta de Caridad promoted the San Juan de Dios as a charitable institution for the welfare of all.

One analyst suggested another, arguably more plausible, interpretation of the motives behind the first Junta de Caridad. He pointed out that Costa Rica's labor shortages – the product of relatively egalitarian landholdings and a low population density – were exacerbated by the exigencies of coffee harvesting, which required a large labor force during three months of the year. Coffee growers needed the few available workers to be healthy and productive, so they set about organizing their own medical services to enable sick laborers to return to work. Although the Juntas de Caridad fostered an image of service to the community, they were also addressing the growers' own need for coffee pickers. Their self-interest is evident in the fact that the Juntas de Caridad existed only in the coffee-growing regions of the country, where the coffee-dependent population would make primary use of their services. Costa Rica's initial efforts to organize medical services were based, in part, on the cycles of coffee harvesting in addition to humanitarian motives for treating increased malnutrition and disease.

There are other interpretations for the emergence of urban, hospital-based medical services. The consolidation of wealth and power among coffee processors and exporters gave rise to the professionalization of medicine in Costa Rica as the affluent began to travel and study abroad. By the 1850s, Costa Ricans trained in Europe and the United States began to practice medicine in their homeland (Lachner Sandoval 1902: 38–9). Doctors returning from training in the United States and Europe wanted to work in well-equipped hospitals. They also wanted to be guaranteed their exclusive right to practice medicine. Part of their attempt to control medical practice can be seen in the history of laws against *curanderismo* (traditional healing practices). In 1818, before independence from Spain, Governor Urrutia in Guatemala (the central seat for the entire Central American region) banned the sale of all medicines or poisons not prescribed by "professors." In 1833 a Costa Rican organization combating a smallpox epidemic in Heredia prohibited the practice of *curanderismo* without its permission. By the 1830s, all *curanderos* practicing in Costa Rica were supposed to be licensed. Although licensing implied control by the medical profession over the traditional healers, at least it allowed the *curanderos* a place in the health care network. In 1887, however, the Protomedicato (later to become the Costa Rican Medical Association) canceled all extant *curanderismo* licenses and refused to grant more (Lachner Sandoval 1902: 38–40). As in the United States during the early twentieth century, Costa Rican physicians competing with *curanderos* for the patronage of the sick rallied their forces to discredit and expel non-professional healers. The delegitimation of *curanderos* was also consonant with the Liberal modernizing ideology of late nineteenth-century Costa Rica: *curanderos* were old-fashioned and unscientific and had no place in modern society.

When analyzed in terms of community participation in health, laws against *curanderismo* can be seen as a step away from participatory medicine. The Protomedicato outlawed the traditional right of citizens to obtain medical care of their own choosing and banned *curanderos* from legally plying their trade. By limiting the ranks of medical practitioners, physicians were asserting control over the range of choices available. By invoking their edict unilaterally, without public input or a referendum on the issue, they informed the public that doctors would assume exclusive control over health policy decisions. In fact, well into the 1950s most Costa Rican health policy decisions limited public participation in health by placing health decisions strictly within the purview of physicians and the state.

Medicine in Costa Rica's central plateau was controlled by the coffee interests until the 1920s, when the state slowly began to take a more active role in the provision of health services (Trejos Escalante 1963: 102–6). Not coincidentally, the increasing involvement of the central government in health paralleled the declining power of the coffee oligarchy in Costa Rican politics. In the early 1900s, "The once-unified and omnipotent aristocracy was now beginning to break up and lose its control over the political system" (Seligson 1980: 46). The coffee elite became complacent, content to allow their wealth to accumulate rather than risking their economic well-being by diversifying into other markets

(Bell 1971 : 6). The *cafetaleros* stopped financing social welfare programs, preferring instead to allow groups such as the Rockefeller Foundation – whose representatives were "socially acceptable to the elite" (Bell 1971 : 8) – to devote themselves to social development. The coffee oligarchy eventually lost much of its power to the emerging middle class of professionals and white-collar workers employed by the state.

The state's ability to assert its power over coffee growers in the 1930s can be seen in its regulation of coffee prices and the Juntas de Caridad. The state abandoned its laissez-faire policy toward coffee production in the 1930s Depression era. Coffee-processing plants had previously been free to set their own prices without governmental interference. Then, in 1933, the state created an oversight committee to regulate prices paid to coffee producers (Seligson 1980: 36). The state assumed greater control over health care in the coffee regions in 1936, when the Legislative Assembly created a state organization to supervise budget allotments to the Juntas de Caridad, which by this time had begun to administer hospitals in major provincial towns throughout the country. The new Consejo Nacional de Salubridad (National Health Council) changed the nature of the Juntas, transferring control away from the coffee interests and putting it in the hands of doctors working within the state apparatus. The prospect of losing control over the Juntas upset some deputies from the outlying provinces, who insisted that regional hospitals would suffer (*La Tribuna*, November 3, 1936). Of course, their political power would undoubtedly also suffer under this centralization of the health system. Proponents of the Consejo said that the new plan would be more responsive to the public interest and that it would distribute funds according to "scientific criteria" (*Diario de Costa Rica*, November 6, 1936). Dr. Antonio Peña Chavarria, writing in the Annual Report of the Ministry of Health, applauded the decision, saying that the Juntas de Caridad "had functioned as delegations of Political Power since 1845" (Ministerio de Salud, Memoria 1936: 54). Both of these examples show the state taking control from the coffee interests in deciding national affairs.

Health has been used as a political symbol in Costa Rica throughout this century, as seen in these examples from the 1930s. Then as now, health was ranked on a moral plane above politics, and politicians impugned their opponents' motives by asserting that they had politicized health issues. For example, when Dr. Peña Chavarria blasted the Juntas de Caridad as bastions of political power, his subtext was that health should not be subject to political considerations. On the other side of the political spectrum, one deputy complained that he would vote against creation of the Consejo, because

[t]he reports that President Cortes has given to the press about this matter were degrading to the congress, because they attributed the opposition of some deputies to personalistic or partisan considerations. I categorically deny that my congressional actions have ever been based on partisan interests or on anything other than the good of the republic. (*Diario de Costa Rica*, November 6, 1936)

Each of these men tried to outdo the other in professing an altruistic concern for the public health.

Further evidence for the early politicization of health work comes from 1932, when a debate took place about whether the Department of Public Health should become a cabinet ministry subject to political appointment. Solon Nuñez Frutos, then Secretary, favored the change. He said:

It does not matter if they make the position of Minister of Health a political position. Social protection is not just political, it is supremely political. A Minister of Health might fall just as a Minister of Development or Agriculture, but for however short his career might be, his work can be more valiant than that which he might do for many years under lesser political and social conditions. (Ministerio de Salud, Memoria 1932: 7)

Nuñez was one of the few politician-health planners to acknowledge explicitly the political nature of health care. Furthermore, his opinion set the stage for institutionalizing the political nature of health. The contradiction, of course, is that politicians continue to maintain that health is an altruistic concern, but underneath the moralistic veneer health was and still is a partisan matter.

Even under state control, health services continued to favor coffee-growing regions. Dr. Nuñez, who became the first public Minister of Health in Costa Rica, directed the Rockefeller Foundation's hookworm campaign in Costa Rica's coffee-growing regions and studied in the United States at Johns Hopkins University, then the foremost medical institution in the hemisphere (Ministerio de Salud, Memoria 1932). As late as 1936, the Ministry of Health's annual report included a special section on "hygiene in the coffee zones." It reported that an epidemiological investigation had detected a correlation between increased child mortality rates and the coffee harvest season, ostensibly because children were not adequately fed or nursed while their parents and older siblings were busy picking coffee. In response to this finding, the Ministry arranged for day care centers to be set up in Tres Ríos (a coffee-growing region in the central plateau) during harvest months to insure that children there would receive adequate care (Ministerio de Salud, Memoria 1936).

The period from 1930 to 1960 witnessed a slow, gradual shift in the nature of Costa Rican health services as the state assumed ever greater responsibility for providing medical care, and coffee and banana interests withdrew. Rosenberg argues that health and social services were neglected during the 1930s:

Throughout the critical period of the 1930s in Costa Rica, the social question was systematically neglected at the level of public policy for a number of reasons: (a) the lack of competitive political parties that might employ social welfare as a political force; (b) the absence of a populist movement that might use social programs as a means to mobilize the masses; (c) the rural orientation of the small, well-organized Communist party; and (d) the continued political domination of Costa Rican politics by the traditional coffee oligarchy. (Rosenberg 1981: 281)

Rosenberg is certainly correct that the health-related policy initiatives of the 1930s were minor compared with those of the 1940s, when social security reforms were enacted. Health was not totally neglected, however. During the 1930s, the state asserted greater control over health care by curtailing the power of the Juntas de Caridad, challenging the health conditions existing on United Fruit's plantations, and establishing the Unidades Sanitarias, forerunners of the contemporary rural health posts.

Nuñez was responsible for pushing a bill through the Legislative Assembly to create rural health centers (Unidades Sanitarias) in the early 1930s. This state-sponsored infrastructure, modeled after the County Health Units of the United States (Ministerio de Salud Memoria 1930–1: 32), would replace the official town doctors (Médicos del Pueblo). Town doctors had been on the government payroll since a law authorizing their employment was passed in 1894. They were paid for providing medical care to the sick in small towns without other medical services. Nuñez apparently felt that town doctors were not earning their salaries, and that the government was subsidizing unscrupulous physicians:

[I] think it is very nice and humane to help the professionals, especially in these times when the profession is so strapped, in which people because of their poverty do not solicit medical services and if they do solicit them do not pay for them; but the state should demand of those it protects at least a minimum of work in relation to the salaries they receive. (Ministerio de Salud, Memoria 1930–1: 33)

The Unidades Sanitarias were an expensive project, especially during the Depression, but the legislature felt the expense was justified even though local communities did not contribute to the effort. Nuñez said:

The efficient organization of these units requires a budget increase of many thousands of *colones*, because the effort to obtain the collaboration of the

Municipalities and of individuals has failed. (Ministerio de Salud, Memoria 1930–1: 32)

In contrast, subsequent rural health programs would be predicated on the communities' willingness to assume at least a portion of the costs.

Changes in the state's role in health care during this period were related to the changing Costa Rican political system. In the early part of the twentieth century the ideology of popular participation began to become an important political symbol. This was evident in the 1910 election of Ricardo Jiménez Oreamuno, the first presidential candidate in Costa Rica to seek support from rural areas (Vega Carballo 1981: 304–5). As President, Jiménez eliminated the electoral college and substituted direct elections (albeit with limited suffrage).

Thus began a revolution of popular participation which was to weaken further the grip of the aristocracy ... By the first quarter of the twentieth century Costa Rica was finally emerging into the modern world. In the course of a few short years her isolation from the once-irrelevant ideologies of popular participation and socially responsive government dissolved. (Seligson 1980: 47)

Still, the kind of popular participation which emerged in the 1910s was based not on direct participation of citizens in the business of governance, but on the citizens' right to elect officials who would represent them in day-to-day decision-making. For the disenfranchised rural citizen, this new parliamentary democracy did not greatly affect involvement in politics, since rural *caciques* (political bosses) continued to rule local affairs. Nevertheless, popular participation began to assume unprecedented importance as the dominant social ideology.

Despite the attempts to convince citizens of the participatory nature of government, the health care organizations established in the 1920s and 1930s had little or no participatory component. The Secretariat of Public Health (antecedent to the Ministry of Health) was established in 1922 and the Instituto Nacional de Seguros (National Insurance Institute), which covers work-related accidents and illnesses, in 1924. Apart from a few educational programs undertaken by public health officials, archival documents from this period rarely mention the need for community input; certainly there were no institutionalized mechanisms for involving communities in health.

It is possible to infer the vision of community participation prevalent at the time by noting what health officials did not say. For example, in 1932, Nuñez spoke of the need for "collaboration" (*colaboración*) to get the Sanitation Department functioning. The work would come to naught, he said, "unless they have the ample, intelligent, and sincere cooperation of all social institutions." He specifically mentioned the need for collaboration on the part of the highest officials of the Republic, local leaders, doctors, schools, and of the Rockefeller Foundation, but he did not mention the need for the collaboration of community members. The community's role, ostensibly, would be to comply with the programs set up by these other groups, and to benefit from the health improvements Nuñez anticipated.

Collaboration is also mentioned in the report sent to the Ministry in 1939 by the operator of the dispensary car on the Atlantic railroad:

> The collaboration of the authorities and of important citizens has allowed great intensification of the work, but I should make special mention of the dedicated, spontaneous collaboration of the teachers along the Limón Circuit…A special paragraph should be dedicated to the managers of the Northern Railway who have allowed the Dispensary Car to travel on *extra trains*, even though the Company-Secretariat contracts specify that the Car should travel only on *regular trains*. (Ministerio de Salud, Memoria 1939: 424; emphasis in original)

The dispensary car operator apparently did not expect community members to become actively involved in his health care efforts. Collaboration – meaning facilitation, material assistance, and political favors – was expected, however, from local leaders, and was conspicuous in its absence. The sanitary engineer assigned to Siquirres in 1938 complained bitterly of the local officials' lack of cooperation. Some of his planned projects were not completed, he said,

> due undoubtedly to the disharmony among some employees, and their lack of cooperation or progressive spirit. For example, the municipal officer [*jefe político*], in spite of all the notes I have sent him, is incapable of stopping all kinds of animals from wandering freely through the streets, turning over garbage cans and scattering garbage all over. (Ministerio de Salud, Memoria 1938: 276)

Eventually, *colaboración* came to mean money. As early as 1940, it became clear that "collaborating" communities were those that provided money and labor for state-sponsored initiatives. This attitude was manifested by a representative (*diputado*) from the Legislative Assembly, who petitioned for a budget increase for the Ministry of Health.

> From the very beginning of our [anti-malarial] work, we have been faced with empty accounts. At the same time, we are faced with the anxiety of all the people who are asking us for better development of public hygiene…We receive constant petitions for cooperation from municipalities and Juntas de Protección Social which are building health clinics and emergency and maternity facilities. Do not believe, fellow Diputados, that these municipalities and important members of our rural areas arrive to ask the assistance of the State with their hands empty. Each town comes with a sum of money which represents a large

economic sacrifice ... Then it is worth asking, if these groups contribute their own funds to build a project for the common good, is it possible that the State would not respond as is its obligation by supporting their generous plans? (Archivo Nacional Congreso 1940, no. 19267)

Health services of the 1920s and 1930s were provided in paternalistic fashion, with the state proposing and acting on health initiatives presumed to be in the best interests of rural communities. The paternalistic ideology had distinct advantages, in enhancing access to health services, over the health programs initiated in the late 1800s when the coffee oligarchy ruled. People had greater access to health care in rural areas, and health policy came to be decided by a broad range of people. Nonetheless, participation in daily health programs was limited to doctors, public employees, local political leaders, and foreign development agencies. The people affected by the programs were given no part in the planning, execution, or evaluation of the services they used.

Although the base of involvement in health and in politics was not as broad in the 1920s and 1930s as it later became, Costa Rican elected representatives were adamant that authoritarianism would not be permitted. They were not willing to let the executive branch of government operate unilaterally any more than they were willing to let the coffee oligarchy continue to rule the country. Their insistence on participating in the political process is seen in the debate over creation of the Juntas Patrióticas (Patriotic Assembly) in 1928. A staff member at the Ministry of Health told me that these Juntas were a forerunner of community participation in health.

The Juntas Patrióticas were created by executive decree on May 22, 1928 by recently inaugurated President Cleto González Víquez. Their responsibilities, according to the decree, were "to watch over compliance with the laws, observance of the norms of public morality, and the order and progress of the locality." A Junta would be established in each locality, comprising three members hand-picked by the President, their identities unknown to one another. Each member was to give confidential monthly reports to the President "about the course of public business in his jurisdiction" (Colección de Leyes y Decretos 1928: 215). Congress opposed the decree vigorously, some saying it was unconstitutional. A newspaper reporter said of his interviews with Congressional representatives, "They told us, furthermore, that this law should rather be called the Network of Spies ... It promises to be an interesting issue because the law will certainly cause great commotion in the country" (La Tribuna, May 31, 1928). Other articles and letters appearing in the paper over the following week called the Juntas "spy dens," or "a secret service." The Congress said it would not allow "anonymous juntas" to

carry out any duties. In response to opposition, the President rescinded
the decree before any Juntas were appointed. The person who told me
about the Juntas Patrióticas admitted they were "short-lived, because
they were created with a political tinge." He did not say, however, that
the Juntas Patrióticas had been an executive attempt to circumvent the
power of Congress, nor did he say that they would have entailed a hunt
for political infidels in rural areas of the country. Several lessons can be
drawn from this example: (1) the political network of the central plateau
was gradually being extended into rural areas, so that regional political
power bases were becoming critical to national leaders; (2) elected
Congressional representatives were strong enough to triumph over the
executive branch, an indication of the strength of the parliamentary
democracy; and (3) government organizations were expected to be public
and accountable. It is not surprising, given the many competing
meanings attributed to the concept, that the Juntas Patrióticas have
become incorporated into the historical record as precursors to contemporary community participation in health.

The limits on grassroots participation in health were already evident in
the early decades of the century. Physicians acquired increasing control
over health policy in the central plateau, while in the lowland plantations
the workers resorted to confrontational tactics to draw attention to their
health and medical needs. As the state assumed control over health
services, doctors who would make "scientific" policy decisions were
charged with protecting the public health. The community's role was
extremely limited throughout this period, with only occasional mention
of the need for *colaboración*. Community involvement was channeled
toward modes of participation acceptable to the state, such as active anti-
communism (during and after the 1934 banana strike in Limón) and
compliance with sanitary regulations. As state health institutions were
consolidated in subsequent years, the space available for active, genuine
community participation in health grew increasingly restricted.

Costa Rican health institutions

The Costa Rican health system today has two principal branches (see
Low 1985 for a discussion of differences between them). The social
security agency, Caja Costarricense de Seguro Social (CCSS) is the
larger and more widely utilized health institution, providing curative
care for salaried workers since the 1940s. In the 1970s plans to
"universalize" CCSS coverage allowed unemployed, self-employed,
and indigent citizens onto the CCSS rolls (see Casas and Vargas 1980;
Rosenberg 1983; Jaramillo 1984). The CCSS spent 70 percent of total

health expenditures in 1988 (Ministerio de Salud, Memoria 1988: 75) and employed over 90 percent of the nation's doctors (Ministerio de Salud 1981: 151). The CCSS is financed in large part by employers, who in 1987 paid an additional 19 percent above their employees' salaries into the fund. Employees paid 9 percent, deducted from their salaries, and the state added, from its own coffers, 1·25 percent of total salaries paid in the country. Costa Rica's medical system is nationalized; that is, private, fee-for-service medicine is legal but in 1980 accounted for under 15 percent of medical consultations. Health officials estimate that around 85 percent of citizens were covered by the CCSS as of the late 1980s. The state was then making efforts to sign up uninsured citizens, most of whom are indigent rural residents living in isolated areas of the country.

Despite being the most important medical institution in the country, the CCSS has no programs or mechanisms to stimulate community participation. It has never had a community participation component, and the people I interviewed seemed to think it never will have one. The only state institution which has actively promoted community participation in health has been the Ministry of Health, which spent just 16 percent of the total health budget in 1985 (Alvarado Aguirre 1987: 149). From 1973 to 1987, the Ministry of Health's Rural Health Program was responsible for ensuring preventive care (vaccinations, nutritional surveillance, prenatal care, environmental sanitation, the monitoring of child growth and development, and education) in rural areas of the country; the Community Medicine Program provided a similar function in impoverished urban areas. In 1987 these two branches of the Ministry were combined to form the Division of Primary Health Care. The Ministry of Health is financed by the central government, with an unascertainable percentage donated by international agencies in material and technical assistance. The exact amount of foreign assistance in the Ministry's health budget was a politically sensitive issue, but the Minister of Health told me in 1989 that 5·6 percent of the Ministry's budget came from foreign sources between 1986 and 1989, with 3 percent designated for improving water and sanitation supplies. In other words, he insisted, only 2·6 percent of the total health budget came from foreign aid (Mohs 1989: personal communication). This figure seems low, but the Minister's statements show how important he considers economic self-sufficiency in health financing.

Since the early 1970s, the Ministry of Health has used the primary health care strategy, emphasizing the need to extend basic health coverage to the most remote areas of the country. The Rural Health Program, which has primary responsibility for this endeavor, is the only division within Costa Rica's health institutions which has actively promoted community participation in health (Bonilla Masis 1981). The relatively new primary health care approach was not unique to Costa Rica; it became popular throughout Latin America after an influential meeting of Ministers of Health held in 1972.

Meeting of Ministers of Health of the Americas, 1972

The 1970s were a decade of revolutionary changes in rural health care, especially in Latin America. When the Ministers of Health of the Americas met under the aegis of PAHO in Santiago, Chile, in 1972, the Allende government there was in the process of revamping the health system to allow better access for all sectors of society. The desire for change must have been contagious, for in Santiago the Ministers decreed that health was a right of every citizen, and that states were responsible for insuring that right (PAHO 1973). That meeting stimulated Latin American governments to design and implement comprehensive, state-sponsored rural health programs of the kind later championed by the World Health Organization and UNICEF under the banner of primary health care.

The document which resulted from that meeting (PAHO 1973) was one of the first to state that community participation should be a central component of plans to extend health services, and it is frequently cited as one of the catalysts of PHC in Latin America. However, the idea was not then new or unprecedented, but a reflection of trends already in progress. The military junta in Panama which seized control in 1969 made popular participation the centerpiece of all its community de-velopment efforts, in an attempt to win support from marginal sectors of society (La Forgia 1985 : 56). A private program in Mexico, called Project Piaxtla, had generated enthusiasm among local residents and health workers since it began in 1963. A pilot project in community medicine had also begun in 1970 in San Ramón, Costa Rica. The "Hospital Without Walls," as it was known, inspired many similar programs throughout Latin America, including Costa Rica's own rural health network.

The Santiago meeting was not the principal impetus for starting primary health programs in Costa Rica, yet the Ministers helped create an international climate favorable to efforts already underway in Costa Rica. Nonetheless, the desire to claim personal credit for the plan was perhaps inevitable. An ex-Minister of Health whom I interviewed made it sound as though Costa Rica's ideas for an expanded rural health program were unique. He explained that since the 1960s, a network of hospitals and clinics had been constructed along the Pan American highway and secondary roads. This left the inhabitants of dispersed rural communities, approximately 40 percent of the population, unserved by the national health system. The government, he said, decided to remedy the situation by creating two programs: the first was the CCSS universalization effort mentioned earlier, which entailed transferring all hospitals and medical personnel from the Ministry of Health and other miscellaneous agencies to the CCSS; the second was the creation of a rural health program, which would be controlled by the Ministry of Health (Ministerio de Salud 1978).

Costa Rica's rural health program was not nearly as unique as the ex-Minister would have had me believe. Nearly all the Latin American countries were starting virtually identical programs in the early 1970s, encouraged to act on humanitarian impulses by the international funds available for such programs as well as by the prospect of gaining additional domestic political support for their efforts. Costa Rica's health officials point to the country's success in implementing such an ambitious program, highlighting the domestic contributions to the program. But when compared with other programs initiated at the same time in other Latin American countries,

Surprising similarities exist in the format and structural details of many of these different government health programs – surprising until one realizes that nearly all of them are aided and monitored by the same small complex of foreign and international agencies: WHO/PAHO, AID, IDRC, UNICEF, FAO, Milbank Foundation, Rockefeller Foundation, Kellogg Foundation, etc. (Werner 1976: 5)

The international backdrop to the Costa Rican situation is an important key to understanding the community participation component of the rural health program, but it would be imprudent to judge international health initiatives by looking solely at the motivations and interests of the donor agencies. State politics are equally important in assessing how the international edicts are interpreted and implemented.

Partisan politics

In the context of a supportive international climate, Costa Rican political factionalism was equally important in determining when, why, and how community participation came to be a central feature of the rural health program in the late 1970s. Given the history of political partisanship seen in community development programs like the Juntas Progresistas in the 1950s, it is not surprising that political considerations were also central to the evolution of primary health care. By the 1980s Costa Rica had evolved a strong two-party political system, structured around a regularly elected executive branch (the presidency is limited to one four-year term) and a Legislative Assembly made up of 57 elected delegates representing all existing political parties. The Partido Liberación Nacional, a Social Democratic party, is associated with the late José Figueres Ferrer, three times President and political luminary who headed the party from its formation in 1951. Liberación, as it is known, traditionally favors a strong state role in production and finance, publicly owned businesses, and nationalized public services. Under PLN leadership after the civil war, banks were nationalized, the army was abolished, and an extensive state apparatus was constructed. Today the PLN owes its support largely to middle-class public employees who depend on state enterprises for their livelihood. The PLN has been opposed by a shifting coalition of parties, most recently by the Social Christian Partido Unidad Social Cristiana, known as Unidad or, more commonly, by the surname of the party's presidential candidate (e.g., "Carazistas" after Rodrigo Carazo or "Calderonistas" after Rafael Angel Calderón Fournier, son of former President Rafael Angel Calderón Guardia). Unidad promotes free-market economic policies and re-duced state involvement in the public sector. Competition between Liberación and its opposition sets the parameters of political discourse in the country, although at any given time five or six additional parties vie for a small share of power. The executive office of government has rotated between Liberación and the major opposition party since the 1948 war, a fact which Costa Ricans offer proudly as evidence of democracy in action.

Several factors led to the creation of an ambitious rural health program in Costa Rica during the 1970s (Valverde 1972; Vargas 1977). Health was fast becoming the most popular international development issue, which meant that funding and technical assistance would be available to countries seeking to improve their rural health programs. Community participation was an even more important trend in the early 1970s, because of AID's Title IX mandate (described in Chapter 3) and PAHO initiatives emphasizing the concept. Within Costa Rica, PLN leader José Figueres, elected President in 1970 for the third time, came into office with ambitious plans to revamp the health system. His administration concentrated on universalizing services within the social security system, but also initiated efforts to build a rural health network. The rural health program grew swiftly and efficiently under the subsequent PLN administration of Daniel Oduber (1974–8), spurred by generous inter-national financing and the solid political commitment of the Partido Liberación Nacional. Because the PLN controlled the executive office of government from 1970 to 1978, the party had eight years to solidify its reorganization of the nation's health system. Between 1973 and 1978, the government built 218 rural health posts throughout the country (Ministerio de Salud 1981: 112), staffing them with nursing auxiliaries and newly trained *asistentes de salud* (community health workers).

The first efforts to involve local communities in the primary health program were perfunctory, strictly utilitarian, and not institutionalized. They were designed to help the government carry out its plans quickly and inexpensively. For example, mobile medical teams were sporadically sent into rural areas to dispense pills and advice; sometimes jeeps with dental chairs mounted in the back seat would arrive in rural towns. All such efforts relied on some local coordination to inform prospective patients of upcoming visits. By the 1970s, rural health care became more systematized. The Ministry of Health first divided the rural zone into health "areas," each one to be covered by two paraprofessional health workers. They chose locations for the health posts and visited the communities to explain the program, asking community members to provide a space which could be used until a health post was built. Then, as one former Ministry of Health employee explained, the Ministry formed health committees in each area.

Why? To help out the health post. Because there were a few things that we told the communities they would have to provide, for example, alcohol and other basic necessities. This was very important, because this way the community felt the obligation to seek contributions, so they themselves would help out the health post. This way the people were working for the community, and the community was completely informed of what was happening... From that 'emerged communities organized for their own activities.

The gentleman who told me this had been involved in the Ministry of Health during the administration of President Oduber, from 1974 to 1978, when the major achievement of the primary health program was building rural health posts and training rural health workers. Those four years are not known particularly for their efforts to enhance community participation in health, but he was speaking to me in 1985, when community participation in health had taken on much greater significance than when he left office in 1978. He therefore wanted to claim retroactive credit – both for himself and for the PLN – for making community participation a feature of Costa Rica's rural health program. An indication of the attitude toward participation during the early stages of the rural health program is evident in comments made by the PAHO representative, to the effect that community participation in health would be important only to underwrite and publicize programs designed and implemented from above:

The participation of the community takes on great importance in the initial stages of organizing programs on the local level, not only in the construction of health posts but in divulging the advantages to the populace that will result from the program. (Villegas 1978: 19)

Toward the end of that administration, the Ministry of Health listed the isolation and passivity of rural communities as the greatest barriers to participation in health.

Someone who came into the Ministry of Health during the subsequent (1978–82) administration of Rodrigo Carazo gave a different interpretation of community participation between 1974 and 1978. He said the Oduber administration of 1974–8 had been motivated by a desire not to promote community involvement in health, but to build as many health posts as possible to show local communities (in concrete terms) its commitment to primary health care.

They saw the need to create physical facilities, but knew that none of their budgets would finance such an ambitious plan. So they looked to the communities to donate land and materials to build the posts. For about the first five years of the history of community participation in health, community input was restricted to the physical structures. Then, once the infrastructure was in place, they didn't know what to do with the communities. So they thought, well, the communities can keep on supplying some materials, cleaning the health post, painting it, doing the maintenance work. Basically the whole epoch employed a utilitarian concept of participation. Communities subsidized the state. The moment the Ministry ran out of syringes, or cotton, the community would be asked to provide it. Totally utilitarian. It was a fairly primitive concept of what we considered to be community participation.

The competitive tone detected in these two accounts derives from partisan rivalries. The 1978–82 administration of Rodrigo Carazo, of the Partido Unidad Social Cristiana, placed community participation in health at the center of its social agenda. This infuriated PLN members, who credited their own party with restructuring the health system, and who resented attempts by the opposition to "steal" issues from the PLN social agenda.

The community participation program of the late 1970s was designed to benefit the administration then in office more than the rural communities. If by promoting community participation in health an administration could gain international approval and financing while thwarting the political opposition, and if these were among the primary motives for establishing such a program, then the implications for evaluating community participation in health are serious: impediments to effective community participation should not be sought solely within rural communities, nor among the technical or bureaucratic details of program organization, but in the structure of Costa Rican politics and the cycles of international development policy. The fate of community participation in health has to be seen in the context of long-standing rifts between Costa Rica's two major political parties.

Partisanism, DINADECO, and community participation

The struggle between the Partido Liberación Nacional and the Partido Unidad Social Cristiana to govern rural development policy was in progress well before primary health care appeared on the scene. The partisan squabbling which surfaced in response to Carazo's community participation programs had its roots, according to some observers, in earlier debates over DINADECO (Dirección Nacional de Desarrollo de la Comunidad; National Directorate of Community Development). DINADECO is an integrated rural development agency, created in 1967 to coordinate the community development projects of separate government agencies. Local DINADECO units, called Asociaciones de Desarrollo, are composed of community members granted *personería jurídica*, the legal status to dispense municipal development funds. The Asociaciones de Desarrollo have remained in effect since 1968 as the only community groups with juridical power.

The idea to create one central governmental office to oversee community development dates back to 1958, when the Costa Rican Ministry of Health requested technical assistance from the United Nations to teach a course in community development (Campos and González 1977: 5). The United Nations encouraged the creation of rural community development projects throughout the late 1950s (see p. 39), so they gladly sent representatives to discuss the possibilities of community development in Costa Rica. The first meeting, held in 1959, was attended by representatives of numerous national agencies, but also by international agency representatives from CARE, UNESCO, the International Cooperation Administration (also known as Point Four, a U.S. bilateral aid program), and the Economic Commission on Latin America. A working group continued meeting through the early 1960s, with additional members attending from the Pan American Health Organization and from other countries (Campos and González 1977: 10–11).

Although discussions about the need for a Costa Rican community development office began in 1959, DINADECO was not legally constituted until 1967. This was the same time that Title IX legislation was being enacted in the United States, and some of the same rhetoric was used by politicians in both countries. As early as 1963, Costa Rican

President Francisco J. Orlich (PLN) drew an analogy between governmental support for community development and the vitality of Costa Rica's democratic system. He talked about the need to

[c]reate an administrative environment which will allow the strengthening of public civic sentiment, to the point where the local concept of democracy entails not just a horizontal sense of what the communities should demand of the Government, but a vertical sense of awareness of the obligations and responsibilities of individuals toward their neighbors, their Government, and their Nation. (Campos and González 1977: 11)

President Orlich's vision did not mention the role of partisan politics, but in its formative stages care was taken to keep DINADECO activities free from political contamination. A pilot project was finally approved by Congress in 1965, but no community-level work was conducted in late 1965 or early 1966 because the office did not want its actions associated with the presidential campaign then in progress (Campos and González 1977: 26).

Despite such precautions, DINADECO came to be seen as a PLN program. A bill to create the national office of DINADECO was proposed to Congress in 1966 by PLN congressman Armando Arauz, passed into law, and signed by President José Joaquín Trejos of the anti-PLN party, Partido Unificación Nacional (PUN). DINADECO never received the active cooperation of the Trejos administration, however, perhaps because the President "never really understood the concept of community development," but also because "the doctrine was identified with the more liberal Partido Liberación Nacional and seen pragmatically as a politically useful instrument" (Livingstone 1973: 70). Furthermore, PLN Congressmen were unwilling to assist the program in its early years, since they did not want to do anything which might keep the PUN in power for another four years (Campos and González 1977: 52).

DINADECO became even more clearly identified with the PLN under the subsequent administration of PLN President José Figueres, beginning in 1970. Figueres, in addition to enacting extensive health reforms, gave greater powers to DINADECO. He appointed a new Director, José Luis González Ramos, who had once worked with the Ministry of Health on an Alliance for Progress program to take medical services to underserved areas (Campos and González 1977: 36). With a $500,000 grant from AID and technical assistance from AITEC (Acción Internacional Técnica, a New York-based group subcontracted by AID), DINADECO grew rapidly between 1970 and 1974.

DINADECO continued to be favored by the 1974–8 administration of PLN President Daniel Oduber, according to one former DINADECO employee with whom I spoke. The Ministry of Health even developed plans to coordinate community participation in health by using DINA-DECO promoters: "the function of the DINADECO promoters, together with personnel from the Rural Community Health Program, is to organize communities so they can broach community development problems" (Villegas 1978: 19). As a result of the attention given to DINADECO by the PLN party, opposition administrations were loath to support the program. This was the situation when Carazo became President in 1978. In the words of one ex-Ministry of Health official, "Politics is very influential here. And because of that, DINADECO lost considerable influence from 1978–82."

DINADECO was unacceptable to Carazo's administration because it was associated with the PLN, yet community participation and rural development were essential to Carazo's national development agenda. Carazo needed to find another forum for community development to stay in favor with the international donor agencies and rural residents. People who worked within Carazo's administration said they intended to support individual consciousness-raising and community development by creating a new ministry. The proposed Ministerio de Promoción Humana (Ministry of Human Promotion) would replace both the Ministry of Culture and DINADECO. One Carazista told me their goal was not to eliminate DINADECO, for "DINADECO was to have been the backbone of the Ministry of Human Promotion." But when Congress opposed the creation of a new ministry, the plans were scrapped. In the meantime, DINADECO "began to spring a few leaks"; its work was "inadvertently" paralyzed while its staff waited in vain for the new ministry to be created.

The Carazista interpretation put the blame for DINADECO's downfall on the PLN-controlled Congress, rather than on deliberate neglect by the Carazo administration, as charged by PLN sympathizers. PLN members identified strongly with the DINADECO program and looked suspiciously at any attempt to change its character, especially when the reformer happened to be a member of the opposition party. The Carazistas, on the other hand, had always been skeptical of DINADECO's goals and charged that the organization was politically motivated. They accused the PLN of using DINADECO to extend its political influence in the countryside. Some said the Carazo administration set up the community participation in health program precisely to circumvent the power of DINADECO in rural regions. For the same reason, some PLN officials immediately opposed community participation in health, which they saw as a deliberate attempt to undermine DINADECO. Nevertheless, PLN Congressmen would have been unwise to criticize community participation in health too vociferously, both because their own party had begun the program and because criticism would have been imprudent given the enthusiastic international climate. If they waited until Carazo's term was finished, they knew they would be able to dismantle the program if their party won control of the executive office in 1982. In the meantime, though, the Carazo administration was forging ahead with its plans to build a strong national network of committees to promote community participation in health.

Popular participation during the Carazo administration

Carazo's inauguration speech revolved around "human promotion" and "popular participation." Both phrases, it was clear, would become watchwords of his administration. Carazo described human promotion as the process of making each and every Costa Rican into "an agent of national development," making all citizens conscious of their inherent capacity to change society and their need to accept responsibility for their own actions. He described popular participation as the permanent hallmark of democracy, investing every citizen with both the right and the obligation to participate in the government's work (*La Nación*, May 9, 1978).

When the new administration's plan to create a Ministry of Human Promotion fell through, the philosophy was transferred intact to the Ministry of Health, where the Unidad de Participación Popular (UPP) (Popular Participation Unit) was created under the auspices of the Rural Health Program. The terminology reflected the extent of politicization: while the international health literature refers to "community participation" (in Spanish *participación de la comunidad* or *participación comunitaria*), more critical analysts and some opposition political groups prefer "popular participation." Midgley described the difference this way: "While [popular participation] is concerned with broad issues of social development and the creation of opportunities for the involvement of people in the political, economic, and social life of a nation, [community participation] connotes the direct involvement of ordinary people in local affairs" (1986: 23). One's choice of terms, then, is an indication of opposing political allegiances. The political innuendo implied in the choice of terms is even more pronounced in Spanish, where the term *popular* is used to refer to social movements that oppose traditional or oligarchic political interests. Carazo, in a move emblematic of a deep political and philosophical rift over the nature of participation, called his unit "popular" rather than "community" participation. This program, the name implied, would be broad-based, egalitarian, democratic, non-paternalistic, and responsive to citizen needs.

The Ministry of Health was a logical location for a community participation program for several reasons, ranging from pragmatic to nepotistic. It was 1978, the year after the World Health Organization and UNICEF sponsored the Alma Ata Conference where community participation had emerged as a fundamental principle of primary health care. Carazo was thus capitalizing on the Alma Ata rhetoric. In addition, the health posts constructed during the previous eight years offered a nationwide, grassroots infrastructure where Ministry of Health employees could base their operations. This, according to one interviewee, was a feature DINADECO could not offer. He also said the Ministry of Health did not suffer from DINADECO's political stigma; rather the Ministry was "one of the most beloved images for community members, who felt that it was one of the few institutions which *transcended* politics."

The Carazo administration's decision to work through the Ministry of Health was also influenced by Carazo's choice for Vice-Minister of Health, a man married to the daughter of the Director of the well-known Hospital Without Walls program in San Ramón. Since 1970, the experimental program in San Ramón had taken health professionals into the communities to provide health services, based on the philosophy that good health necessitated outreach. Special dispensation had been given to the experimental program by previous governments, so that in 1978 San Ramón was the home of the only public hospital in the country not subsumed under the CCSS during the universalization process. In San Ramón the rural health posts, semi-urban health centers, and the hospital were all under the same chain of command, instead of being divided between the Ministry of Health and the CCSS as they were in the rest of the country. The Hospital Without Walls had been very successful in organizing and motivating communities through an integrated rural development model (Serra and Brenes 1983; Braveman and Mora 1987). This model, with some modifications, became the prototype for Carazo's national program to enhance community participation in health.

The San Ramón Hospital Without Walls program was established in 1970 by Dr. Guillermo Ortiz Guier, a surgeon and poet with an active commitment to community health. Dr. Ortiz took physicians, nurses, and other health professionals out of the hospital and into the rural communities to treat illness and, more importantly, to address the causes of illness in the community. Over the years, surrounding communities responded favorably to the program, and started a strong base of grassroots health activities (Ortiz 1978). When Carazo came into office in 1978, he wanted to extend the San Ramón health model to the rest of the country, but he could not convince Dr. Ortiz that he should leave his work in San Ramón to join the Ministry of Health. So he found a substitute, a person who could guarantee that the Ministry would emulate the San Ramón model. He chose Dr. Jorge Arias Sobrado, a physician trained in community medicine in Uruguay (another country with a progressive health system), who was married to Dr. Ortiz's daughter. With Dr. Arias working in the Ministry of Health, a closer relationship between San Ramón and national policy would be assured, and the symbolic association between health and democracy could be further exploited. *La Nación* repeated this connection: "With the intention of extending participatory democracy, President Carazo adopted the experience of the Hospital Without Walls in San Ramón" (*La Nación*, April 19, 1980).

The newly organized UPP (Unidad de Participación Popular) had two mandates: to organize a nationwide network of health committees, and through them to initiate community–government dialogues to address rural development problems. In addition, the UPP arranged to train local health volunteers, called *responsables de salud*, in rudimentary primary care techniques and community organization. Between 1978 and 1981, approximately 2,000 such volunteers were sent to San Ramón for instruction in primary health care and sanitation, then sent home to help out in their own communities. The UPP also organized health committees at local levels wherever rural health posts existed. Local committees were then encouraged to form *cantón* (county)-level health associations and regional health federations. When these were established, the UPP organized and conducted "community diagnoses" with approximately 45 *cantón*-level health associations. Each diagnosis took place over a weekend, bringing together representatives from every existing community organization and from several government ministries to identify problems and solutions to the development quandaries affecting each region. According to the Carazistas, this was a fundamentally different way of working with local communities than had ever existed in Costa Rican government; never before, they told me, had government representatives asked the communities to discuss and rank their needs, or worked out joint agreements to meet the most pressing needs. "It was a great community–State plenary session," said one former UPP employee. The diagnoses reportedly became the forum for unusually frank discussions between government representatives and community members, as community members ranked land tenure, alcoholism, poor roads, and unemployment among their most pressing health problems.

The Carazo administration based its entire rural development strategy on the work of the UPP, talking about it as a means to change the dominant political ideology of the country. Carazo's appointees included visionaries intrigued with the political ramifications of increasing community awareness of social and economic inequalities. In their eyes, popular participation in health was much more than a means to improve health; it was a way to transform the Costa Rican political structure. Through popular participation, one Carazista told me, individuals could become masters of their own destiny. Their goal, he said,

was to create a consciousness among the people of how they could organize themselves. But organize for what? To create a popular structure capable of lifting itself up alongside the administrative structure of government, to establish a parallel relationship of equal to equal. Health would be the initial pretext, but we also wanted to make sure that the school was functioning well, that bridges were built, that roads were improved.

The concept of community participation *per se* was not enough to generate great national enthusiasm or political support. Quite apart from whether any substantial benefits would be realized by those who participated, the concept had to be linked on an ideological level to nationally cherished symbols which would rally people behind the government's strategy. The Carazistas chose (deliberately or not) to link community participation with health and with democracy. The match was well chosen on both counts. *Democracia* is Costa Rica's hallmark, used to refer both to the country's membership in an international community of like-minded nations, and to its unique political heritage when compared with the other countries of Central America. *Democracia* is used to explain the country's stability and civility; and to justify a trace of nationalistic superiority. Costa Ricans may not have been motivated to support community participation on its own merits, but its equation with *democracia* immeasurably increased the moral weight of the program.

While community participation on its own was nothing new in the history of Costa Rican political rhetoric, the idea of communities participating with government to improve *health* was compelling, for health and democracy are important symbols in the Costa Rican context. Individual health waxes and wanes throughout the life span, thus health is elusive and its pursuit requires constant vigilance. Just as democracies are said to be under constant threat of communist takeover, health too is endangered by lurking pestilence. Democracy is equated with health, communism with scourge and illness.

Health – as a symbol and as the condition of physical well-being – has always claimed the attention of Costa Ricans, although there are indications that this value orientation may be changing. When Low (1985: 70) surveyed patient satisfaction with health services, "traditional" families expressed a more explicit concern with health than did "less traditional, more modern" families who, presumably, could take good health more for granted. Her findings imply that an explicit concern with health may decrease as disposable income increases, health services become more accessible, and the health profile of the population improves. Nonetheless, an anthropological maxim holds that attitudes change more slowly than behaviors; health and well-being (*bienestar*) remain the focus of anxiety and concern even as Costa Ricans become objectively healthier.

As people have come to assume that health is a state function (Foucault 1973: 18–20), health has evolved into a nearly universal symbol of good government. Governments, therefore, are increasingly held accountable for health. Accountability amounts to more than the actions taken to guarantee health, for a government must not only act but must also convince the populace that it cares about health. The Carazistas were perfectly aware of this. One of them told me, "We used health as a pretext for reaching the local people." They portrayed an image – consumed by a health-conscious public – of themselves as health promoters. They recognized the symbolic power they wielded when talking about health: "We utilized health as a value; an expansive, universal, and comprehensive value." They deliberately chose health as their catalyzing symbol.

Carazistas insisted that community participation would strengthen Costa Rica's democracy. They said that democracy could not be taken for granted, for it was a process to be practiced daily. Their speeches emphasized that Costa Rica needed to move beyond "formal" democracy, which consisted simply of going to the polls every four years. Many Costa Ricans sympathized with this argument: they saw their country convulsed by political enthusiasm on election day, but otherwise felt removed from the political process. The community participation program would be the route to participatory democracy. It would be a forum for enabling local leaders, fostering community dialogue, and raising political consciousness in the countryside. In so doing, the program would revitalize Costa Rica's political system by fostering new, locally chosen and legally authorized leaders who would eventually become local political representatives. No longer would the political representatives be chosen by the party leadership, but by the communities themselves. This, the Carazistas said, would destroy the fiefdoms of the political *caciques* who ran the countryside. "When we went out to talk with local leaders," one Carazista told me, "we refused to sit down with the *cacique*. We talked with the representatives the community had chosen. This was very damaging to the political leadership, to the traditional *caciquismo*." Popular representation is the hallmark of democracy, he told me, but Costa Rican political candidates have traditionally been chosen in anti-democratic fashion, based on their wealth or political connections. The anti-democratic process becomes institutionalized, he said, when politicians deny the legitimacy of organized, participating communities. In contrast, the Carazistas said they held the key to participatory democracy; community participation in health would bring about a peaceful social revolution.

The Carazistas adopted radical rhetoric that led some politicians to question the wisdom of the community participation program. Wasn't it dangerous, they wondered, to grant so much power to rural communities? Wouldn't communities seize the opportunity to rise up against the state? Wouldn't participation undermine the politicians' power and lead the country toward socialism? The Carazistas, in contrast, saw their program as a means to circumvent revolution and maintain social peace. As one prominent Carazista told me:

Under a socialist system, the end result is that the state has the last word. Under our program, the end result is the responsible exercise of liberty... It seems to me this is the vaccine against any kind of extremism, because it simply allows each person the responsible development of his own personal capacity. There is not a dictatorship in the world which hasn't fed on the ignorance of its people... Precisely the antidote to socialism is for us to have the people living and reiterating their own rights and convictions.

The Carazistas' vision of community participation was not radical, he insisted, because it sought to strengthen, not overturn, the political system. Proponents said that Costa Rica's democracy would be less susceptible to subversion if the government listened and responded more sincerely to people's needs.

This optimistic political vision was marred by a conspicuous lack of consensus within Carazo's own party. Carazo's liberal social policies appeased those on the left wing of the Partido Unidad Social Cristiana, while his conservative economic policies satisfied those on the right. In general, though, it should be remembered that Unidad's platform had historically been hostile to community participation in government decision-making, and Carazo's UPP program represented a radical departure from this legacy. As one observer put it, Carazo was a moderate leftist of Social Democratic extraction even though his advisers were from the center-right. "Odd bedfellows," he said. It may not be so odd if we consider that many of Carazo's supporters, and Carazo himself, were ex-PLN members. And the coalition Carazo headed was an unlikely amalgam of disgruntled ex-PLN reformists, 1940s-era Calderonistas, and ultra-rightist businesspeople. In this political context, the popular participation program has to be seen as a historical anomaly, which gained a political toehold only because a few high government functionaries actively promoted the idea ("although," as one jaded observer said, "perhaps not with much ideological clarity").

Carazo-era politicians, UPP employees, and even some Liberacionistas I interviewed were adamant that Carazo's popular participation program was free from partisanism and political favoritism. The Carazistas cited these facts as evidence of their openness: among the 45 *cantón*-level health associations which were created, 30 presidents were Liberacionistas, five were Communists, and only ten were from Unidad. The President of the national health confederation was a Liberación leader from San Ramón, and the Vice-President was a socialist leader from Guanacaste. One former UPP employee who was neither PLN nor Unidad told me, "It was completely paradoxical. They [the Carazistas] never tried to instill any political militancy, nor was there any manipulation of the community organizations for electoral ends. Quite the contrary, the majority of cantonal associations were headed by Liberacionistas, yet this was a program of Carazo's government." Even a Liberacionista who worked in the Ministry of Health under the subsequent administration said, "Their motives were honest and good; there was never any intention on their part to politicize the issue." Carazistas insisted that the organizational structure of participation never became the patrimony of any faction or political party. Certainly they thought the government should be involved in promoting participation, "but without assuming paternalistic, 'statist', or partisan attitudes" (*La Nación*, April 19, 1980). In the words of one of Carazo's health functionaries, "Our program was not going to impose patterns but to raise consciousness [*concientizar*] that they could make their own decisions. This formative process obviously had a high degree of indoctrination, but the indoctrination directed people towards participation, not toward our cause or any political project."

Their political openness, however, was punctuated by opportunistic jibes at the PLN. In 1978–82 press accounts and 1985 interviews, Carazistas frequently contrasted their participatory strategy with the "interventionism and paternalism" supposedly practiced by the Liberacionistas. For example, the Vice-Minister of Culture was quoted in the newspaper saying that Costa Rica's democracy embraced and enhanced participation: "the State should be neither totalitarian, nor interventionist like that of the Social Democrats" (*La Nación*, April 19, 1980). An influential political appointee in Carazo's Ministry of Health told me their program would allow people to manage their own development agendas, without waiting passively to receive help from paternalistic programs of the sort which typified the PLN political philosophy. A member of Carazo's cabinet argued that the country had had excellent legislation promoting community participation, but that "from 1949 to the present, it has been manipulated traditionally as a political instrument of the Partido Liberación Nacional." Sincere as they may have been in their intentions to keep their program free from partisanship, some Carazistas could not resist the opportunity to contrast their supposedly altruistic goals with those of their political opponents.

Carazo's administration was left with little time to worry about its social agenda after 1980, when the country's economic crisis became acute. Carazo is remembered today mainly for "bringing the Chicago boys" – and economic havoc – to Costa Rica. Promoting free enterprise at a time of world depression forced Carazo to borrow heavily from foreign banks and international lending agencies. In the last two years of the Carazo administration, the economy fell into ruin (Fallas 1982). The foreign debt tripled between 1978 and 1984, and between 1979 and 1984 "the GNP per capita declined 13 percent, open unemployment increased by 69·5 percent, consumption of basic food items declined by 37·4 percent, the currency was devalued by some 550 percent, and imports declined by 48·3 percent and exports, by 11·6 percent" (Céspedes, DiMare, and Jiménez 1985, cited in Seligson and Gómez 1989: 164).

In spite of its economic woes, the administration continued to use the rhetoric of popular participation to assert its commitment to Costa Rica's health system and to participatory democracy. The rhetoric masked a number of policy contradictions. The Vice-Minister of Health, who had headed the community participation program, became ambassador to France in 1981. To insure that the UPP program would not be dismantled after the Vice-Minister left, Carazo requested that its offices be moved to the presidential palace, where it would presumably be safer. The fact that Carazo could not trust the Ministry of Health to safeguard the program was, in the words of one informant, "another example of the fundamental contradictions it [the UPP program] generated within the party's governing team." In the countryside, meanwhile, budget cuts forced several health posts to close or to operate without the requisite staff, while no funds were available to train rural health workers (Morgan 1987b). Thus while the government continued to assert its commitment to community participation and rural health care, in the context of a severe economic crisis it simultaneously cut services and bowed to internal party pressures to curtail both programs.

Community participation in health was opposed by middle-level technocrats and bureaucrats who feared that direct dialogue between local communities and state institutions would eliminate their public sector jobs. Some expressed their opposition by refusing to recognize the state–community agreements put together during the community diagnoses; consequently some of the work promised by the state was never completed, causing the government to lose credibility. Professional privilege and status also worked against the program. One national planner reportedly criticized the program by saying he had studied for 12 years and gone to London to get a planning degree, only to have his post usurped by illiterate peasants. Many doctors were opposed, especially when UPP employees suggested that community members might evaluate physician performance (Mohs 1988: 29–31). In short, several important and extremely influential sectors of Costa Rican society opposed Carazo's program.

The community participation program had not been a response to needs expressed either by Congressmen or by organized social movements. Rather, it was the pet project of a small group of politicians who suddenly found themselves in a position to realize their plans in a way that would bring them international prestige. The program ultimately fell prey to one of the factors which allowed it to flourish for a time: active support from the highest echelons of government. Liberacionistas were obliged by their own sense of partisan rivalry to oppose the program. They were driven toward this position precisely because their political opponent, Rodrigo Carazo, had given the program top billing and because Carazo's Vice-President had been actively and publicly involved in facilitating the UPP process.

A last-ditch effort to save the program took place in the last days of the Carazo administration. The occasion was the inauguration – amid great fanfare in the Costa Rican National Theatre – of the Confederación Nacional de Salud (National Health Confederation). It was April 17, 1982, just three weeks before PLN President-elect Luis Alberto Monge would be sworn in. The Confederation comprised local and regional health association representatives from around the country. The inauguration was attended by Dr. Hernan Acuña Monteverde, Director of the Pan American Health Organization in Washington, D.C., as well as the PAHO representative in Costa Rica, Dr. Emigdio A. Balbuena V, and President Rodrigo Carazo (*La República*, April 17, 1982). Around the same time, President Carazo passed an executive decree giving the President of the Confederation the right to sit – with full voting powers – on the Consejo Nacional Sectorial de Salud, a policy-making board comprising the leaders of Costa Rica's governmental health institutions.

This would be the first time that community interests were represented officially at such a high level of decision-making. Another executive decree left by Carazo proclaimed that the 17th of April henceforth would be celebrated as "Popular Participation Day." Then Carazo's term ended.

The demise of community participation in health, 1982–6

By the time President Luis Alberto Monge of the Partido Liberación Nacional came into office in 1982, the political context of health care had changed considerably since the last PLN administration. The country was in a severe economic recession. Poverty rates had risen from 25 percent in 1977 to 71 percent in 1982 (Castro 1983) and social unrest was growing. Currency had been devalued in 1980, loan payments halted in 1981, and the International Monetary Fund was calling for social service cutbacks. The country grew dangerously dependent on foreign aid and debt relief packages; in 1985 it was estimated that $600 million – almost $2 million per day – was being injected into the economy from abroad (Sanders 1986: 5). Doctors went on strike in early 1982 demanding a salary increase, the cost of importing medications rose by 400 percent, and numerous rural health centers were closed. Spiraling health costs and allegations of low-quality care set off a national debate about the wisdom of state-sponsored medical care, with some sectors arguing for the "reprivatization" of services.

Within this economic context, and given its partisan prejudice, the Monge administration was not inclined to give high priority to Carazo's community participation program. If national-level politics had been Monge's sole concern, he might have disbanded the program on the spot. But community participation was still popular among international development agencies, and Costa Rica was more dependent than ever on their support. Furthermore, Costa Rica had acquired an international reputation for excellence in primary health care which necessitated some semblance of community participation. It would have been imprudent for the incoming administration to eliminate all vestiges of participation in health. The new administration instead retained the program in letter but not in spirit. By deliberately neglecting the program, they managed to eliminate it gradually, and in 1985 the Ministry of Health closed the division which had been dedicated to community participation.

The process of "cutting off the oxygen" to community participation in health took place on several fronts simultaneously. First, the Director of community participation appointed in 1982 had political connections but no prior UPP experience. His first act in office was to change the name of the program, because he did not like the sound of "popular" (as opposed to "community") participation. This was a man who saw communists lurking throughout the state apparatus. He explained:

because *participación popular* sounded a lot like Vanguardia Popular [the name of Costa Rica's Communist party], see? That program definitely had enthroned "reds." Their offices were used to meet with people from the Farabundo Martí [a reference to the Frente Farabundo Martí de Liberación Nacional, the armed wing of the Salvadoran rebels]. I was the first to take the reds out of power there. It had to be done, kaput.

He was not the only one to cite communistic tendencies as a justification for eliminating the program. Monge's Minister of Health told me he also felt that the UPP was infiltrated by communists and needed to be purged. Their allegations are rather ironic, considering that Costa Rica's Communist Party was then at one of the weakest points in its history (Solís 1989). Nevertheless, the new Director, with the backing of the Minister, renamed the program Promoción y Fomentación de la Comunidad (Community Promotion and Fomentation), or PROFOCO. Unfortunately, his virulent anti-communism blinded him to the benign, democratic social reforms which had motivated many UPP employees under Carazo.

Second, the Monge administration refused to recognize the community participation infrastructure set up during Carazo's term. Cantonal and regional health associations were not given a place within the Ministry's operations, and the National Confederation of Health was completely ignored, as though it had never existed. Local health committees – which predated Carazo – were still encouraged, but their sole function was to maintain the rural health posts. No mechanisms were created for health committees to interact with higher levels of the Ministry of Health. No community representative was permitted to sit on the Consejo Nacional Sectorial de Salud. The Liberacionistas also ignored Carazo's presidential decree establishing "Popular Participation Day."

Third, the Ministry of Health cut PROFOCO's budget allotment. The government continued to pay the salaries of UPP (now PROFOCO) personnel as long as they worked for the Ministry, but the majority soon found other jobs. PROFOCO received no budget at all from 1983 until the program was disbanded in 1985. When I visited the PROFOCO offices in early 1985, an employee literally borrowed a pencil from me while remarking ruefully on PROFOCO's economic plight.

Fourth, the PLN administration began to lobby openly against the San

Ramón Hospital Without Walls, which had been the prototype for Carazo's community participation program. They argued strongly that the San Ramón hospital should be placed under CCSS control, along with all the other hospitals in the country. Supporters of the Hospital Without Walls saw the PLN stance as retribution for San Ramón's key role in Carazo's health programs. Others said that the PLN position was motivated by fear that the San Ramón example had become potentially too disruptive at a time of economic crisis, when social unrest was increasing throughout the country. They pointed out that San Ramón's local health committees had moved beyond health issues to indict poverty, unemployment, and landlessness as among the major causes of disease. Through the Hospital Without Walls program, communities were organized to combat malnutrition, to improve roads and water systems, to bring electricity to unserved areas, to make sure children were vaccinated, and to organize agricultural cooperatives (Ortiz 1978). PLN health officials said it was unfair for the San Ramón hospital to stay under the auspices of the Ministry of Health when all other public hospitals had been transferred to the CCSS. Sectors of the San Ramón population favored the proposal to have the hospital administered by the CCSS (*La Nación*, November 30, 1984), but others (including all the regional health committees) were adamantly opposed (*La Nación*, November 25, 1984). Early in January, 1985, the PLN got its way. San Ramón's hospital was transferred to the CCSS and given a new director (*La República*, December 16, 1984), thus severing its preventive community health outreach programs from hospital services. As one Ministry of Health worker put it, "the hospital now has walls."

Fifth, the Monge administration created an alternative institutional mechanism, supposedly to facilitate community participation in health. The Juntas de Salubridad y Seguridad Pública (Health and Public Security Commissions, hereafter JSSS) were created by executive decree in April, 1983 (*La Gaceta*, April 25, 1983). The administration justified the JSSS as a step toward integrating the preventive services offered by the Ministry of Health with the curative services provided by the CCSS. "Integration of services" became the Monge administration's health priority, much as community participation had been the health focus of the Carazo administration. The Minister of Health reasoned that the JSSS would facilitate the process of integration in each *cantón*. Each JSSS would consist of seven members: local medical directors of the Ministry of Health and the CCSS, the municipal president, and four community representatives. The latter would not be elected, but chosen by the Minister of Health from a list of ten recommended by the communities.

Critics of the JSSS (and there were many among the people I interviewed) argued that the model was retrogressive compared with what Carazo had instituted. According to one skeptical Ministry employee, the plan had been retrieved from a dusty archive at the CCSS, an institution never noted for its attempts to involve communities in health care. The JSSS were denounced as undemocratic, since the communities could not elect their own representatives and nominees could be rejected unilaterally by the Minister of Health. Because the JSSS operated only in cantonal seats, isolated rural communities were rarely represented, nor were mechanisms set up to solicit opinions or feedback from those who used the rural health posts. The responsibilities of the JSSS were never clearly delineated, so many of the busy people designated to sit on the Juntas felt their time was being wasted. Many cantons thus complied with the order as a condition of integrating services, but abandoned the Juntas soon afterward. There was no penalty for discontinuing a JSSS, since no state institution was charged with overseeing or evaluating the organizations. According to one PROFOCO employee, 81 JSSS were created in 1984, only 20 of which were still functioning in 1985. The JSSS might have succeeded on one count: getting functionaries from the two separate state health institutions – the CCSS and the Ministry of Health – to sit in one room and talk with each other. As forums for community participation in health, however, the JSSS were completely useless.

The PLN was charged with maliciously and undemocratically destroying a valuable, internationally respected community participation program. They responded that Carazo's program had been a politically motivated attempt to duplicate DINADECO's community development functions. DINADECO, it will be remembered, had been seen as a PLN program. One state employee told me that Carazo had intended to set up an equivalent rural power base which could be manipulated by Unidad just as DINADECO was supposedly manipulated by the PLN.

Carazistas were especially sensitive to criticisms that they had been looking for an alternative to DINADECO. They said such comments were excuses given by the PLN to justify dismantling the community participation program. One former UPP employee said:

The newly-appointed PLN Minister of Health had political prejudices, of partisan nature, against the community leaders. He chose to believe those who said it was a political project with roots in the electoral campaign. But I don't accept their assertions that this program was political; all programs are political. Every one. Sure, the program had its objectives, its vision, and all that is political. But it was never intended to influence the elections. Nonetheless the Minister told us he didn't want to hear anything more about popular participation, that even the name was disagreeable [Unidad de Participación Popular]. He said the name sounded ideologically dangerous. And this despite the fact that the program came from an eminently democratic party.

There were charges and countercharges that community participation was manipulated for partisan purposes, and indeed it seems that partisanism was one salient reason for the program's demise in July 1985, when PROFOCO was officially disbanded. The few lingering personnel were transferred to another unit of the Ministry of Health, where they would no longer have anything to do with participation. Between 1985 and 1987, neither the Ministry of Health nor the CCSS sponsored any programs to enhance community participation in health.

Primary health care – as a PLN-identified program – continued to be nurtured under the Monge administration. The rural health program was resuscitated after the setbacks it suffered during the economically disastrous final years of the Carazo administration. Additional rural health workers were trained to augment services in the countryside, and additional funds were solicited from international donor agencies to amplify primary health programs. Yet now the programs were operating without a community participation component, without one of the elements judged by the World Health Organization to be essential to effective primary health care.

Costa Rican health officials knew that the *rhetoric* of participation continued to be important, even though they had abandoned the strategy. For that reason, health documents issued during the Monge (1982–6) and Arias (1986–90) administrations continued to assert that community participation was an integral component of Costa Rican Ministry of Health programs (see Jaramillo 1987; Ministerio de Salud, Memoria 1988: 40). Monge's Minister of Health, in his influential treatise on Costa Rica's health problems, wrote that a "model of community participation should be promoted to the maximum as one of the fundamental priorities for change" (Jaramillo 1984: 54) and "all individuals within each community should try to participate in the health care decisions affecting themselves and their families, to the full extent of their individual potential and together as communities" (Jaramillo 1984: 93). Community participation was a feature of the integration plan jointly published by the Minister of Health and Executive Director of the CCSS (Jaramillo and Miranda 1985: 57). Although community participation in health ceased to have any practical reality, the fact that it still carried rhetorical significance in the international health community was not lost on Monge's health officials.

Perhaps for this reason, the Ministry of Health halfheartedly allowed community participation to be revived in 1987, under the heading of the

Programa Nacional de Participación Comunitaria (National Community Participation Program). This program was funded externally, by the Pan American Health Organization and UNICEF; like other such financially dependent programs, it was fated to disappear because it did not have access to a permanent budget line within the Ministry of Health. Unlike its predecessors, this program was managed by the Department of Social Work rather than by the rural health or PHC divisions of the Ministry. Its duties pertained only to the health sector, and not to housing, agriculture, employment, or other sectors. There was, in other words, no attempt at intersectoral coordination, the need for which is discussed in much of the Costa Rican PHC literature (see Villalobos 1989). The program identified and targeted three priority needs for its work: garbage disposal, water, and latrines. According to the Director of the program, whom I interviewed in 1989, the program employed just three people to promote community participation, and these three divided their time among other social work responsibilities.

Not only did the duties of the participation program change, but the philosophy of the program shifted as well. *Autogestión* (self-motivation) or *autocuidado* (self-care) began to dominate the rhetoric of participation. The idea, although not stated in such blatant terms, was to shift responsibility for health matters from the state to the communities, especially in the area of environmental sanitation. When I asked the director how local health committees were integrated into the program, she replied that her employees worked mainly at the level of regional health centers rather than the dispersed rural health posts where the health committees were located. The health committees still existed, she said, in their time-honored role of changing light bulbs and painting the health posts, "which is also a form of participating." Programmatic, personnel, and financial limitations forced the program leaders to spend their time training doctors and rural health workers rather than working directly with local communities. When judged against the popular participation programs of Carazo's era, this program was an obvious step backwards.

Conclusion

The Costa Rican state has been involved in the provision of health services for 60 years now, and debates over the appropriate nature of state involvement continue. Some Costa Ricans argue that the state apparatus is too cumbersome and costly to provide efficient health services for all citizens (see Morgan 1987b). The answer, they feel, is privatization (also euphemistically referred to as "economic democratization") of health services. On the other side of the debate are those who argue that state control over health services is the only way to insure fair and equitable access to medical care regardless of ability to pay. For-profit medicine, these critics argue, would inevitably make it more difficult for poor people to obtain high-quality medical care or preventive services.

Like most health policy debates in Costa Rica, the current debate over privatization is conducted largely without popular input. Initiatives are introduced, weighed, and decided by politicians, health planners, and representatives of international agencies without consulting local constituencies. Whatever the outcome of the debate, new programs and policies are likely to be presented as *faits accomplis* to consumers, without resort to anything resembling community participation in decision-making (see Shallat 1989).

The anti-participatory nature of health planning should not be surprising given the historical record. Since the early days of the United Fruit Company and Rockefeller Foundation medical programs, the opinions of local communities have been largely irrelevant to health planners. The only exception to this trend was during the late 1970s and early 1980s, when a short-lived but apparently sincere effort was made to open a state–citizen dialogue about health and rural development needs. Paradoxically, though, Carazo cannot claim sole credit for this initiative. His popular participation program would not have received such concerted attention had it not been for the strong support and financial backing of foreign aid agencies. The proverbial timing was right. The Alma Ata Conference coincided with the election of a President eager to build his populist image by appealing to rural supporters. The international agenda fitted well with Carazo's platform. It was a serendipitous combination of events, then, that allowed community participation in health to achieve such (temporary) prominence.

Nonetheless, if there is a historical pattern in the events related in this and earlier chapters, it is a decided lack of community involvement in rural health decision-making despite the high-sounding rhetoric. Carazo's participation program was something of an aberration, and partisan disputes were not the only reason it failed. Over the years, Costa Rica's rural social structure has incorporated several impediments to greater participation by the poor. Inequitable land tenure patterns, the *caciquismo* of local power elites, state paternalism, the physical mobility of the poorest strata in the form of constant migrations, and the continued dependence of poor people have created a situation in which it is difficult for the state and the rural poor to collaborate on rural development projects. The participation strategy envisioned by Carazo's UPP team was based on an egalitarian philosophy of rural social structure which would have put rural community members on an equal footing with state functionaries. Ideally, they would have worked together, side by side, to resolve health and development problems. This level of egalitarianism was unacceptable not only to paternalistic bureaucrats within the state apparatus, but to rural elites who benefited from the status quo. The members of one rural community, meanwhile, seemed to take this all in their stride.

6 La Chira: participation in a banana-growing community

On days when there is *corta* (cutting), the men who cut bananas rise at 4 a.m. to dress quickly. Their tee-shirts and shorts are permanently stained with black juice from the banana trees. A truck passes at 4:30 to drive them to the plantation three miles away. By the first light of day they are already at work in teams of two, measuring the hanging stalks of fruit with a calibrator to check whether the bananas are the right size for shipping to Germany, or Italy, or the United States. If the bananas are the right size, one man stands underneath the stem with a cushion on his shoulder (to avoid bruising the fruit), while the other cuts the stem with two or three swift swings of his machete, taking care to avoid hitting his teammate. The carrier hauls the 60 to 90 pound stalk to an overhead cable gridwork that crisscrosses the plantation. Together they hang the stem from the cable and go back to find another. When they have collected 25 stems, another worker comes by and hitches himself to the front of the line. He is the sweat-drenched human tractor who pulls the fruit to the central packing plant (*empacadora*).

The women get up at 5 a.m., fix a breakfast of bread and coffee, and get their children up and dressed. The truck passes again at 5:30 to pick up the women and the few men who work in the packing plant. By the time they get to work, the first stems of bananas are coming in from the fields, ready to be cleaned, inspected, selected, cut into bunches called "hands" (*manos*), labeled with Dole or Chiquita stickers, packed into boxes, and loaded onto refrigerated boxcars. When they reach the port, the boxcars are loaded directly onto a container boat bound for Europe or the United States. The length of the workday depends on how many boxes of bananas headquarters ordered; a large cutting, 3,000 boxes, may keep the packing plant staff working until 7 p.m.

Except for the plantation maintenance staff – the ditch diggers and pesticide sprayers – people work only when there is *corta*. It could be two days a week, or it could be every day (except Sundays) for two weeks. Everyone enjoys the lazy days when there is no *corta*; then they can go fishing or scrub the laundry or visit a neighbor to see if she might give

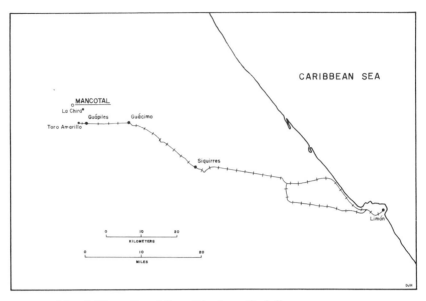

Map 2 The railroad from Limón to Guápiles

them some ripe avocados or *juplones*. But they only get paid for the days they work.

I chose to work in La Chira (the pseudonym means "banana flower") after consulting with officials in the Ministry of Health in San José and Guápiles. The Director of Rural Health helped me pick a site that would fulfill my criteria: somewhere in Limón province (the poorest and most rural province in Costa Rica), in a banana region (to incorporate the history of United Fruit Company's health programs), typical of other communities in banana regions in terms of ethnicity, age structure, male–female ratio, and problems of community health organization. As banana-growing communities go, the 700 residents of La Chira are more independent than those in a company town, and more dependent than people who live in the larger urban centers of Guápiles or Siquirres. I chose the canon of Pococí, located in the lowlands northeast of Turrialba volcano, 100 kilometers west of the Atlantic port of Limón and a four-hour bus ride from San José. Guápiles, the center of Pococí, is now a rapidly growing city of 11,000, but for most of the past 60 years the area was a sparsely inhabited, isolated backwater.

At the time of the Spanish Conquest the area around Pococí was inhabited by Guetare Amerindians. Remnants of their rich material culture survive today in worked gold ornaments, ceramic pots and figurines, carved stone metates, and jade pendants which are excavated and sold (illegally) by local residents. The indigenous peoples of the Pococí region disappeared hundreds of years ago, victims of disease and warfare when Spanish settlers arrived in the late sixteenth century.

Judging by what historical information is available, the region remained sparsely populated until the 1880s, when bananas were first planted by the North American, Minor Keith, for his nascent export industry (Stewart 1967). A railroad was built in the 1880s to haul bananas from Guápiles to Limón, the Atlantic port. For the next 100 years (until around 1980), the railroad remained the only link to the rest of the country. The main rail line linked San José to Limón via Siquirres, so the line from Siquirres westward to Guápiles was a spur not heavily used. When a road was finally built connecting Guápiles and Siquirres, it took several hours to traverse by auto. Cars had to cross the rivers on bridges built for trains; as late as 1979 the trip reportedly took four hours. The road was paved around 1981 and the same trip now takes 20 minutes. Guápiles was thus an inaccessible and undesirable place to live, in the eyes of most Costa Ricans, until 1981. In 1987 a new road was opened north out of San José to Limón, passing right by Guápiles and greatly easing the trip between Guápiles and San José, which now takes just over an hour by car.

The canton of Pococí, which included what are now the two cantons of Guápiles and neighboring Guácimo, was formed on September 19, 1911, under the administration of President Ricardo Jiménez (*La República*, October 16, 1965). The United Fruit Company was active in the region before the turn of the century; in fact, a banana plantation in Guácimo was abandoned due to disease in 1913. In 1934, the Company turned over 10,000 hectares of land to the state, in the Siquirres, Guápiles, and Pococí regions (Archivo Nacional Congreso 1935).

There are two theories about the origins of the word Guápiles: the town was either named after a wealthy landowner's hacienda, or after the indigenous word (Guapes) for the two rivers which pass through the region. Now known as the Toro Amarillo and the Chirripó, these rivers are part of the reason why Guápiles stayed isolated from the rest of the country for so many years. During the rainy season the rivers become violent, unpredictable channels carrying runoff from the Irazu and Turrialba volcanoes to the sea. Bridges are still washed away frequently when the rivers overflow their banks, and landslides are common.

When I arrived in Guápiles, the Rural Health Supervisor helped me select a community for a case study of participation in health. I wanted to live in a village with a rural health post, less than 1,000 inhabitants, electricity, and an average (or at least not atypical) panorama of participation in health. After narrowing the possibilities, he took me to

La Chira, located about 8 kilometers northwest of town along a bumpy dirt road.

La Chira is a town located in the municipality of Guápiles. The community is home to about 650 people who live along the road leading from Guápiles to the inland banana plantations. The region was created administratively in 1930, after the United Fruit Company had abandoned its holdings: "the government divided the area into two colonies and distributed the land to heads of family. One of these colonies became the municipality [central Guápiles] and the other was named [La Chira]" (Instituto Nacional de Vivienda y Urbanización [INVU] 1980: 13). Today most residents work in one of the nearby banana plantations. This is not, however, a company town in the traditional sense: most families own their own homes and small plots of land. Workers commute daily to the banana *fincas*, many of which are owned by independent absentee landowners who have long-term contracts with the multinationals to buy their fruit. The distinction between "independent" and "company" *fincas* is not, however, as clear-cut as it might appear. The labor relations manager at one of the multinational offices told me that independent owners sometimes front for the multinationals to avoid labor strife (because unions are often more antagonistic toward multinationals than toward independent owners). In fact, some of the "independent" *fincas* around La Chira are deeply mortgaged to the multinationals.

La Chira is served by all basic public utilities: electrical lines were installed around 1977–8, and the single public telephone was installed in 1976. A potable water system was introduced into the area with the banana industry in the late 1960s, because the packing plants require a steady supply of clean water. Now, however, the 20-year-old water system has taken on more customers than it can supply, and most La Chira homes are without water every morning. Consequently, water was cited as a major problem by community residents. Transportation is the other major problem. Although La Chira is close to Guápiles, a trip to town was a major undertaking in 1985 when I lived there. Few residents own cars, and the bus passes on its way into town just three times daily, at 6 a.m., 3 p.m., and 7 p.m. Owners of the private bus company know that the public wants more frequent service, but they refuse to make more trips because the roads are so poor. Plantation owners have no incentive to invest in road improvement because all bananas are shipped directly from the plantations by rail. In 1985, La Chira residents considered road improvement to be one of the community's top priorities; by 1988 the road from La Chira to Guápiles was paved.

La Chira's profile of salient community problems corresponds with what was found in all of Pococí in 1974, when a government-sponsored

Table 1. *1984 population census*

	No. of Housing Units	Men	Women
Costa Rica	544,094	1,204,401	1,204,832
Limón province	40,645	86,539	79,686
Pococí	10,251	22,871	20,798
Guápiles	2,589	5,564	5,493
La Chira	144	359	298
Jiménez	696	1,383	1,321
Rita	2,749	6,373	5,435
Roxana	1,349	3,032	2,745
Cariari	2,652	6,062	5,379
Colorado	216	457	425

community survey revealed the following patterns: 14 communities cited roads and 14 cited potable water as their most important problems; 11 cited electricity; five cited health; three cited education, two cited markets, and one each cited the need for a rural guard post, latrines, and a community hall (Instituto de Fomento y Asesoría Municipal [IFAM] 1974).

Table 1 shows the number of household and sex-specific populations for the municipality of Guápiles, the community of La Chira, other communities in the region, the province, and the nation. La Chira, like some of the other banana-growing regions in Pococí, has more men than women, reflecting the predominantly male nature of the industry.

Other data from a 1982 government report show the canton of Pococí to have a 15 percent illiteracy rate (compared to about 10 percent nationally) and 7 percent unemployment rate. The birth rate in 1982 was 38/1,000, just slightly higher than the 30/1,000 reported nationwide. There is some discrepancy over the infant mortality rate, reported in one document as 51 per 1,000 live births and in another as 21/1,000. The Director of the Guápiles hospital reported it to be 11/1,000 in 1985, considerably lower than the national average of 18/1,000. Likewise the crude mortality rate is reported in one document as 5·7/1,000 and in another as 4·0/1,000, while the national average is 3·9/1,000. Twenty-three percent of people who live in Pococí have migrated there from other areas of the country; 33·8 percent of the population is economically active (IFAM 1982; Jaramillo 1984).

In 1974, a government survey reported that 38 percent of homes in the canton of Pococí had potable water; Pococí thus ranked lowest on a 4-point national scale designed by the agency. Twenty-five percent had

Table 2. *Leading causes of death in Pococí canton (1984)*

Death	Rank	%
Symptoms and ill-defined conditions	1	14·7
Diseases of the respiratory system	2	8·3
Certain causes of perinatal mortality	2	8·3
Other accidents including belated effects	3	5·5
Diseases of the digestive system	4	4·6
Tumors of the lymphatic and circulatory system	4	4·6
Chronic heart disease	5	3·7
Tumors of the digestive system	5	3·7
Accidental falls	5	3·7

Source: Ministerio de Salud, Region Huétar Atlántica, 1984. Diagnóstico de Salud, Provincia de Limón, San José, Costa Rica, p. 15.

electricity (also lowest on the national scale), and 81 percent had toilets (including latrines), making Pococí third on the 4-point scale (IFAM 1974). This situation has improved considerably since 1974, although current figures for the canton level are not available.

When health workers surveyed sanitary conditions in La Chira in 1984, they reported that of 128 occupied houses, 121 had indoor potable water. Only two families drew their water from streams, and five were without a regular source of water. Ninety-six homes used toilets with septic tanks, and 30 used latrines. Garbage disposal was perhaps the most pressing sanitation problem, since only 30 houses had access to public garbage collection services. Forty-one families buried their garbage, 50 burned it, and seven dumped it in rivers or pastures.

Pesticide intoxication is a serious but largely undocumented problem in all banana-growing regions of the country, and Pococí canton is no exception. Exact numbers of cases are impossible to obtain because hospitals do not record the diagnoses of patients seen on an outpatient or emergency basis (categories which comprise most pesticide intoxication consultations). An obligatory report is supposed to be filled out for each pesticide intoxication and sent to the Ministry of Health, but in practice the system does not work. There is a National Center for Control of Intoxications which does statistical analysis of reported cases; unfortunately, reporting is left to the discretion of the affected. A study done by that unit in 1988 found 731 cases of intoxication for Pococí canton in 1987. That same year, there were a total of 683 cases for the entire country reported to the Centro de Intoxicaciones and 193 to the Ministry of Health. Underreporting is obviously a serious problem (Dr. Roberto Castro Córdoba, Ministry of Health: personal communication).

Epidemiological and ethnomedical profile

Health services are generally adequate according to La Chira residents. This perception derives from their feeling that health is not among their major "felt needs." They consider themselves healthy, especially in comparison to nearby settlements without running water or indoor plumbing. "There," they say, "the children are laden with worms." Parasites are considered a sign of poverty from which few La Chira children suffer. Today's grandparents report that many of their children died young (12 out of 15 in the case of one couple), but these days people cannot even recall the last time a child died. Residents feel they are well served by medical facilities and they rarely complain about the quality of care.

Ethnomedical beliefs in La Chira follow the general patterns outlined by Richardson and Bode (1971) and Low (1982, 1985). Religious healing is not as evident in rural La Chira as it appears to be in the cities, although some La Chira residents said they prayed to Dr. Moreno Cañas to heal grave illnesses (see Low 1982). The hot/cold dichotomy and *nervios* are common etiologic explanations in La Chira, and *pega* is a common ailment. *Pega* is described as a stomach or intestinal blockage (Simpson 1988). Symptoms include loss of appetite and an inability to urinate, defecate, or vomit. Several older La Chira residents – not considered specialized *curanderos* – treat *pega* by vigorous massage, sometimes administering a purgative to induce vomiting. Some pregnant La Chira women still consult empirical midwives called *parteras* (one or two of whom practice clandestinely in Guápiles), but virtually all births take place in the Guápiles hospital. Costa Rican anthropologist Marta Pardo reminds us (1984) that *automedicación*, or ethnomedical self-care, needs to be understood not as ethnological esoterica, but in a political-economic context in which medicine is a commodity; in other words, she says, *automedicación* is a response to the particular set of economic and ideological conditions which characterize Costa Rican capitalism.

Most medicine is secularized and local concepts of disease follow biomedical rationale. In 1985, the itinerate Ministry of Health doctor posted to Guápiles told me his consultations are composed of the following: family planning, maternal and child health problems, skin diseases, respiratory problems like bronchitis and asthma, and some leishmaniasis in areas where land is being freshly cleared. Pesticide intoxication, he said, is a big problem in the hospital emergency rooms.

A nutritional research branch of the state-run Asignaciones Familiares published a study of the nutritional status of banana workers. Findings showed that the three most important determinants of nutritional status were: (1) income and buying power; (2) labor instability and insecurity; (3) migration. The cost of the basic food basket in banana regions was 17 percent higher than the minimum wage in 1980. Migration was a cause of discontinuity in health records, lack of prenatal care and follow-up, and continuity of care. This was caused by the 3-month layoff rule, according to which workers have no labor guarantees (Tristan 1980).

Community organizations in La Chira

Twelve community organizations exist in La Chira. Some are mandated by the state, others are locally organized. La Chira has no local corporate identity except for the Asociación de Desarrollo (Development Association), the government-mandated branch of DINADECO. The Asociación de Desarrollo is subsidized by state funds channeled through the municipality. Its members are the only community residents invested with *personería jurídica* (legal authority). Other state-mandated organizations include the health committee, nutrition center committee, school board, and school parents association. In large part the organizational structure of the community is imposed from the top down by government ministries which oversee local development projects.

There are, nonetheless, a few committees organized around sports or specific *ad hoc* community projects. These include a soccer team, committee to build a local library, committee to improve one local street, committee to lobby for construction of a Guardia Civil delegation in La Chira, and committee to lobby for electricity and water to serve six new houses in Barrio Nuevo. There are two religious committees: one for the Catholic church, one for the evangelical Church of God.

Of the 268 La Chira residents over the age of 13 surveyed during my stay (out of a total population of 657), 77 percent have never served on any community organization or committee. Of the 61 adults who had ever served, 27 (10 percent of those surveyed) were currently serving. The committees most frequently represented were the school board (with 19 people citing former membership), the Asociación de Desarrollo (11 former members and four current members), and the health committee (with nine former members and six current members). (Current membership on the health committee was undoubtedly over-represented, even though this was a random sample, because the six committee members live in three households.) No one cited serving on the Rural Guard committee nor the Barrio Nuevo committee; these may have been defunct at the time of the interview, or the committees may have consisted of only one or two people.

Evangelicals (who comprise a small number of families in the community) do not, on principle, serve on community committees. They say they do not associate formally with other community members and do not contribute to the betterment of the community *qua* community. Their efforts, they say, are directed toward serving their church.

Except for religion, participators did not seem to differ significantly from non-participators. Women made up 43 percent of those interviewed who had ever participated, and women were represented on every committee with the exception of the Asociación de Desarrollo and the sports team. Perhaps it indicates their lower status that women did not serve on the only legally invested organization in La Chira, but everyone agreed that women were free to serve on the Asociación de Desarrollo if they wanted. The more acceptable options for women, however, were as members of the school, health, or nutrition committees.

Employment and the banana industry in La Chira

Bananas are a notoriously unstable crop; this was even more true in 1900 than it is today. Then, as now, Pococí offered a prototypical banana climate: alluvial soils, and ample rainfall and humidity (the annual average humidity is 89 percent). But the fruit planted then was susceptible to Panama disease (controlled today through chemical spraying and disease-resistant varieties). At the beginning of the century, small areas were planted intensively with bananas for brief periods (averaging ten years), until Panama disease forced plantations to be abandoned in favor of new lands (Strouse 1970: 80). The Pococí region was subject to United Fruit's monopolistic buying policies; if the Company decided to buy from other, more profitable regions, growers could not sell their produce. By 1930, United Fruit had abandoned the "Old Line" region between Siquirres and Guápiles, leaving only a smattering of poor, independent farmers and ranchers. In contrast to other areas in Limón province, cacao farming did not fill the void left when the banana company pulled out.

Unlike its holdings closer to the port, United Fruit sold or returned to the government all of their lands north and northwest of Siquirres. This, coupled with the peripheral location of the Old Line zone, and the subsequent economic retrogression of the area, made land values sink. These low land values then acted as a magnet when the new wave of banana production started early in the 1960's. (Strouse 1970: 88)

Consequently, Pococí remained economically and geographically isolated until the next boom cycle, in the mid-1960s.

La Chira exists in its present form today only because North Americans and West Europeans eat bananas. Before the mid-1960s, only a few families lived in the area. They had come from Heredia and Turrialba in the late 1940s and early 1950s to eke out a living planting corn and raising cattle. But most residents moved to La Chira around or after 1968, when the second regional banana boom began. They came from areas of chronic unemployment, like the northwestern province of Guanacaste, and from Turrialba, where the population had grown to exceed the demand for coffee pickers. Most came as unskilled, often illiterate, members of Costa Rica's growing migratory agricultural proletariat. In La Chira the men work planting, cutting, and hauling bananas, cleaning drainage ditches, spraying fungicides, and maintaining equipment. Women work in the banana packing plant or as domestics, caring for other women's children. A few families own commercial establishments; now there are two bars, two *pulperías* (general stores), a pool hall, and a butcher shop. Some farm their own land or raise dairy cows, and a handful work for the state, teaching or cooking in La Chira's elementary school.

La Chira residents are subject to chronic unemployment and under-employment because the community depends so heavily on the banana industry as a source of employment, and because the financial stability of the banana industry is so tenuous. In 1985, 75 percent of the workers at Mancotal (a pseudonym), the closest *finca* and major source of employment, held secure, permanent jobs. The remainder were occasional laborers, hired for a maximum of three months and then fired. Under a legal arrangement worked out with the state, banana *finqueros* (*finca* owners) are required to extend labor guarantees and benefits only to those employees kept on payroll longer than three months. Increasing numbers of banana workers therefore work for three months and then get laid off. The law allows the companies to rehire the same workers after a one-month hiatus, but people who work under this arrangement are never sure whether or when they will be rehired. The effects of the "three-months" rule can be devastating on families without other sources of income, although there are obvious benefits for the Company. Laborers are complacent and not prone to organize, since "trouble-makers" are certain not to be rehired. One of the top managers at Mancotal told me, "the people who 'have record' [i.e. have permanent jobs] don't work quite as hard, they play around a lot. In contrast the new people, for fear of being fired without benefits, for fear of not ever being rehired, well, they work quite a bit harder." In addition, the policy creates a permanent excess of cheap labor in the vicinity. The *finqueros* need a stable and permanent labor force, but they have little incentive to keep many employees for longer than three months, except for those who had been on payroll before the law went into effect. Young people, in particular, have trouble finding work. They compete with friends and relatives for scarce, low-paying jobs outside the plantations. In the past, many migrated in search of work.

Today, however, young people are inclined to stay in La Chira in hopes of a better future. At the time of my fieldwork, they knew that a new highway through Guápiles would soon link San José and Limón and offer a faster, less treacherous course between the capital and the only Atlantic port. "The city of Guápiles will, in the future, be the major administrative center of the Atlantic region" (INVU 1980: 3). The urban population of Guápiles was 6,040 in 1976, but one government agency anticipates that it will grow to 20,000 by the turn of the century (INVU 1980: 3–4). Entrepreneurs are beginning to diversify from bananas to *pejivaye* (a hard, starchy fruit which grows on palm trees, considered a delicacy), heart of palm, ginger, and other high-priced food crops. Land speculators have moved in and helped foster an aura of economic optimism. Many young people in La Chira are counting on the road to bring them jobs in the near future.

The fact that La Chira currently depends so heavily on bananas as a source of work determines, to a large degree, the class composition of the population. The majority of families (53 percent of the 77 I surveyed) have at least one member employed in the *fincas*. *Bananeros* are, by definition, working class. The only professionals who live in La Chira are one nursing auxiliary and two unmarried teachers. Anyone who aspires to more or who acquires technical training usually leaves, either to find work or a more affluent social network. Even the manager of the Mancotal banana plantation commutes form Guápiles rather than live in nearby La Chira. This phenomenon makes La Chira a fairly homogeneous community, manifesting few of the sharp class divisions which characterize communities in other parts of the country. Yet it also makes La Chira an unstable community, for few jobs are available to the children of banana workers raised there. Availability of jobs has not kept pace with population growth, and few children of banana workers acquire the education needed to move into skilled labor in the cities. Scarce banana work is almost their only option at present.

The United Fruit Company is frequently cited as the classic illustration of foreign dependency in Central America (see Kepner and Soothill 1936). Even today, with United Fruit's power mitigated by the presence of competitors and nationally owned subsidiaries, the degree of dependence on the world market is nowhere more evident than on Pococí banana plantations. When Europeans and North Americans reduce their banana consumption, when bananas can be purchased more cheaply from countries other than Costa Rica, or when oversupply causes lower prices, the people of La Chira are told not to report to work. Residents of the village thus subsidize the multinational banana companies by absorbing market inconsistencies.

The world banana market is inherently unstable, and the companies have used this fact to their advantage. The major companies that operate in Costa Rica – BANDECO (owned by Del Monte), Standard (owned by Castle and Cook), and the Compañía Bananera de Costa Rica (a subsidiary of United Brands, formerly the United Fruit Company) capitalize on the market's image of insecurity and vulnerability to justify requests for concessions for their employees and the state. Their campaign for favorable profit margins has taken several forms in recent years: systematic attempts to eliminate contentious labor unions; organizing of pro-management labor associations; a successful lobbying campaign to reduce government export tariffs; massive layoffs; reducing risks by turning more of their holdings over to independent producers; and continual threats to pull out of Costa Rica. Such gloomy predictions are occasionally offset by promises of economic revitalization and growth, often when foreign aid becomes available. For example, when AID and the Inter-American Development Bank extended credit for a plan to increase banana exports in the Atlantic region in 1985, the companies responded enthusiastically, calling for the state to reduce export tariffs in exchange for the companies' commitment to increase the acreage under cultivation (*La Nación*, September 16, 1985). The companies promised 8,000 new jobs and millions of dollars in additional foreign revenue. This constant vacillation between optimism and despair is evident in La Chira, where banana workers worry constantly whether Mancotal will even exist from one month to the next.

Costa Rica's banana industry experienced an economic downturn between 1980 and 1985. Despite stated plans to increase production, companies have frequently cut back the number of their employees, diversified to reduce their risks, and requested government concessions. For example, Standard Fruit – citing fiscal problems on the part of its parent company, Castle and Cook – abandoned 1,500 hectares of bananas between late 1984 and 1985, leaving 800 workers unemployed (*La Nación*, August 29, 1985). In December, 1984, Standard approached the government to ask for local credit, the postponement of certain payments, and cancellation of taxes levied by the state (*La Nación*, December 25, 1984). In February, 1985, the papers published a rumor that Standard Fruit Company intended to abandon the country's two largest plantations – Río Frío and Valle de Estrella – leaving well over 6,000 workers unemployed (*La República*, February 5, 1985). Subsequently, between

400 and 600 Standard employees in Pococí were laid off and 600 hectares of lands in Río Frío were abandoned (*La Nación*, February 26, 1985; *La Nación*, February 24, 1985). In May, 1985, a hurricane destroyed a significant portion of the banana crop in the Pococí region. In the following weeks, the companies threatened to lay off thousands of workers if prompt economic assistance from the government was not forthcoming (*La Nación*, June 11, 1985). In 1984, United Brands used a divisive 72-day strike in its Golfito plantation as an excuse to close the plantation, putting 1,000 employees out of work and plunging the area into an economic depression. Many observers agreed that the Company's decision to pull out was based on purely economic factors: a world surplus of bananas; diminishing west coast markets, and competition from Ecuador. Within Costa Rica, however, "violent community labor unions" were blamed for the strike and for United's decision to leave. This event helped solidify opposition to labor organizing in other plantations around the country.

Labor organizing and the Asociación Solidarista

The organization of labor on the banana plantations around La Chira is relevant to our discussion of local participation in community affairs, to the extent that participatory options available at work affect the form of organizing in the community and vice versa. Aggressive union activists are not likely to be involved in passive, utilitarian organizations in their off-hours. Since 1980, the labor organizations around La Chira have been characterized by pro-management syndicates and diligent suppression of alternative labor options. Dissent is discouraged, and workers are permitted to participate only in prearranged workshops and activities. This type of organization promotes compliance, paternalism, and reliance on outsiders for direction. It is not conducive to fomenting grassroots initiative, consciousness-raising, or self-motivated community action of the kind which had been advocated through the Ministry of Health's community participation program.

Banana workers in La Chira have a restricted number of carefully managed options through which they are permitted to channel work-related concerns. The system was first explained to me by an agricultural engineering student studying banana cultivation. In the La Chira region, he said, people tend to be more aggressive and violent than in large company towns like nearby Río Frío. Communist labor unions (the so-called *sindicatos rojos*, or red unions) infiltrate the plantations and encourage people to strike by promising improved working conditions. Their true agenda, he said, is to achieve socialism by breaking the companies, therefore they must be stopped. Despite claims to the contrary, he said, the red unions do not care about workers. As proof he cited the aftermath of the 1984 strike in Golfito: 10,000 families without work, in dire straits without the electricity and housing provided by the company. What could be done, I asked, to avoid the infiltration of red unions in the banana sector? The answer, he said, lies in the Asociación Solidarista, a conformist social movement associated with the Costa Rican Catholic church. Each banana *finca* sets up a chapter, financed by contributions from workers and employers. The Asociación runs cooperative stores and offers low-interest loans to workers. Membership in the Asociación is voluntary, but he told me that workers who did not join would be suspected of communism and fired at the first opportunity. The red unions cannot penetrate the Asociación Solidarista, he said, because of another anti-communist strategy: the companies compile and circulate across the nation a computerized blacklist of known and suspected communist agitators (Bourgois 1989: 12). These lists are pooled, so that someone fired for labor organizing from BANDECO, for example, will not be able to get work on Standard plantations.

The idea for an Asociación Solidarista was first proposed by Alberto Marten in 1947 (just prior to the civil war of 1948), when the realignment of social classes in Costa Rica was at an acute stage. Marten proposed a new system of labor organization encompassing a pact of solidarity between workers and management, a peaceful, non-confrontative means to resolve labor conflict. The Asociación gradually gained significant support in the central plateau, but for many years it could not survive in banana regions, which had historically been the province of more radical labor organizations. In 1978 and 1979, the relatively young Pococí plantations were affected for the first time by a series of strikes. In response, the Federación Solidarista del Atlántico (FASBA) was established in 1980 to promote Solidarismo on the banana *fincas* of Guápiles. According to two chroniclers of the movement, FASBA "seems to be a serious effort to defeat the Costa Rican union movement in areas where the movement has been historically, geographically, and socially dominant ... its intention is to rob the working base of unionism by acting as a federation of anti-union workers" (Blanco and Navarro 1984: 189). This interpretation is borne out by events which took place on the Mancotal plantation between 1978 and 1985.

Nineteen seventy-eight was a confrontative period in the banana plantations in Pococí and Guácimo. The active local union, Sindicato de Trabajadores Agrícolas y de Plantaciones de Pococí y Guácimo (STAPPG), was an affiliate of the Communist Party union, the Confederación General de Trabajadores (CGT). Support for leftist politics was growing stronger: in the 1978 presidential elections, 14·3 percent of voters in Pococí voted for the communist-led coalition, Pueblo Unido. Pococí thus ranked fifth among the nation's 40 municipalities in the percentage of votes for Pueblo Unido that year (*Libertad*, March 3–9, 1978). Since its creation in 1969, STAPPG had been fairly effective in organizing the region's banana workers. In 1978 STAPPG claimed 1,500 members, collective bargaining contracts on 35 *fincas*, and affiliates on 40 plantations (*La República*, September, 26, 1978). The union's strength became obvious in June, when two large plantations went on strike and others were disrupted by work stoppages.

Labor agitation in the Atlantic was countered by a fierce anti-communist propaganda campaign waged by the owners, the government, and the press. *La Nación*, the leading daily, carried a seven-part series lambasting communist labor unions in all sectors of the economy (see *La Nación*, July 2, 1978). The Sindicato Nacional de la Empresa Privada (National Private Enterprise Union [SINDEP]) ran a full-page ad, titled "Unionism is in the hands of professional agitators," stating that "irresponsible and misdirected unionism" is attempting to "insure and exacerbate class struggle and create social and economic chaos, where the principal protagonists in the drama are professional Marxist-Leninist agitators interested only in forcing their imperialist ideology on the sacred interests of this country" (*La Nación*, July 2, 1978). The administration of Rodrigo Carazo, inaugurated just a few months earlier in May, was determined to thwart the labor strife by dealing harshly with union organizers.

Both major strikes in Pococí were settled just days before Mancotal declared a strike in early July (*Libertad*, June 9–15, 1978; *La Nación*, July 5, 1978). STAPPG called the strike when management refused to reinstate 14 workers who were dismissed without benefits in reprisal for their participation in a work stoppage two months earlier. That work stoppage, in turn, was prompted by protests against the creation of a pro-management union designed to circumvent STAPPG's bargaining power. The North American absentee owner of Mancotal refused to reinstate the 14 workers or to negotiate with STAPPG. He was described by the communist newspaper as a rabid anti-communist gringo who created a pro-management union to eliminate STAPPG. He told the newspapers he would only negotiate with the SITRABATE, the pro-management union (*La Nación*, July 7, 1978). The owner's position was supported at higher levels: a judge in Limón declared the strike illegal, the central government sent police to escort non-strikers back to work, the strikers were routed, and the union's demands were not met (*La Nación*, July 8, 1978).

STAPPG had infuriated local *finca* managers and members of government by bringing in outsiders to participate in the strike, and by advocating violent, confrontational tactics. Immediately after the strike ended, the Ministry of Justice petitioned to have the union declared illegal. The petition was finally granted in 1982, when the Ministry of Work and Social Security, Department of Social Organizations, passed a resolution to dissolve STAPPG. The union was found guilty of "directing acts of violence against workers of the *finca* [Mancotal], invading the land and permitting other strangers to do so with the intention of making the workers leave the SITRABATE union and join the STAPPG union, while at the same time impeding their legitimate work by imposing a forced strike" (*La Gaceta*, January 27, 1983).

In the wake of the 1978 strikes the organizational alternatives available to banana workers were deliberately channeled to favor management. While they worked to disband STAPPG, pro-management groups simultaneously joined forces to promote the establishment of Asociaciones Solidaristas on banana plantations in Pococí and Guácimo. In 1980 they called a convention, the Congreso Bananero Solidarista, with the intention of expanding Solidarismo in the banana zones. Two hundred representatives attended from Guápiles and Sixaola (another banana-growing region in the southeast). At this convention:

Suggestions were given for how to combat the union movement, which for them is a "pseudo-labor" movement. The entrepreneurs were going to "suggest" that workers assert their legal rights (a highly unusual move) such as the struggle for housing, medical services, the creation of consumer cooperatives, longer vacations, etc. This was a tactic for them, a "defense mechanism" against banana unionism. (Blanco and Navarro 1984: 208)

Mancotal's owner was known throughout the region as, in the words of one Guápiles resident, "a man who saw a communist behind every tree." Not surprisingly, then, Mancotal was one of the first *fincas* in Pococí to establish an Asociación Solidarista, in 1981. The Director of Labor Relations at Standard Fruit Company's offices in Guápiles told me that the Asociación Solidarista had been extremely effective in eradicating union activity in the region since 1981. Nonetheless, some *fincas* were slower to organize than others. According to a 14-year veteran at Mancotal, treasurer of the Asociación and respected resident of La Chira, other *fincas* balked in setting up Asociaciones,

because the red unions were very strong. The red unions attacked the Asociación because they said that it was a way for the patrons to divide the workers and do what they wanted with them. Later people began to see that, quite to the contrary, the Asociación had a lot of guarantees. For example, the patron donates a certain amount of money and the worker donates a percentage of his salary; as the interest builds up the worker sees his capital multiplying…The unions are needed, but they must be democratic. We don't like the red unions. We attack them because they are involved with politics, with communism…The red unions are terrible.

At Mancotal, he told me, the red unions were broken after the 1978 strike, which was very violent. The red unions look for violence. In the southwest [near Golfito], he told me, the red unions left the company with no option but to abandon the region. Many displaced workers showed up at Mancotal, looking for jobs. "Many," he said, "are workers who had previously been active in the communist unions, but no one will give them work. They look high and low, but can't find work for good reason, because they have created havoc in the *fincas*."

Participation in the Asociación is not mandatory, for, as the treasurer said, "in free Costa Rica everyone has the right to their opinion." Nonetheless, some believe that workers who choose not to join the Asociación may be communist sympathizers and, as my agronomist informant told me earlier, they might likely be fired at the first opportunity. Managers would rather see all workers conform by joining the Asociación. From the workers' perspective, too, joining the Asociación was perceived as the prudent thing to do. Some of the Mancotal laborers I spoke with said they felt obligated to join even though they didn't like the Asociación. Others told me, tight-lipped in response to my persistent questions, that it was taboo to talk about unions.

Most residents of La Chira with whom I spoke would, when asked, profess support for the Asociación Solidarista, although I did hear occasional grumblings about nepotism, favoritism, and workers' entitlements being withheld. Except among members of the executive board, however, I never heard anyone express enthusiasm for the Asociación. Rather, the general attitude was complacent and compliant: membership in the Asociación was considered necessary to keep a job at Mancotal. People who did not work there could afford to be more critical. One woman told me the red unions defended workers' rights better than the Asociación, even though, she said, she abhorred communism. A Ministry of Health worker in Guápiles told me that Solidarismo seemed to function better than domination by the red unions, even though Solidarismo was not in the workers' best interests because it used workers for the political ends of those in control. A La Chira resident, who had been fired from a nearby banana plantation for complaining about discrepancies between men's and women's wages, told me the Asociación Solidarista is taking advantage of the workers, but no one can do anything about it because they fear for their jobs. Specifically, she said, the executive body of the Asociación at Mancotal comprises a closed circle of people (many of whom are related through blood or marriage), and workers are unable to affect the composition of the board. Her observations echo Blanco and Navarro's assertion that the executive boards are chosen in conjunction with plantation managers. Executive boards tend to include administrative and management staff who hold their present positions precisely because they have collaborated with management objectives. While the Asociaciones profess an ideology of worker–management harmony, this assertion is contradicted by the fact that Asociaciones are invariably formed at management initiative and operate with little worker involvement in decision-making (Blanco and Navarro 1984: 191). She also said that the Mancotal Asociación is run without financial accountability, and that workers never receive the dividends they are promised. Furthermore, she said that the cooperative store owned by the Asociación is run by members of a single family who are suspected of corruption because the store's financial accounts are kept confidential.

The Asociación store presents an interesting case. When I asked La Chira residents about the benefits of membership in the Asociación, they often mentioned the low prices to which they were entitled through the Asociación store. Yet when I compared the prices of household staples at the Asociación's cooperative store with those of the one other store in town, the private store's prices were just 0·7 percent higher; a difference equivalent to 8 cents on a total bill of $10. In other words, the Asociación store did not offer significant savings to its members who shopped there.

What could the Asociación do for the workers, I wondered, given the financial uncertainty of the banana industry? I asked the treasurer of the Asociación about the future of the Mancotal operation. He said, "The situation is a bit serious. I think they are going to have to abandon the *finca* [after another three or four years]."

I asked, "Can the Asociación do anything to help?" His response was telling.

The only path open to us in this case is to talk with the workers, to convince them that they must do everything possible to help the company. Try to work well, don't mishandle the fruit, be fair with their work, and increase productivity. The Asociación is obligated to help the company; by helping the company the worker will always have a job. In contrast the union is different. The union organizers say, okay, we should be getting such-and-such a price for this work, and if the company doesn't give it, they grumble and go on strike. Instead of benefitting both parties, they damage both parties because when work stops the bananas are ruined, Sigatoka disease sets in – there are a whole series of problems.

When it comes time to lay people off, he said, the permanent workers will be fired first. The administration hopes this will increase productivity on the plantation; it would undoubtedly also increase joblessness, poverty, and insecurity in the region.

Participation in labor vs. health

Participation is defined differently by groups and individuals depending, in part, on their relationship to the monied classes. This is true for participation in labor organizations and in health programs. As an example of the relationship between labor organization and the ideology of participation in health, I will compare two men, both of whom were active in the government's program to enhance community participation in health, and both of whom held strong opinions about labor organization on the banana plantations.

When Carazo began to promote community participation in health in 1978, Don Esteban (a pseudonym) was working with DINADECO as a community organizer. He was temporarily transferred to the Ministry of Health, where he wrote many of the documents and pamphlets detailing the community participation program philosophy. He acknowledged that participation in health has often been limited to utilitarianism. Participation, he wrote, must be considered in its political context, for competing political factions will understand participation to mean different things. The same document states that health is "an equitable distribution of the nation's wealth, housing, jobs, education, means of transportation, recreation – that is, health is integral to development" (Ministerio de Salud, Unidad de Participación Popular 1980: 2). Don Esteban's model for incorporating communities into the rural health program went far beyond the utilitarian. He also championed community involvement in: (1) diagnosis and investigation of health problems; (2) definition of strategy; (3) planning; (4) implementation; (5) continuing control; (6) evaluation; and (7) programmatic reformulation of programs.

Don Esteban's vision of the history of health participation included pre-Columbian social organization and sanitation; the importance of the family as the basic unit of organization; the social upheaval, cultural disintegration, and exploitation caused by the Conquest, the relevance of indigenous communities "which still live under conditions of marginality and domination," the role of traditional medicine, and the existence of spontaneous and autochthonous responses to health problems on the part of rural peoples. This expansive approach to history acknowledges that participation is not contingent upon state initiative, but is an ongoing process which changes according to historical contingencies.

When ranked along a continuum of participatory philosophies, the perspective outlined by Don Esteban would fall just to the left of mainstream reformist tendencies. He was obviously aware of the institutional and political constraints inherent in his task, and his documents therefore contain a mix of democratic social reformist rhetoric and technical advice appropriate to the political climate of the late 1970s. Reformist tendencies notwithstanding, Don Esteban's personal history contains a more radical chapter coincidentally pertinent to La Chira. In 1978, he was involved in the STAPPG union strike at the Mancotal plantation. Because of this, he told me, "I was accused of being a red." Perhaps his involvement with the strikers had been politically imprudent, he said, but he remained convinced that Mancotal's owner was a "tyrant" and that the Asociación Solidarista was detrimental to workers' interests. He was motivated by personal conviction to participate in a collective expression of frustration, workers' solidarity, and dissatisfaction with established grievance procedures. Yet this action was defined by the state or company officials as a perversion of legitimate community participation. To strike, in their view, was antithetical to the democratic process, a process which they would reserve the right to define.

Since his early work with DINADECO, Don Esteban had seen popular participation as a tool for attaining a more just society, for arming the community to fight their battles with the state. His vision of participation was broad enough to include a range of grassroots activities, including those not condoned or supported by the state. In sum, Don Esteban was a social critic and activist who chose to work within the system. As an employee of the Ministry of Health, he hoped that his political commitment to social justice and equitable distribution of wealth could influence governmental policy, while perhaps contributing to the empowerment of the rural poor.

This philosophy of participation had little in common with that of another Ministry of Health employee, Don Pedro, who took over the leadership of the Popular Participation Unit when Liberación regained the presidency from Unidad in 1982.

Don Pedro's first act as Director, as I mentioned earlier, was to change the name of the unit, because "*participación popular* sounded too much like Vanguardia Popular," the name of Costa Rica's Communist Party. When I asked Don Pedro about the history of participation, in 1985, he traced it from the first state-sponsored endeavors to involve rural communities in nutrition and malaria control programs in the 1940s, through the rural mobile units of the 1960s, and into the present. The fact that rural people have been "quite receptive" to participation, he said, can be attributed to the country's high literacy rate, the vast sums spent on health and education, and ethnic and linguistic homogeneity.

Don Pedro's version of the history of participation focuses on state initiatives, despite his vocal opposition to paternalism and state-sponsored "give-away" programs. His interpretation of participation – unlike Don Esteban's – leaves no room for spontaneous or confrontative participatory strategies. He limits participation, *de facto*, to compliance with state initiatives.

Under Don Pedro's leadership, PROFOCO published an occasional bulletin detailing its accomplishments and participatory philosophy. One issue consisted of an essay by Father C. M. Solano, an eminent church leader associated with the Asociación Solidarista and one of Solidarismo's most active organizers. The essay, titled "What am I if I don't participate?" exhorts citizens to organize themselves against the impending national tragedy signaled by

acts of terrorism which threaten the internal security of the country; military, political, and journalistic aggression from the exterior [a thinly veiled reference to the Sandinistas then in power in neighboring Nicaragua] which reveal the strength of our adversaries; social problems resulting from economic upheaval; and alarming indicators of decreased production, productivity, and exports. (Boletín PROFOCO 1984)

The nation's ills cannot be remedied by traditional means like paternalism or state involvement, says Father Solano, but by "SOLIDARITY, membership, cooperation, and participation" (emphasis in original). He predicts more serious danger if his call is not heeded: "Our peace, our democracy, our liberty, all the values we Costa Ricans so appreciate are in peril today. But there is still time, time to protect and save ourselves, with everyone's solidarity and participation." Father Solano used the rhetoric employed by the Costa Rican right, appealing to xenophobic fears and anti-communist sentiments as he preached the need for social harmony. The fact that Don Pedro used Solidarismo's literature to buttress his own philosophy of participation is revealing: both Solidarismo and PROFOCO under Don Pedro's leadership were preoccupied with the threat of communism. This could only be avoided, they said, by restricting the participation of Marxists in community organizations. Don Pedro said,

The only way [to limit communist infiltration] is not to allow the participation of communist leaders. To attack and eliminate them. Remove them from the communities. There is no other way … It's the same system used in public health. When you have a rabies epidemic, what you have to do is kill the dogs. Right away. Because if you don't eliminate the dogs, you don't eliminate the rabies. Perhaps it's a bit crude to say it that way, but one has to get rid of the communists because if not there will be problems.

Don Pedro's image of communists as "rabid dogs" (*piricuacos*) was particularly graphic, implying that communism is a scourge that, like any dangerous disease, must be ruthlessly eliminated.

Both the Asociación Solidarista and PROFOCO sought to monitor and control participation in Costa Rica's rural communities. The two organizations shared, for propaganda purposes, the philosophy that social relations should be based on social harmony, satisfaction, nationalism, and peace. They both denied the existence of exploitation or class struggle. Don Pedro said that PROFOCO would work with the Asociaciones Solidaristas in rural areas "to insure that there is harmony... For me, health will come when there is stability, when there is equilibrium. In the social realm, if there is stability, there is peace. And if there is peace, it's because there is justice." The two organizations attained their goals through aggressive lobbying to convince rural communities how lucky they were, and through active repression of "communist-inspired" alternatives. The philosophical implications for community participation are clear: communities needed to be taught their own best interests, because they were incapable of choosing wisely on their own. Communities which chose to oppose state policies were misguided. The philosophy assailed class conflict, defining it as illegitimate and dangerous to the national interest. Nonetheless, certain forms of rebellious demonstration were condoned, provided they fitted within the right-wing ideological framework: Don Pedro says, for example, that "justice should be defended with arms." The problem, of course, is who defines justice. In the end, Don Pedro's philosophy does not entrust communities with the judgment, autonomy, or power to decide for themselves.

These men represent two "ideal types" of health and participation. Don Pedro uses an equilibrium model: health is the absence of disease, participation supports the state. The body, like the organic society, seeks balance and harmony. The etiologic agents of disease (germs) and social disruption (communists) are dangerous interlopers who must be attacked aggressively if harmony is to be restored. Don Esteban's is a more dynamic, conflict-based model, wherein the body struggles to attain or maintain health against various "insults" (Dunn 1975; Villalobos 1989), and where participation is likewise a struggle for ever-greater degrees of representation and accountability in political decision-making. The etiologic agents of Don Esteban's model are legitimate voices calling out for expression; they represent an opportunity for reevaluating and possibly changing the status quo. The two men see the world through fundamentally different epistemological-philosophical orientations.

Health services in the Guápiles region

The first organized health facility in Guápiles was a dispensary built by the United Fruit Company in the early 1900s to serve the banana workers there. Few historical records document the services offered, but if reports from nearby regions are any indication, the wooden "hospital" was probably staffed by one or two United Fruit employees not trained in medicine, who dispensed quinine and referred serious cases to the hospital in Limón. The building was converted into a school in 1920, a few years after United Fruit abandoned the region (*La Prensa Libre*, May 22, 1979). Archival records state that 25,000 colones were allocated in 1934 to build a new school in Guápiles. The Congressman representing the region, Virgilio Chaverri Ugalde, told the Legislative Assembly that the school was in bad shape, that it didn't even belong to the Board of Education "because it was built by the government to be a hospital and when that institution disappeared it was converted into a school" (INVU 1980: 14). According to a long-time resident of La Chira, this building burned down 30 or 40 years ago. From roughly 1920–1960, there were no organized medical services in Guápiles.

The lack of access to medical care seems to have persisted for four decades, while the population – small though it was – suffered from endemic malaria and cutaneous leishmaniasis (*La Prensa Libre*, May 29, 1979). One La Chira resident said, "it was very sad here. Everybody was yellow or white, pale, sick, and thin." Health status began to improve in the 1950s, when the government undertook an ambitious malaria control program. Access to medical services, however, did not improve until the early 1960s, when an influx of migrants arrived to plant bananas. In 1962, the Ministry of Health used Alliance for Progress funds to set up 15 Unidades Sanitarias (Health Units) in rural areas, including Guápiles, to treat the uninsured populace (Ministerio de Salud, Memoria 1962). At around the same time, the CCSS set up a dispensary to treat those insured under the state social security program. The doctor employed by the Unidad was reportedly often absent. A full-time, permanent doctor was not available in Guápiles until 1964, when the CCSS hired Dr. Ricardo Rojas Centeno. In 1966, the CCSS sent another doctor to Guápiles because the number of *asegurados* (insured) had gone up.

State-sponsored health services in Guápiles began to proliferate in the early 1960s. As the state extended its health infrastructure from urban to rural areas, community participation in health was mentioned for the first time as a necessary goal. Objectives listed in the Ministry of Health's 1962 annual report included "to obtain the participation of the community in solving their health problems" (Ministerio de Salud,

Memoria 1962). At this early stage of conceptualization, community participation appeared only under the heading of "objectives," not under "proposals," "methods," or "accomplishments." If statements in the Ministry's reports can be taken at face value, community outreach efforts during this period consisted of educating rural communities to take advantage of Ministry programs and to assist in "filling some of the needs of the Unidades Sanitarias" (Ministerio de Salud, Memoria 1962). "Participation" was limited to the local population's utilization of and support for state-sponsored services.

State-sponsored health services in and around Guápiles evolved in tandem with the banana industry. According to Dr. Rojas, the banana companies did not supply doctors to treat their employees; rather, they contracted with the CCSS to provide curative services. In addition, the Instituto Nacional de Seguros (INS; National Insurance Institute) set up offices throughout banana lands to process claims for work-related accidents. As lands were cleared and plantations established, Dr. Rojas said the CCSS treated many cases of chemical intoxication, and "Gramaxon took many lives here."

State-sponsored health services relieved a potentially enormous burden for the banana companies. If the state had not been willing to assume the costs of preventive care and sanitation and to subsidize curative care, companies would have had to devote substantial resources to the sanitation and health improvements necessary to make the region habitable and profitable. Of course, this was precisely the course followed by the United Fruit Company in the earlier part of the century, but by the early 1960s the predominant business philosophy had changed:

Too many foreign concerns have, in line with traditional practice carrying over from the previous era, usurped local governmental function. Granted, it is often less time- and money-consuming to continue the obligations of the paternalistic employer rather than to rely on others. But once a nationally responsible political authority emerges, and some semblance of specific, differentiated, political institutions develops, the Western enterprise should probably undertake a concerted effort to rid itself of all of these extra-business activities. *Public health and basic education should be a function of the public authority.* If the Western enterprise is seen as competing for public favor with the local government in these fields, it becomes vulnerable to political reprisal. It opens itself to the charge of interference with the process of national political development. *The wiser policy would be the exercise of subtle pressure on local individuals, local groups, and the local government to assume responsibility for these activities.* (Robinson 1964: 134–5; emphasis added)

This was the policy followed by Standard Fruit Company when it began operating in Costa Rica in 1955. Standard was never directly involved in providing medical services the way that United Fruit had been, although

Standard's operations were contingent on the state's willingness to build hospitals, clinics, and rural health posts in banana-growing frontiers. Standard thus claims indirect credit for improving access to medical services throughout the Atlantic lowlands (Fernández n.d.), although the company does not mention that many of these areas would be uninhabited – and therefore would not require medical services – were it not for the prospect of employment in the *fincas*.

The construction of a large CCSS hospital in Guápiles was clearly related to the population growth brought on by banana work. The 84-bed hospital, which opened in 1973, serves approximately 48,000 residents of the cantons of Guápiles and Guácimo (CCSS n.d.). The hospital is the region's tertiary care center. Patients are supposed to be referred from the health posts (run by the Ministry of Health) to the CCSS clinics (outpatient consultation facilities which exist in banana zones of Cariari, Roxana, Ticaban), and then to the Guápiles hospital. In practice, however, many local residents circumvent the first two steps and head directly to the hospital: the 6 a.m. bus from La Chira to Guápiles is timed deliberately to get residents to the hospital in time to make outpatient appointments before the clinics are full.

The alliance between commercial interests and state health care continues today under a number of guises. For example, the CCSS clinics were built to serve banana employees. According to a document I consulted in the Guápiles hospital, the Cariari clinic "attends a population which suffers from intoxication by organo-phosphates and work-related accidents"; and the Ticaban clinic "exists basically to serve one employer, since it is located in a remote area where there is one important banana company" (CCSS n.d.). To cite a more specific example, state health workers are subject to pressure from banana company managers over the issue of paid sick days. Under the terms of banana labor contracts, workers who want to be paid for sick days must submit a voucher, a *comprobante*, signed by a CCSS physician. The Standard Fruit labor-relations manager told me that some "shameless" workers (*sinvergüenzas*) took advantage of this system by showing up at the Guápiles hospital to have physicians sign *comprobantes* when they weren't "really" sick. Physicians would often sign without asking questions, he said, because it would reduce the number of patients they would have to examine. Therefore the company had spoken with hospital management, asking them to be more strict in their allocation of *comprobantes*, thus saving the companies' money and increasing work attendance. He said the companies would like to abolish the *comprobante* policy altogether, but that, once granted, such concessions were hard to revoke. The hospital director, for his part, noted that his outpatient consultation figures were artificially elevated by the collective bargaining clause which entitled workers to one sick day per week provided a *comprobante* is issued, "even when the worker does not present a justifiable medical reason. We have brought this problem to the attention of Company managers and would like to participate with them in seeking a solution to these problems which affect them, the Institution [hospital], and the country" (CCSS n.d.).

The *comprobante* issue illustrates how contradictory the state's role in health care can be. Banana managers would like CCSS doctors to share responsibility for controlling the work force by carefully screening every banana worker who asks for a *comprobante*. From the company's point of view, this is a legitimate request for the state to support company goals: increased productivity leading to greater export earnings. The effect of the policy, however, is to call into question the workers' integrity, trustworthiness, and autonomy, encouraging doctors to distrust workers who seek medical services. The preventive health services offered through the Ministry of Health, on the other hand, have emphasized efforts to empower and educate the common citizenry, to grant the skills necessary for recognizing and treating illness and thereby to have rural citizens assume greater responsibility for health matters. Yet the individual and community autonomy preached by the Ministry of Health is inconsistent with the social control functions the companies would like to see exercised by the CCSS. This is just another example of the contradictions confronting workers and rural residents who use the state-sponsored network of health services: the CCSS perpetuates a hierarchical order of physician superiority which depends for its legitimacy on the subordination and dependency of patients, while the Ministry extols a more egalitarian model emphasizing the self-care, self-motivation, and empowerment of patients and citizens.

La Chira's health committee

The Ministry's rural health program came to La Chira in 1974, when a rural health worker, or *asistente*, named Alban, arrived to work in the community. Accompanied by a nursing auxiliary, Alban set up operations in a small rented house for two years, while the government made arrangements to build a health post on land donated by a local resident. La Chira residents could not tell me why the government had selected their town for building a health post; they were simply informed that it would be built there. Medical consultations in the newly constructed post began in 1976, when the post was visited every two months by a Ministry of Health doctor. The doctor who worked there in 1976 reported that the post at La Chira was "exceedingly uncomfortable." It lacked lights, slides, alcohol, and speculums; furthermore, transportation was difficult. For this reason, Alban usually sent patients to the Ministry of Health center in Guápiles, rather than imposing on health personnel to visit La Chira (Castillo 1976).

Three months after Alban arrived in La Chira, he began asking the "best known" members of the community to serve on the health committee. He did not convoke an *asamblea* (town meeting) to elect members. Rather, he recruited selectively. Maribel, one of the first members, said she and a few women friends told Alban that they would help out "for a few days." They ended up serving for ten years. In the beginning, Maribel said, the health post needed many supplies: curtains, paint, medicines, cleaning materials, kerosene for the refrigerator generator. So the committee members held raffles and bingo games to raise money, and went from house to house soliciting contributions. Their greatest fund-raising success, she said, occurred one year when cattle prices were low. Health committee members convinced ten of the wealthier community members to donate a heifer apiece, which they raffled off to benefit the health post. The committee's main purpose through all these years, Maribel said, was not related to health *per se*. Their purpose was to raise money.

Today's health committee members perceive their role in the same terms. When asked, every member told me, independent of the others, that the committee's major responsibilities included raising money to pay the cleaning woman's salary, utility (light, gas, and water) bills, and maintenance costs. Three out of seven members cited these tasks as the committee's *only* responsibilities. A fourth said the committee should inform the community about upcoming doctor visits to La Chira; a fifth said committee members should make home visits to ask about health problems, make sure the Ministry functionaries are indeed visiting homes as they are charged, check to see whether families need latrines or whether their water is contaminated; two other members said their responsibilities included community education, sanitation surveillance, and referring the sick to Guápiles. The current *asistente* in La Chira corroborated the utilitarian version; he said the committee was responsible for buying alcohol, painting and otherwise maintaining the health post, paying the cleaning woman, and buying medicines and vaccines when the health post ran low on supplies.

The health promoter in Guápiles lamented that communities *think* their only responsibilities are to maintain the health post, whereas he says the Ministry of Health would like them to aspire to higher goals like collaborating with health workers and making house visits. Yet when he appeared at a health committee in La Chira to exhort members to work harder, they did not take him seriously. I observed this interaction at the first health committee meeting I attended in La Chira. The promoter's method consisted of reading to the committee from a pamphlet issued by the Ministry of Health, detailing the functions of a health committee. The pamphlet stated that health committee members should organize the community to support their work, rather than doing all the work themselves. It went on to list the myriad duties and tasks of a health committee. The promoter read for ten minutes, while the seven other people in the room grew increasingly restless. Finally, one of them interrupted him, saying that it sounded great, but would be impossible for them to do even a fraction of the work he listed. Another said they would never have time to do all he said. The promoter responded that the committee needed to rank its priorities, to select one pressing health problem to work on, whereupon one member said that this community had no serious health problems. The promoter insisted they did, citing the overgrown vegetable garden behind the health post. Apparently the committee members did not consider weeds to be a serious health problem; they immediately demurred. "People would never cooperate on such a project," said one woman, "No one cooperates around here. Why, the Asociación de Desarrollo isn't even functioning now. If the people don't care about such an important community organization, why are they going to concern themselves with a little committee like this one?"

Such interpersonal dynamics confused me completely at the time. Why had the promoter been so directive and insensitive to member sentiments, and why had he berated them so? Only later did I realize that his performance had been enacted for my benefit. With my arrival in Guápiles, I had inadvertently jeopardized his reputation (and, for all he knew, his job), because he was the health promoter in charge of community organizing in the Guápiles catchment area. When I chose to work in La Chira, he knew that the health committee there had not met for the past three months, and had just barely functioned before that. Consequently, and unbeknownst to me until several months later, he sent a letter to all former health committee members in La Chira asking their cooperation in reconstituting the health committee. Thus the meeting I attended was the first in nearly four months to be held in La Chira. He wanted to prove to me that unorganized communities were not the result of his incompetence; that I could not fault his sincerity or diligence.

Community members themselves were not quite as anxious to perform for the visiting anthropologist, although they went along with the promoter's efforts to reconstitute the health committee for the duration of my stay in La Chira. When I moved to the capital (as I later discovered), the committee disintegrated once again. From their perspective, lack of participation in the health committee was a fact of life, understandable given their past experience with La Chira's health committee. It would be a mistake to try to understand their lack of participation solely with reference to psychological or community-level factors; rather, their actions must be interpreted as part of a larger political-economic and symbolic complex. For example, people in La Chira offered a variety of explanations as to why committees did not function better: "paternalism" was one of the most frequently voiced reasons, heard from community residents and others. The nursing auxiliary in La Chira complained, "People expect the government to give them everything." Likewise a nursing auxiliary in a nearby town said, "Costa Ricans are passive and paternalistic," and the health promoter in Guápiles said Costa Ricans expect to get everything from the state.

Paternalism is usually discussed in disparaging tones; the word is used to berate and lament the Costa Rican character. People say citizens in a paternalistic society are poorly motivated and lazy, unwilling to work on their own behalf. Yet such are the contradictions of social history and ideology that paternalistic (i.e., state-sponsored) reforms have been a significant, if intermittent, feature of Costa Rican life for the past 50 years. The state has always initiated reforms to avoid social conflict, while also lamenting (and sometimes rescinding) its own role in the process of maintaining social harmony. Solís and Esquivel (1984) argue that the contradictory nature of paternalistic reforms in Costa Rica must be understood as a byproduct of class struggles acted out in political parties. For example, while Carazo was in office, the authors say, his Partido Unidad Social Cristiana comprised an uneasy alliance of moderate reformists and confrontative conservatives. Frictions between them brought Carazo's reformist plans to a standstill and exacerbated the contradictions inherent in social policy (1984: 88). The authors' class-based interpretation can explain why state reformism is pursued at one point in history and not another, but here it would be helpful to understand more about the ideological incongruity between the concepts of paternalism and participation.

Tension between these concepts was stated explicitly in Carazo's inauguration speech when he said, "Paternalism is the negation of human dignity; it converts dignity into an object of assistance but not into the subject of self-actualization." Carazo contrasted paternalism with participation (which, in the early days of his administration, he subsumed under the heading of "human promotion"):

Human promotion [is a philosophy which] trusts in man. Paternalism distrusts him and, furthermore, wants him dependent on the State so he can be manipulated and directed according to the State's interests. Paternalism assumes that there exists a stratum of the population that is incapable of being responsible. (*La Nación*, May 9, 1978)

La Chira's experience with the government's rural health program illustrates the contradictions that surface when Carazo's words are compared with state actions. The state encourages paternalism by undertaking programs – such as rural health – that are designed, financed, and implemented without consulting local communities. As we have seen, even the Ministry of Health's popular participation unit was centrally planned. How could La Chira residents be faulted for not participating in health, given the extent of paternalism that characterized the construction of their own health post?

State paternalism is antithetical to popular participation, yet the concepts coexist, as symbolic inversions of one another, in Costa Rican political ideology: paternalism carries a negative connotation in the popular consciousness but is practised nonetheless; participation carries a positive connotation but is unsuccessful in practice. This dialectic tension explains why paternalism is cited for the failure of community participation programs. It also explains how La Chira residents cope with the contradictions. They are political pragmatists. The health committee is not a high priority for them, and they do not participate enthusiastically on the committee because they know from experience that the program will endure through state paternalism. Their understanding of *participación* is more akin to the *colaboración* state officials spoke of decades earlier; they know their participation is not essential to the program's success. Yet they have internalized the anti-paternalistic sentiment expounded in national political ideology, which explains why they felt guilty enough to reconstitute the health committee when a foreigner showed up drawing attention to their lack of participation.

Only one health committee member in La Chira blamed centralized planning and poor state–local communication for the health committee's low level of motivation. If the health committee were consulted in advance about policy decisions affecting their community, he said, the Ministry of Health would see more enthusiasm from the committee: "but we always end up eating our biscuits after they've burned. We never eat them before they burn, or even get to see how they're going to be made." The other health committee members tended to blame themselves, or their neighbors, for lack of effective participation in health; this was the only person who said the state must assume some responsibility.

Another contradiction which surfaced in La Chira was the discrepancy between ideal democratic selection procedures and actual composition of the health committee. According to Ministry of Health regulations, and consistent with accepted procedures for constituting community organizations throughout Costa Rica, health committee members should be elected at well-attended town meetings. Nominations for each office are followed by secret balloting, and the candidate with the majority of votes wins. The term of office is two years; nepotism is discouraged. The reality, however, is often quite different.

The La Chira health committee was composed of six members: a husband and wife, two brothers, and two sisters. None of the members was elected, because no more than five or six people attend town meetings to elect new health committees. One of the brothers was responsible for recruiting his own brother and the two sisters, while the husband–wife team joined the committee three years earlier. As mentioned earlier, the first La Chira health committee members were not elected either, and they served for ten years. The composition of the current committee may not have been ideal according to the rulebook, but it represented a pragmatic response to prevailing conditions. In the opinion of the members, their current set-up was preferable to having no health committee at all. Nonetheless, I heard the committee president tell the others that it was wrong to "just pick" members without elections, "because it isn't democratic."

Paradoxically, though, the rural health program in La Chira has never been noted for its democratic features. Not once has the committee been democratically elected; the community was given no say in the conceptualization or design of the program; community members had no voice in selecting health workers or deciding program priorities. Communist Party members were not permitted to serve on health committees, thus the political orientation of committee members was restricted in undemocratic fashion. Given this history, health committee members need not have been as wedded as they were to "democratic process"; the fact that they were requires an explanation.

The commitment to the rhetoric of democracy was, in part, a response to virulent anti-communism. Fear of communism was palpable in La Chira in 1985, partly because anti-Sandinista hysteria was fostered by the Costa Rican media and radio. Anti-communism was institutionalized in PROFOCO policy: no communists were permitted to serve on health committees. Knowing this, La Chira residents nonetheless told me that their democratic system was designed to tolerate all political points of view. One man told me that the DINADECO promoter in Guápiles had taken a leave of absence to run for office on the Communist Party ticket.

I asked why a communist would be permitted to work as a community organizer. "This country is a democracy," he said, "so someone can't be denied a job because of his political beliefs. It serves him well, too, since his job is community organization and communities are where communists make the most headway."

The ambivalence expressed at the community level should not be surprising, since it is also evident nationally. Communism has been alternately tolerated and outlawed in Costa Rica, but the national attitude toward it has never been neutral. In 1935–6, anti-communism became a feature of León Cortés Castro's National Republican campaign for president. The candidate presented communism as a threat to nation, family, and religion:

He succeeded, among his followers, in giving "Communism" a sinister connotation, representing it as something far more significant than an interpretation of history, a theory of social organization, or a program of social and economic reform; instead it connotated a mysterious and malevolent power. (Bell 1971: 12–13)

There was a time during World War II when Costa Rica's leaders welcomed Communist Party support for the democratic governments of Latin America. The U.S. and Soviet alliance against fascist Germany was paralleled in Costa Rica by an alliance between Calderón Guardia's administration and the Communist Party, which "was portrayed by its architects as consistent with the united war effort... United States representatives in Costa Rica also seemed to look favorably on the alliance" (Bell 1971: 43). With changes in the international balance of powers after the war, however, and in the aftermath of Costa Rica's civil war, national policy turned against communism.

During the post-war period, anti-communist rhetoric grew way out of proportion to the actual threat of a communist takeover in Costa Rica. Social reforms enacted under Calderón Guardia had taken away many of the Communist Party's causes for complaint, while the Party itself was small and relatively powerless. Nonetheless, anti-communist rhetoric proved effective in mobilizing political opposition (Bell 1971: 56–7), a strategy which continues to be effective today. Then, as now, conservatives blamed the international communist threat as the source of Costa Rica's internal problems. In 1946, the newspaper Acción Demócrata asserted that democratic liberties did not apply to communists:

In the distorted and moralistic view of Acción Demócrata, Costa Rican democratic institutions did not apply to the "reds." Those "bad Costa Ricans" had lost any rights which they had previously shared with their fellow citizens. (Bell 1971: 61)

Something of this sentiment is evident today in the view toward participation in community organizations. In theory, communists are permitted to express their views publicly, consistent with the tenets of participatory democracy. Simultaneously, however, communists are perceived as threatening the very foundations of participatory democracy.

Democracy is offered as the antidote to communism. It symbolizes nationalistic commitment, participation, and duty, but it has negative connotations as well. From the point of view of La Chira residents, democracy is defined more by participation in the electoral process than by continuous involvement in governmental decision-making or accountability. Because voting is the major characteristic of democracy, it carries profound responsibility. Jorge, a young health committee member, explained that he preferred Liberación to Unidad, but that he did not plan to vote in the upcoming presidential elections.

"Why not?" I asked.

"Because I don't want to be responsible for helping elect someone who might make errors. I'm stupid, 'cause I'm not doing anything, right?"

In other words, he does not expect the President to be accountable to the common Costa Rican voter and does not want to delegate the enormous responsibility of governing the country to an unaccountable official. In his case, not voting is an expression of powerlessness and resignation, a means of expressing dissatisfaction with the form that "democracy" has taken. Public apathy over health committee elections is a variation on the same theme. Why should community residents attend a town meeting to elect health committee representatives, when they know the representatives have little decision-making authority and only the most utilitarian responsibilities? Health committee members do not even have enough clout to make accountability an important issue. Jorge would not vote in national elections because the President had too much authority; La Chira residents do not endorse health committee elections because the committee has no authority.

Another symbolic component of "democracy" was utilized rhetorically by the promoter from Guápiles to induce greater participation in the health committee. When the committee members challenged the list of duties he read them at the meeting mentioned earlier, he chastized them for not being more active and for resisting his suggestions. He emphasized the importance of collaborating, and putting aside selfish, individualistic motives. He said, "All together we form a team, a community enterprise. We're reluctant to work together, yet we don't want there to be communism. The communists would come to our houses and *force* us to work for the benefit of the community!" His subtext juxtaposes the Costa Rican system (imperfect though he admits it may be) with a less desirable alternative. Participation is equated with democracy, which in turn is contrasted with communism. "If you don't participate," he implied, "you will regret it later when our democracy is taken away." He put the burden on rural communities to protect and defend their country's political integrity, implying that compliance with state-sponsored initiatives (like community participation in health) would keep the communists at bay.

The lack of community participation in La Chira's health committee is thus a rational, predictable response to the community's experience with state-sponsored social welfare programs. Residents know that the programs will be sustained through government initiative, because state paternalism is ubiquitous and guaranteed. Their participation, therefore, is unnecessary, and is perfunctory when restricted to cursory activities like fund-raising. Yet the notion of participation represents the yearning for a different kind of democracy, one which does not exist in practice. For the residents of La Chira, the idea of participation symbolizes the need for their more thorough representation in government, greater accountability of elected leaders, and greater authority in making decisions which affect their community.

Partisanism and health in La Chira

The last chapter discussed the relationship between political affiliation and health among politicians in the capital, where rural health was a divisive partisan issue. Liberacionistas alleged that Carazo had designed the community participation program to augment his grassroots base of support by stacking health committees with Unidad members. Was this true, I wondered, in La Chira? Was political party affiliation a factor in the composition or functioning of the health committee or the operations of the rural health program?

Partisan tensions were more evident in relations between the municipality and La Chira than within the community. Guápiles, the county seat, was the center of activities for Pococí's elected authorities. Money and technical resources for the entire canton were allocated in Guápiles. La Chira residents sent one delegate to town meetings, but they had to depend on their collective relations with authorities if they wanted to acquire support for public works projects. The municipality was controlled by a strong contingent of Liberacionistas, while La Chira was known as an Unidad stronghold. Of the 267 La Chira adults I surveyed, 97 (36 per cent) favored Unidad, 37 (14 percent) favored Liberación, 132

(49 percent) expressed no preference, and only one favored Pueblo Unido (the socialist party). These figures do not demonstrate over-whelming support for Unidad, but the Unidad supporters in La Chira were well organized and vocal in comparison to their Liberación counterparts. Rafael Angel Calderón Fournier, the Unidad presidential candidate in 1982, had come to La Chira on a campaign swing, and several families proudly showed me photographs of themselves posing with Calderón. Because Unidad supporters were so vocal, Pococí officials may have overestimated their importance in terms of numbers. One Pococí authority (a Liberacionista) was heard to say that La Chira would never obtain support for its road improvement plans as long as it remained a *cueva de mariachis* (den of iniquity; a disparaging reference to La Chira's political reputation).

In the health sector, the rural health *asistente* was the focus of partisan tensions between Guápiles and La Chira. Paco (a pseudonym) was a 35-year-old man who had worked in the La Chira health post for eight years. He was born and still lived in Guápiles, commuting by motorcycle to La Chira. Paco's main passion was not health but politics; he campaigned for Liberacionistas and himself ran for local office on the Liberación ticket in 1985. His ardent support for Liberación affected his relations with the community, and I heard whispered allegations that he was involved in shady dealings. One La Chira resident said that Paco had offered government coupons for powdered milk to poor families in return for their votes. There was, however, a more serious charge against him.

According to several people, 25 bags of cement were donated by the Ministry of Health to construct latrines for people in La Chira's health catchment area. Paco allegedly used the cement to build a house in La Chira, which he then put on the market. Meanwhile, he signed a note saying he would replace or pay for the cement, but a year had passed and he had not followed through on his promise. Several community members were outraged and insisted – at a health committee meeting at which I was present – that Paco be arrested and charged with theft. When the health committee finally persuaded Paco to attend a meeting (he agreed, in part, no doubt, because of my presence), Paco became indignant at their allegations.

I have never robbed one cent from the Ministry or from this community. Quite the contrary, I've given more than my share. I've worked here after hours seeing patients. After nine or ten years here, the Ministry knows that I've always done my job well. And then I get this letter from the secretary of the [health] committee, saying that you were charging me for cement. The idea that you would charge me, after all I've done for this town… We aren't materialists. We should give to the person who serves the community and help that person.

Paco then explained the allegations against him, saying that a political ally in Guápiles had given him 25 broken bags of hard cement to use for the floor of his house. A receipt had to be filled out, however, in the name of a community organization, because giving government cement to an individual was forbidden. So Paco made out the receipt in the name of the La Chira health committee. When one of his political opponents in La Chira found out about this, he was outraged and denounced Paco publicly. Paco said when he explained the situation to the president of the health committee, the president agreed to write a note saying that the committee had lent Paco the cement. That, Paco hoped, would silence the opposition. "Yes, it's true," Paco said, "that I promised to return to you something which was never yours. Yes it's true that I, innocently and with only the best intentions, used the name of the health committee so that I could be given something; it's true."

Paco believes that all attacks against him were politically motivated. If he were accused at all, he said, it was because someone resented his work for Liberación. If the past Asociación de Desarrollo in La Chira discriminated against the health committee, he said, it was because the members (all from Unidad) resented Paco's political affiliation.

Any efforts to have Paco formally charged would have been futile, given his Liberación political connections in Guápiles. Indeed, several La Chira residents did resent the fact that he flaunted his political influence, but they felt powerless to do anything about it. They could only hope, someone said, that he would be fired if Unidad won the presidency in the upcoming elections. Meanwhile, they could avoid him by not using the health post and by not participating on the health committee. This may explain why the La Chira health committee was composed entirely of Liberacionistas, when I had been told in the capital that health committees were bastions of Unidad power.

Partisan politics indirectly affected the functioning of the health committee, mainly through the actions of the *asistente*. People of the same party seemed to have an easier time working together, but no one ever cited political affiliation as a factor in whether they chose to work with the committee. Other considerations were more important to their decisions: the amount of work required, the authority granted to the committee by higher functionaries in the Ministry of Health, and a sense of obligation to community and country.

Discussion

The contradictions in national participation policy are evident in La Chira, where participation is *not* a metaphor for the distribution of political power. In La Chira, a handful of people on the health committee fulfill the perfunctory obligations required by the state, knowing that the state will bear primary responsibility for maintaining existing social welfare programs. They realize that theirs is a paternalistic government which expects but a modicum of cooperation in return for free health services, supplemental feeding programs, primary school education, and miscellaneous public works programs. Because all such services are designed, implemented, and maintained by the state, there is little incentive for local residents to participate actively in government-sponsored programs, especially when sanctioned mechanisms of partici-pation are also imposed from above by state institutions. By not involving community committees in decision-making processes, the state limits both the organizational form and the extent of participation which can be expected of rural residents.

The notion of participation does not have the same symbolic significance in La Chira as it acquired among politicians in the capital. Whereas national politicians respond angrily to charges that they "politicized" or "manipulated" participation, similar charges are not levied against communities, nor are they heard in La Chira. Community residents are charged only with not actively supporting government-sponsored efforts to enhance participation. The irony of this is not openly discussed in La Chira – that is, no one talks about the paradox of how government co-opts, expropriates, and passes judgment on what is supposedly a grassroots process – but the end result is that community residents do not feel that allegations of non-participation impugn their democratic credentials in the same way that politicians feel they do.

The low level of participation found in La Chira, and the acquiescence in government initiatives, does not mean that community members passively accept whatever programs are imposed from above. They are actively concerned to see that government programs meet their needs, and they complain bitterly when cutbacks are effected. Two examples can be cited to show La Chira residents making their voices heard.

Two months after I had left La Chira for San José, I happened to be in the Legislative Assembly building one morning. There I ran into two young women who had accompanied a group of eight La Chira residents lobbying to get their local stretch of road improved. Personal con-gressional lobbying was a big step for a contingent of small-town citizens who lived a four-hour, $4 bus ride from San José. I never learned the specific outcome of the visit (although the road was paved in 1987), but their lobbying strategy indicated that they had chosen to work within mainstream political channels. The second example was less conformist.

As I mentioned earlier, the potable water system serving La Chira was

inadequate to meet the demand, for the population had grown substantially since the system was installed. The people I spoke with
expressed unanimous concern about the lack of water, but survey
respondents were divided about how to cope with the problem. Forty-
seven percent agreed with the statement that not paying the water bills
was a just means of expressing their dissatisfaction, while an equal
number disagreed and 6 percent had no opinion. One house had a sign in
the window saying, "I don't pay for water."

A movement to address the water issue was organized in Guápiles by
a DINADECO employee (who was also running for office on the
Vanguardia Popular [Communist Party] ticket). He once came through
La Chira in a car with a megaphone, advising people not to pay their
water bills. One of the few La Chira residents actively involved in the
water protests told me he was skeptical of the government's promises to
improve the system. "Those are just campaign promises," he said. It was
his opinion that "the little guy is going to have to fight for things, because
he's the one being asked to pay the bill … The previous governments had
smooth sailing (*vinieron cosechando viento*), but from now on it's going to
be stormy."

Ultimately a group from Guápiles and surrounding towns decided to
demonstrate their frustration by blocking the highway leading to
Guápiles. Two men from La Chira participated in the blockade. One of
them later told me that the Guardia (police) had come in to remove the
protestors even before state negotiators came to discuss the situation.
"That wasn't right," he said. "The people in charge don't want us to
complain, but democracy doesn't work that way. Displays of dissatisfaction should be accepted as a part of democracy in action, but
Costa Rica is democratic only as long as people don't complain."

When I asked health officials and politicians in the capital whether
water protests could be defined as a form of community participation in
health, they invariably said yes. Government documents sometimes
profess a similar tolerance for active protest:

The population of Guápiles is not apathetic. On the contrary, they have the spirit
to get ahead. They organize themselves to plan for the future in search of better
living conditions, in their personal lives as well as for the good of the community.
On certain occasions the population has risen up in strikes, which doesn't imply
that they are a violent people. Rather, they have done this with dignity and
because circumstances merited the action in search of justice for the canton.
(INVU 1980: 89–90)

Yet the state would not tolerate a road blockade as a legitimate means of
expressing community concern. Demonstrations were antithetical to the
vision of participation promoted by the government; they were, rather,

a sign of communist-inspired violence. This is an example of how participation was defined selectively by state institutions, and how participation approved by the state could be identified by juxtaposing it to communism. Any popular action involving confrontational tactics was suspected of being sponsored by communists and thus labeled illegitimate, regardless of who else may have been involved or whether their concerns were valid.

The distinction between passive, acquiescent community participation and active, contentious communism surfaced often: a press headline once announced "Reds infiltrate [community] committees in the south" (*La Prensa Libre*, March 25, 1985). The article implied that communist agitators were attempting to take over the leadership of local committees. A community leader was quoted saying, "Our movement is completely democratic. Precisely for this reason we cannot accept the infiltration of communists." It is a unique interpretation of democracy which does not allow the free exchange of ideas and open participation of people from different political parties.

Another example occurred closer to La Chira, at a meeting I attended with representatives from the Ministry of Health and the Caja, who met with health workers from a nearby town to discuss the integration of health services. No community representatives were present. Discussion centered around the need for a new clinic and ways to involve the local community in the process of asking for and contributing toward the project. A member of the local Asociación de Desarrollo showed up, uninvited, towards the end of the meeting. When briefed on the conversation, he said that the quality of services was much more important to community residents than the physical plant of the clinic. He went on to argue, rather vehemently, that the community was not presently receiving the services it deserved, given the amount of social security they paid. Health officials at that point tried to convince him that his community needed a new clinic. He insisted that service was more important. The officials changed tactics. The regional director of the Ministry of Health began to belittle his community, saying they did not fulfill their responsibilities (like cutting the grass around the health post). The regional director of the Caja argued that people in the community must take responsibility for their own health by quitting smoking, for example, because they were costing the state a fortune in unnecessary medical expense. When the community representative said that he was tired of hearing government promises, the Ministry of Health official said these problems had to be worked out *together*, to which the community leader replied, "then it would have been nice if we had been invited to this meeting." The next day, a doctor who had been present at the meeting told me that the Congressional representative from that district was a member of the Communist Party, and "that's why they fight so much." In other words, grievances attributed to communist sympathies could be dismissed.

In summary, there is some evidence of active, grassroots resistance to government inaction. People do actively challenge state initiatives and make their demands known. To be effective and worth the effort, however, protests and active resistance must occur when they are most likely to result in constructive (from the community's point of view) solutions or government concessions. The economically depressed, red-baiting climate of 1985 was not particularly conducive to this type of resistance. Involvement in protest demonstrations rendered one suspect of having communist sympathies, and suspected communist sympathizers were fired and blacklisted from the banana plantations. This policy had two effects: first, prudent banana workers were not likely to risk their jobs by discussing union organizing; second, union organizers or other activists would be forced to leave the community in search of work and would therefore be less likely to have an impact on other facets of community organizing. With the banana industry in financial straits, most workers felt lucky to have their jobs. This was not the time to risk their economic security by demonstrating dissatisfaction; as one informant said, the best thing they could do was to help the banana companies. His philosophy reiterated the organizational principles of the anti-participatory organizations gaining adherents in the region. Many rural residents saw the promise of security and equilibrium in the Asociación Solidarista or, increasingly, the evangelical Protestant church. These organizations grew as the recession became more acute, job possibilities became more scarce, and anti-communist sentiment became more entrenched. At this particular point in history, La Chira residents were understandably anxious to guard their material resources and reputations, which would have been jeopardized by doing anything perceived as disrupting the status quo.

Political economists of health stress global economic forces and cultural imperialism as the major determinants of ill health in the Third World (see Doyal 1979; Elling 1981). While certainly the effects of global dependency and imperialist policies are important elements of health status in Latin America, critical analysis has dwelt almost exclusively on the deleterious effects of international capitalism (Morgan 1987a). But this sort of economic determinism is not subtle enough to account for the history or political-economic contingencies of any single country. Understanding the dynamics of the capitalist world system will not tell us why the metaphors of health and democracy were so compelling in the Costa Rican context, or why participation became the center of such controversy. For that we need to look both inside and outside national boundaries, at the linkages among local history, class structure, and interest-group politics within the context of international dependency. This study has focused much of its analytic gaze on national politics, but that discussion has been purposely sandwiched between larger and smaller levels of analysis. We are forced constantly to look back and forth from the intrigues of the capital city to the bureaucratic and political tangle of international aid, from the partisan battles of San José to the micro-politics of La Chira's inhabitants, acting on motivations of duty or guilt or vengeance. Unlike other political-economic studies of health that acknowledge only the dichotomy between capitalist protagonists and exploited victims, this book has emphasized the mediating role of the state.

Community participation in health is indisputably a noble goal, worthy of the concerted attention it has received in international health circles. Equally indisputable, however, is the fact that community participation is a powerful concept with revolutionary potential. Governments that promote participation assume the obligation to listen and respond to their citizenry, to accept criticism, to negotiate, and to work toward substantive sociopolitical change. In Costa Rica, a sustained effort to increase participation in health would have necessitated a

159

redistribution of decision-making power as politicians, bureaucrats, and local elites shared control with other constituencies. To respond adequately to mounting community demands, the state would have been obligated to take action against poverty and landlessness, thereby alienating the powerful landowners, businessmen, and international financiers whose support is essential to political stability. As these contradictions became more apparent, participation was redefined, maligned, and eventually dropped from the roster of state-sponsored initiatives.

Many international health experts assumed, especially in the heady, optimistic days of the mid-1970s, that community participation programs would effect social transformations, as if the concept itself contained some transcendent power. They assumed that participation could be equated with democracy and, by implication, that programs designed to enhance participation would function best in states with electoral democracies. In less democratic regimes, they hoped, a focus on participation in health might rub off on the political realm, bringing about more democratic, participatory political formations such as those of the United States and Western Europe. They presumed that the United States and the states of Western Europe truly do encourage effective and active participation, an arguable proposition in itself. They further implied that one mission of the international agencies is to proselytize for the Western democracies, again an arguable proposition. Nonetheless, they did base their vision of participation on the presumed superiority of Western values. As Stone (1989: 207) says, "[C]ommunity participation, regardless of its humanitarian or even its practical merits, may be creating an international arena for the expression of Western cultural values."

Ethnocentric political agendas are but one of the problems of foreign aid illustrated by this case. Even so-called humanitarian foreign assistance is usually dispensed (or withheld) according to political criteria. Bilateral and multilateral donors are motivated by their business, military, and ideological interests when allocating aid monies. Allotted funds, furthermore, are restricted to specific programs that have already been approved. The strings attached to aid monies limit the ability of recipients to devise their own development agendas and priorities, or to build local technical capacity for identifying and solving local problems. Ultimately, foreign monies often finance "technical" (rather than political) solutions to development problems, thereby avoiding (and even obfuscating) the underlying structural causes of disease, poverty, and social inequality.

Even as international experts predicted and hoped for a more democratic world, they continued to insist that community participation was primarily a technical, not a political, concept. Because they rarely acknowledged the political nature of global health initiatives, they implicitly legitimized and reinforced existing sociopolitical formations. One limitation inherent in global health efforts is that the World Health Organization "must work *for*, *with*, and *through* governments, each being responsible for the health of its own nationals" (Brockington 1975: 175; emphasis in original). International health agencies are constrained from addressing directly the relationship between sociopolitical formation and health services. They cannot say, for example, that primary health care improvements in Nicaragua were directly attributable to the Sandinista revolution and overthrow of the Somoza dynasty. Therefore, their power to effect substantive change is limited not only by an ideological-political bias in favor of Western democratic formations, but by the institutional structure of the organizations that forbids involvement in "politics."

Programmatic edicts from Geneva or Washington are designed collectively by health representatives from less-developed countries, but once adopted and disseminated as international mandates, they must be reanalyzed in each country to assess national priorities and program feasibility *vis-à-vis* existing class alliances, political power structures, economic viability, and the degree of dependence on international agencies. The final interpretation and implementation of international edicts may therefore differ significantly from what the agencies originally envisioned. National-level health programs are designed to modify and improve health status in ways which support domestic political priorities and do not challenge the political status quo. Consequently, international health policies enacted within a particular country can, at best, mirror pre-existing social and power relations at the national level.

There is an implicit tension, then, between the global concerns of international health agencies and the concrete realpolitik of nation states. The latter seek to protect their own assets, safeguard political authority, accumulate capital, and maintain social harmony. This is true even of the so-called "democratic" states, whose leaders project an exaggerated image of responsiveness and accountability to their citizens. This ideology belies the darker, less participatory side of a "democratic" regime like Costa Rica's, which is controlled by an ever-shifting assemblage of merchants, financiers, technocrats and landed elites who attempt to monopolize political debate (see Edelman and Kenen 1989a, 1989b). No wonder, then, that the issue of participation so gripped the nation's politicians.

Many Costa Ricans blame the failure of community participation on partisan rivalries. Indeed, they had ample cause to believe that partisanism could account for the program's demise: political bickering over the fate of DINADECO (described in Chapter 5) was just one example of how party loyalties influenced politicians' attitudes toward community organizing. Yet the program's demise cannot be attributed solely to partisanism, because too many groups within each party opposed it from the start. Conservative physicians, paternalistic state bureaucrats, and anti-union managers of banana plantations opposed the program not just because of party loyalties, but because they perceived it as a threat to their control over traditionally subservient rural populations.

Although partisanism played an unmistakable role in sealing the fate of community participation, the program was further limited by the country's political and socioeconomic hierarchy. Leading power holders of both major political persuasions were reluctant, even forthrightly unwilling, to share decision-making power with the rural poor. Threatened by the prospect of having masses of illiterate peasants becoming aware of the extent and source of their oppression and being offered the organizational skills to make demands on the state, elites and middle-class bureaucrats found ample reason to oppose community participation.

Community participation should not be viewed solely as an instrument of state legitimation, although San Ramonenses would attest to the social control elements evident in the structure of participation programs. Rather, participation is a microcosm of competing opinions concerning how best to create and maintain the Costa Rican political structure. To this extent, this study, while focused on the health sector, contains within it an implicit critique of Costa Rican political culture. If Costa Rica's leaders will not tolerate more than a modicum of political participation, then the country's prized elections are a poor indicator of popular will. Elections are merely one manifestation of democracy, but elections held every four years cannot substitute for popular participation in quotidian political discussions and decisions.

At another level of analysis, we must explain the cyclical, sometimes capricious health policy trends implemented in less-developed countries over the past four decades. That phenomenon must be explained by looking, once again, at the role played by international health agencies. Less-developed countries draw the symbols, slogans, and plans for their national health programs from international agency initiatives. Because they depend on international agencies for technical assistance, funding, and prestige, national health policies are designed to reflect international policy trends, technological developments, and global politics. The state does, however, interpret and refine the concepts of international agencies, phrasing them in a Costa Rican idiom to make them consistent with national political priorities. This is how community participation became entwined with other pivotal political symbols in the domestic struggle for power.

The dialectical nature of international health policy was evident in the dilemma facing Third World states during the late 1970s. Health officials and politicians were forced to direct their discourse on participation at two audiences simultaneously: local constituencies and representatives of international agencies. They had to convince both audiences that they were complying with international policy while also upholding national values. For the message to appeal to domestic audiences, participation had to resonate with symbols and values cherished by the *Ticos* themselves. Using the appropriate rhetoric was equally important when addressing international audiences, because rhetoric could mask flaws in implementation (as when the Monge administration continued to advocate participation even after it had dismantled the programs). The rhetoric of participation was just as important, indeed sometimes more important, to winning international acclaim as were the actual programs.

If Costa Rica's experience with health participation seems to ascribe a small role to rural citizens, it is because the fate of the program was determined more by national and international factors than by anything rural communities did or did not do. Microanalytic studies of community participation may blame community passivity, ignorance, or cultural barriers for inadequate levels of participation, yet Costa Rican communities consistently complied (at least nominally) with government mandates. Divisiveness within the central government, not the rural communities, posed the more formidable barrier to program implementation. Nonetheless, when international health experts evaluate community participation, they tend to focus on whether or not communities are "cooperating" with government-sponsored initiatives. In La Chira, however, all state-approved mechanisms of community participation were imposed from outside community boundaries, including the Asociación Solidarista, Asociación de Desarrollo (DINADECO), and rural health committees. Because communities did not have the prerogative to define what constituted participation, grassroots actions such as the water strike and labor strife were not recognized by the state as legitimate forms of participation. Communities clearly do participate in popular development projects and social movements of their own choosing. When they do not support government-sponsored initiatives, they have rational reasons for rebelling.

In La Chira, the symbolic contradictions of participation were acute at the community level. For example, community members voiced an irreconcilable contrast between paternalism and participation. They knew they could depend on the state to act paternalistically, just as they knew that only perfunctory compliance with participation programs was required. Politicians, on the other hand, assailed paternalism even though their policies were paternalistic, and encouraged participation even though their policies were anti-participatory. Politicians also associated health with democracy, saying they wanted to strengthen health and democracy by fighting disease and communism (or the disease of communism). At the same time, paradoxically, many politicians insisted that health was above politics, and that they personally were interested only in the public welfare. Residents of La Chira found it difficult to accept the argument that participation in health was a weapon against communism, or indeed that communism posed a significant threat to democracy as they experienced it. The opinions of La Chira residents illustrated many of the contradictions inherent in the concept of participation as it was wielded by politicians in the capital and by international health planners.

Community participation in health seemed like a good idea when international health planners introduced it in the 1970s. But the Costa Rican case shows how difficult, if not impossible, it is to predict the outcome of international health initiatives. Even the most sympathetic, amenable countries cannot be expected to comply automatically with international mandate. And even if they do, resistance from below can affect the agencies' willingness to pursue particular policies. Local peoples thus affect international health policies, although their influence may be voiced indirectly, through state intermediaries. For example, states unwittingly sowed the seeds of discontent by inviting community participation in health. The process entailed several steps. First, state employees taught organizational skills to people who had no recent history of communal efforts. Then they taught communities how to diagnose their own problems, acknowledging that land tenure and unemployment may be the fundamental causes of illness. They showed that politicians could be held accountable for solving their problems, if only people were sufficiently well-organized to make their demands heard. Community members quickly learned the most effective pressuring tactics: road-blocks, strikes, boycotts, marches. The very act of organizing a community committee, one informant said, is the equivalent of "arming the community" to organize themselves outside of institutional limitations. This presented a problem when the government realized that community participation had outgrown its ability to control it. The situation was exacerbated when the economic climate worsened and the government found itself promoting community–government dialogue when it literally could not afford to respond to community demands.

The economic crisis facing Costa Rica between 1980 and 1983 brought increasing popular pressures on the government. As real wages and buying power declined, labor unions frequently chose to strike, block roads, or otherwise express dissatisfaction with forced austerity. This posed a serious challenge to a political structure based on harmony and *paz social* (social peace), forcing state officials to choose between repression and reform. The dilemma can be illustrated by a minor incident that transpired during the 1985 dry season, when water scarcities around the country sparked numerous demonstrations. The head of the Rural Guard said he dreaded the prospect of direct confrontation: " I am very aware that the Rural Guard are peasants themselves, and we cannot submit this country to a confrontation between peasants" (*La Nación*, April 25, 1985). Another government official said, "The Government must redouble its efforts to attend quickly to the citizens' demands, to avoid turning them into political problems simply because of carelessness or lack of attention" (*La Nación*, April 25, 1985). Despite these appeals, an April 1985 water strike in the San José suburb of Guadalupe was broken up by police who used tear gas and billy clubs against demonstrators. In the days following the strike, however, there was abundant water in Guadalupe. The tension between reform and repression had become acute.

Contradictions such as these surface repeatedly as Costa Ricans juggle the more confrontative forms of popular participation with an equally powerful desire for social equilibrium and peace. Similar tensions were evident in the health program. A Ministry of Health official told me in 1981 that doctors complained that rural communities were becoming too active, too critical of rural health services. This is what happens, he said, when communities begin to participate actively in health matters: they learn to complain when the doctor arrives late and long waiting lines prevent patients from being seen. He said doctors are instilled with an *ideología dominante*; they feel superior to their patients and object to being criticized. This is an example, he said, of what participation can mean in the Costa Rican context, and how elites can come to abhor it. Traditionally, he said, participation has meant going to vote at the polls, but not selecting the candidates. "Participation is *not* complaining about the service; that's bad, and those who do are called communists." The pattern by now is familiar: participation is allowed and even encouraged within governmentally defined limits, but once the invisible boundary is breached, participation becomes a disease, a threat to the social fabric.

Under these circumstances, it is reasonable to ask whether community participation is necessary at all. If prevention is the best cure (to apply a health-related maxim to the political realm), then politicians might find it prudent to forgo participation entirely, thereby reducing the possibility of creating unrealistic expectations and fomenting social unrest. This, as we have seen, is the path of choice for many governments. The health planner might phrase the same question differently, asking whether participation is necessary to improve health. There is remarkably little evidence that health will improve more quickly, effectively, or permanently with formal, government-sponsored participation than without it, despite all that has been written about the process of implementing and measuring participation (Agudelo 1983; Rifkin 1985; Palmer and Anderson, 1986; Rifkin, Muller, and Bichmann 1988). In addition, there is considerable evidence that Costa Rica has improved its health indices dramatically with only half-hearted and sporadic community involvement. Like the politician, then, the planner might conclude that participation is expendable. The equity-minded critic of participation-cum-cooptation might concur. Ugalde, for example, writes, "in spite of the promotional efforts made by international agencies there are no success stories of community participation in Latin American health programs" (1985: 45). He suggests that community participation is not essential for improving health, but rather that community participation programs have "produced additional exploitation of the poor by extracting free labor,... contributed to the cultural deprivations of the poor, and... contributed to political violence by the ousting and suppression of leaders and the destruction of grass-roots organizations" (1985: 43).

For those who view health as more than the absence of disease, who believe that health is the outcome not just of universal access to medicine but of adequate sanitation, access to gainful employment, positive working conditions, and freedom from institutionalized injustice, then the health of the poor improves as people resist the forces that perpetuate inequality. This kind of participation has always existed. It is not imposed from outside, either by well-meaning governments or reform-minded liberals, but is necessarily *ad hoc*, spontaneous, unpredictable. No amount of international technical support or foreign assistance, no proliferation of government institutions can succeed in bringing it about. It is not a product to be imposed or measured or plotted, but a continual process of social change. As such, it is inevitably political, dialectical, and contested. It will always find adherents, both at home and abroad, and it will always meet resistance. The current international fad promoting participation-for-development will fade, but people will always participate.

References

Acuña Ortega, Victor H. 1984 *La huelga bananera de 1934.* San José: CENAP-CENAS.

Adams, Frederick V. 1914 *Conquest of the Tropics: The Story of the Creative Enterprises Conducted by the United Fruit Company.* Garden City, N.Y.: Doubleday.

Adams, Richard N. 1968 Testimony on Title IX in Survey of the Alliance for Progress, Subcommittee on American Republics Affairs, Committee on Foreign Relations, U.S. Senate, Hearings, 90th Congress, 2nd session. February 27, 28, 29 and March 1, 4, 5, 6, 1968, pp. 204–25.

1979 The structure of participation: a commentary. In *Political Participation in Latin America*, Volume II: *Politics and the Poor*, ed. Mitchell A. Seligson and John A. Booth, pp. 9–17. New York: Holmes and Meier Publishers.

Agency for International Development 1975 *Implementation of "New Directions" in Development Assistance.* Report prepared by AID to the Committee on International Relations on Implementation of the Foreign Assistance Act of 1973, 94th Congress, 1st session. July 22, 1975. Washington, D.C.: U.S. Government Printing Office.

1980 *Health Sector Policy Paper.* Washington, D.C.: Agency for International Development.

1982 *Health Sector Policy Paper.* Washington, D.C.: Agency for International Development.

Agudelo C., Carlos A. 1983 Community participation in health activities: some concepts and appraisal criteria. *Bulletin of the Pan American Health Organization* 17(4): 375–86.

Akin, John, Nancy Birdsall, and David de Feranti 1988 Financing health services in developing countries: an agenda for reform. *Pan American Health Organization Bulletin* 22(4): 416–29.

Alford, Robert R. 1975 *Health Care Politics.* Chicago: University of Chicago Press.

Alvarado Aguirre, Roberto 1987 Analisis de la organización y funcionamiento de las políticas de salud a través de los programas materno-infantiles en centroamérica. El caso de Costa Rica, I etapa. Unpublished manuscript funded by the Instituto Centroamericana de Administración Pública and the Ford Foundation.

Archivo Nacional Congreso 1932 Informe de la Comisión Legislativa. Archivo Nacional Congreso No. 18674, November.

1935 Archivo Nacional Congreso No. 17386.

1940 Archivo Nacional Congreso No. 19267, July 5.

Baer, Hans 1982 On the political economy of health. *Medical Anthropology Newsletter* 14(1): 1–2, 13–17.

1989 Towards a critical medical anthropology of health-related issues in socialist-oriented societies. *Medical Anthropology* 11: 181–94.

Bamberger, Michael 1988 *The Role of Community Participation in Development Planning and Project Management.* Economic Development Institute Policy Seminar Report No. 13. Washington, D.C.: The World Bank.

Bandow, Doug (ed.) 1985 *U.S. Aid to the Developing World: A Free Market Agenda.* Washington, D.C.: The Heritage Foundation.

1986 More bang for the foreign aid buck. *New York Times*, April 6, p. 23.

Behrhorst, Carroll 1975 The Chimaltenango development project in Guatemala. In *Health by the People*, ed. K. Newell, pp. 30–52. Geneva: World Health Organization.

Bell, John Patrick 1971 *Crisis in Costa Rica: The 1948 Revolution.* Austin: University of Texas Press.

Bergsma, Hotze 1980 Comments. In Debaters' comments on *Inquiry into Participation: A Research Approach* by Andrew Pearse and Matthias Stiefel. Popular Participation Programme Occasional Paper, Report No. 80.5, p. 71. Geneva: United Nations Research Institute for Social Development.

Birdsall, Nancy 1989 Thoughts on good health and good government. *Daedalus* 118(1): 89–117.

Black, George 1988 *The Good Neighbor.* New York: Pantheon Books.

Blanco, Gustavo and Orlando Navarro 1984 *El Solidarismo.* San José: Editorial Costa Rica.

Boletín PROFOCO 1984 No. 7. San José: Ministerio de Salud.

Bonilla Masis, Oscar 1981 *Desarrollo de la comunidad: políticas sanitarias y participación comunitaria en Costa Rica.* San José: Ministerio de Salud.

Booth, John A. and Mitchell A. Seligson (eds.) 1978 *Political Participation in Latin America*, Volume I: *Citizen and State.* New York: Holmes and Meier Publishers.

Bossert, Thomas 1984 Health-policy innovation and international assistance in Central America. *Political Science Quarterly* 99(3): 441–55.

Bourgois, Philippe I. 1989 *Ethnicity at Work: Divided Labor on a Central American Banana Plantation.* Baltimore: Johns Hopkins University Press.

Braveman, Paula and Fernando Mora 1987 Training physicians for community-oriented primary care in Latin America: model programs in Mexico, Nicaragua, and Costa Rica. *American Journal of Public Health* 77(4): 485–90.

Brockington, F. 1975 *World Health.* 3rd edition. London: Whitefriars Press.

Brown, E. Richard 1979 *Rockefeller Medicine Men.* Berkeley: University of California Press.

Bulmer-Thomas, Victor 1987 *The Political Economy of Central America since 1920.* Cambridge: Cambridge University Press.

Caja Costarricense de Seguro Social [CCSS] n.d. Cobertura de la salud en el cantón de Pococí. Unpublished document from CCSS hospital in Guápiles, Pococí, Costa Rica.

Campos Jiménez, Carlos María, and José Luis Gonzalez Ramos 1977 *Notas y documentos del desarrollo comunal en Costa Rica*. San José: DINADECO, Ministerio de Gobernación.

Casas, Antonio and Herman Vargas 1980 The health system in Costa Rica: toward a national health service. *Journal of Public Health Policy* 1: 250–79.

Casey Gaspar, Jeffrey 1979 *Limón: 1880–1940, un estudio de la industria bananera en Costa Rica*. San José: Editorial Costa Rica.

Castillo Gutiérrez, Alexis 1976 Estudio de Guápiles. Unpublished report on file in the Ministerio de Salud library, San José.

Castro Gutiérrez, Marlene 1983 *Economic Development and Nutrition in Costa Rica*. College of Human Resources, Title XII Program Publication No. 9, University of Delaware.

Cereseto, Shirley and Howard Waitzkin 1986 Capitalism, socialism and the physical quality of life. *International Journal of Health Services* 16(4): 643–58.

Céspedes, Victor Hugo, Alberto DiMare, and Ronulfo Jiménez 1985 *Costa Rica: Recuperación sin reactivación*. San José: Academia de Centroamerica.

Cohen, Abner 1974 *Two Dimensional Man*. Berkeley: University of California Press.

Cohen, John M. and Norman T. Uphoff 1977 *Rural Development Participation: Concepts and Measures for Project Design, Implementation and Evaluation*. Cornell: Rural Development Monograph No. 2. Published by the Rural Development Committee, Center for International Studies, Cornell University.

Cohen, Selina (ed.) 1980 Debaters' comments on *Inquiry into Participation: A Research Approach* by Andrew Pearse and Matthias Stiefel. Popular Participation Programme Occasional Paper, Report No. 80.5. Geneva: United Nations Research Institute for Social Development.

Colección de Leyes y Decretos 1928 Primer semestre. San José: Imprenta Nacional.

1944 San José: Imprenta Nacional.

Collier, Peter and David Horowitz 1976 *The Rockefellers: An American Dynasty*. New York. Signet.

Confederación Superior Universitaria Centroamericana (CSUCA) 1980 Revista Centroamericana de Ciencias de la Salud 17 (September–December).

Davidson, Judith R. and Steve Stein 1968 Economic crisis, social polarization, and community participation in health care. In *Health Care in Peru: Resources and Policy*, ed. Dieter K. Zschock, pp. 53–77. Boulder, Colo: Westview Press.

DeKadt, Emanuel 1982 Community participation for health: the case of Latin America. *World Development* 10(7): 573–84.

DeWalt, Billie and Pertti J. Pelto 1985 *Micro- and Macro-Levels of Analysis in Anthropology: Issues in Theory and Research*. Boulder, Colo: Westview Press.

DeWitt, R. Peter, Jr. 1977 *The Inter-American Development Bank and Political Influence, with Special Reference to Costa Rica*. New York: Praeger Publishers.

Diario de Costa Rica 1936 November 6, p. 5.

Djukanovic, V. and E. P. Mach (eds.) 1975 *Alternative Approaches to Meeting Basic Health Needs in Developing Countries*. Geneva: World Health Organization.

Donahue, John 1986 *The Nicaraguan Revolution in Health*. Granby, Mass: Bergin and Garvey.

Doyal, Lesley 1979 *The Political Economy of Health*. Boston: South End Press.

Dunn, Frederick L. 1976 Traditional Asian medicine and cosmopolitan medicine as adaptive systems. In *Asian Medical Systems*, ed Charles Leslie, pp. 133–58. Berkeley: University of California Press.

Edelman, Marc 1983 Recent literature on Costa Rica's economic crisis. *Latin American Research Review* 18: 166–80.

Edelman, Marc and Joanne Kenen (eds.) 1989a *The Costa Rica Reader*. New York: Grove Weidenfeld.

1989b La Culture politique du Costa Rica: militarisme, antimilitarisme et recherche d'une solution de paix en Amerique Centrale. *Les Temps Modernes* 44 (517/18): 309–47.

Elling, Ray H. 1981 The capitalist world system and international health. *International Journal of Health Services* 11: 21–51.

1989 Is socialism bad for your health? Cuba and the Philippines: a cross-national study of health systems. *Medical Anthropology* 11: 127–50.

Escalona, Mario 1980 La participación popular en salud. *Revista Centroamericana de Ciencias de la Salud* 17: 191–204.

Fallas, Carlos Luis 1978 [1941] *Mamita Yunai*. San José: Libreria Lehmann.

Fallas, Helio 1982 *Crisis económica en Costa Rica*. San José: Editorial Nueva Década.

Fernández, Mauro n.d. [circa 1981] *El auge bananero en Costa Rica*. San José: Standard Fruit Company.

Forman, Shepard 1979 The significance of participation: peasants in the politics of Brazil. In *Political Participation in Latin America*, Volume II: *Politics and the Poor*, ed. Mitchell A. Seligson and John A. Booth, pp. 36–50. New York: Holmes and Meier Publishers.

Foster, George 1982 Community development and primary health care: their conceptual similarities. *Medical Anthropology* 6: 183–95.

1987 World Health Organization behavioral science research: problems and prospects. *Social Science and Medicine* 24(9): 709–17.

Foucault, Michel 1973 *The Birth of the Clinic*. New York: Vintage Books.

Fournier Facio, Arturo 1974 La United Fruit Company y las huelgas bananeras. Thesis, Universidad de Costa Rica, Facultad de Derecho, No. 3156.

Freire, Paulo 1970 [1968] *Pedagogy of the Oppressed*, trans. Myra Bergman Ramos. New York: Seabury Press.

Fruchtbaum, Harold 1988 W.H.O. needs it? *The Nation*, January 9.

Gaceta, La 1954 Contract between United Fruit Company and the Costa Rican government, Law No. 1842, published December 28.

1983 January 27, No. 19, pp. 8–9. April 25, p. 1.

Geertz, Clifford 1973 Ideology as a cultural system. In *The Interpretation of Cultures* by Clifford Geertz, pp. 193–229. New York: Basic Books.

Glick, Philip M. 1957 *The Administration of Technical Assistance: Growth in the Americas*. Chicago: University of Chicago Press.

Green, Linda Buckley 1989 Consensus and coercion: primary health care and the Guatemalan state. *Medical Anthropology Quarterly* 3(3): 246–57.

Gudmundson, Lowell 1986 *Costa Rica Before Coffee.* Baton Rouge: Louisiana State University Press.

Hamer, W. M. 1954 Unpublished letter to S. C. Baggett, June 4, in author's files.

Hancock, Graham 1989 *Lords of Poverty: The Power, Prestige, and Corruption of the International Aid Business.* New York: Atlantic Monthly Press.

Hapgood, David (ed.) 1969 *The Role of Popular Participation in Development: Report of a Conference on the Implementation of Title IX of the Foreign Assistance Act, June 24–August 2, 1968.* Cambridge, Mass.: MIT Press.

Hatch, John W. and Eugenia Eng 1984 Community participation and control: or control of community participation. In *Reforming Medicine: Lessons of the Last Quarter Century*, ed. Victor W. Sidel and Ruth Sidel, pp. 223–44. New York: Pantheon Books.

Heggenhougen, H. K. 1984 Will primary health care efforts be allowed to succeed? *Social Science and Medicine* 19(3): 217–24.

Heggenhougen, Kris, Eustace P. Y. Muhondwa, Patrick Vaughn, and J. Rutabanzibwa-Ngaiza 1987 *Community Health Workers: The Tanzanian Experience.* Oxford: Oxford University Press.

Hollnsteiner, Mary Racelis 1982 The participatory imperative in primary health care. *Assignment Children* 59/60: 35–56. Geneva: UNICEF.

Instituto de Fomento y Asesoría Municipal [IFAM] 1974 *Estudio de servicios básicos en 30 cantones*, Part I: *Resumen cantonal.* San José: IFAM.

1982 *Información básica sobre la municipalidad de Pococí.* San José: IFAM.

Instituto Nacional de Vivienda y Urbanización 1980 *Plan regulador de Guápiles.* San José: INVU.

Inter-American Development Bank, Social Progress Trust Fund, Annual Reports, 1962, 1965, 1969.

Janzen, John M. 1978 The comparative study of medical systems as changing social systems. *Social Science and Medicine* 12: 121–9.

Jaramillo Antillon, Juan 1984 *Los problemas de la salud en Costa Rica.* San José: Ministerio de Salud.

1987 Changes in health care strategies in Costa Rica. *Pan American Health Organization Bulletin* 21: 136–48.

Jaramillo Antillon, Juan and Guido Miranda 1985 *La integración de servicios de salud.* San José: Ministerio de Salud y Caja Costarricense de Seguro Social.

Joseph, Stephen C., M.D. 1980 Testimony prepared for the International Health Act of 1980. Hearings before the Subcommittee on Health and Scientific Research of the Committee on Labor and Human Resources. U.S. Senate. 96th Congress, 2nd Session. July 2, 1980. To consider S. 1424, the International Health Act of 1979.

Justice, Judith 1986 *Policies, Plans, and People: Culture and Health Development in Nepal.* Berkeley: University of California Press.

Kepner, Charles David, Jr. and Jay Henry Soothill 1935 *The Banana Empire.* New York: Russell and Russell.

1936 *Social Aspects of the Banana Industry.* New York: Columbia University Press.

Klouda, Antony 1983 'Prevention' is more costly than 'cure': health problems for Tanzania. In *Practising Health for All*, ed. David Morely, Jon E. Rohde, and Glen Williams, pp. 49–63. Oxford: Oxford University Press.

Lachner Sandoval, Vicente 1902 *Gaceta Médica de Costa Rica* 7(2): 38–40.

La Forgia, Gerald 1985 Fifteen years of community organization for health in Panama: an assessment of current progress and problems. *Social Science and Medicine* 21(1): 55–65.

Libertad 1978 Zonas bananeras son el fuerte de la izquierda. March 3–9; Huelgas y paros en todo Guápiles. June 9–15, p. 3.
    1984 December 14–20, p. 10.

Lipsky, Michael and Morris Lounds 1976 Citizen participation and health care: problems of government induced participation. *Journal of Health Politics, Policy, and Law* 1(1): 85–111.

Livingstone, Richard C. 1973 Desarrollo de la comunidad en Costa Rica, 1968–1972: una historia interpretativa. In *Notas y documentos del desarrollo comunal en Costa Rica*, ed. Carlos María Campos Jiménez and José Luis Gonzalez Ramos, pp. 58–95. San José: DINADECO, Ministerio de Gobernación.

López, José A. 1930 The lower class of tropical American patients. *United Fruit Company Medical Department Annual Report* 19: 163–7.

Low, Setha M. 1982 Dr. Moreno Cañas: a symbolic bridge to the demedicalization of healing. *Social Science and Medicine* 16: 527–31.
    1985 *Culture, Politics, and Medicine in Costa Rica*. Bedford Hills, N.Y.: Redgrave Publishing.

McCamant, John F. 1969 *Development Assistance in Central America*. New York: Praeger Publishers.

MacLeod, Murdo J. 1973 *Spanish Central America*. Berkeley: University of California Press.

Martin, Patricia 1983 *Community Participation in Primary Health Care*. Primary Health Care Issues Series 1(5). Washington, D.C.: American Public Health Association.

May, Stacey and Galo Plaza 1958 *The United Fruit Company in Latin America*. New York: National Planning Association.

Mesa-Lago, Carmelo 1985 Health care in Costa Rica: boom and crisis. *Social Science and Medicine* 21(1): 13–21.

Midgley, James 1986 Community participation: history, concepts, and controversies. In *Community Participation, Social Development and the State*, by James Midgley et al., pp. 13–44. London: Methuen.

Midgley, James with Anthony Hall, Margaret Hardiman, and Dhanpaul Narine 1986 *Community Participation, Social Development and the State*. London: Methuen.

Ministerio de Salud, Memoria Anual. San José, Costa Rica. 1929, 1930–1, 1932, 1936, 1938, 1939, 1962, 1977, 1988.
    1978 *Costa Rica: extensión de cobertura de los servicios de salud en el marco del desarrollo socio-económico*. San José: Ministerio de Salud.
    1981 *Salud en Costa Rica: evaluación en la década de los años 70*. San José: Ministerio de Salud.

Ministerio de Salud, Región Huetar Atlántica 1984 *Diagnóstico de salud, provincia de Limón.* San José: Ministerio de Salud.

Ministerio de Salud, Unidad de Participación Popular 1980 *Manual de metodologías y técnicas, plan nacional de participación popular en salud.* San José: Ministerio de Salud.

Ministers of Health of the Americas 1984 Priority health needs in Central America and Panama. Manuscript.

Mintz, Sidney 1977 The so-called world system: local initiative and local response. *Dialectical Anthropology* 2: 253–70.

Mohs, Edgar 1988 *La reforma del sector salud en Costa Rica durante la década de los 70.* San José: Ministerio de Salud.

Monge Alfaro, Carlos 1966 *La Historia de Costa Rica.* 13th edition. San José.

Morales, Julio O., Nevin Scrimshaw, and Antonio M. Arce 1953. Health systems. In *Turrialba: Social Systems and the Introduction of Change,* ed. Charles P. Loomis et al., pp. 135–56. Glencoe, Ill. Free Press.

Morgan, Lynn M. 1987a Dependency theory in the political economy of health: an anthropological critique. *Medical Anthropology Quarterly* (n.s.) 1(2): 131–54.

1987b Health without wealth? Costa Rica's health system under economic crisis. *Journal of Public Health Policy* 8(1): 126–51.

1989 "Political will" and community participation in Costa Rican primary health care. *Medical Anthropology Quarterly* (n.s.) 3(3): 232–45.

1990 International politics and primary health care in Costa Rica. *Social Science and Medicine* 30(2): 211–19.

Morsy, Soheir 1990 Political economy in medical anthropology. In *Medical Anthropology: A Handbook of Theory and Method,* ed. Thomas M. Johnson and Carolyn F. Sargent, pp. 26–46. New York: Greenwood Press.

Muhondwa, Eustace P. Y. 1989 The role and impact of foreign aid in Tanzania's health development. In *International Cooperation for Health: Problems, Prospects, and Priorities,* ed. Michael R. Reich and Eiji Marui, pp. 173–206. Dover, Mass.: Auburn House Publishing Company.

Muller, Frederik 1979 Participación popular en programas de atención sanitaria primaria en América Latina. Thesis, Universidad de Antioquia, Facultad Nacional de Salud Pública, Medellín, Colombia.

1983 Contrasts in community participation: case studies from Peru. In *Practising Health for All,* ed. David Morley, Jon E. Rohde, and Glen Williams, pp. 190–207. Oxford: Oxford University Press.

Muscat, Robert J. 1984 AID private enterprise policy dialogue: forms, experience and lessons. Prepared for the President's Task Force on International Private Enterprise. First Concurrent Resolution on the Budget, Fiscal Year 1985. Hearings before the Committee on the Budget, U.S. Senate, 98th Congress, 2nd session. February 21, 1984, Volume IV, pp. 242–51.

Nación, La 1978 Presidente Carazo: deseamos contruir una nación fundada en la dignidad humana. May 9, pp. 11–13A.

Aumenta la hegemonia comunista en sindicatos democratas se debilitan. July 2, p. 13A.

Otra huelga en Pococí. July 5, p. 6A.

174   References

Guardia Rural protegerá a trabajadores de finca [Mancotal] que deseen laborar. July 7, p. 8A.
Volvió la normalidad a finca bananera [Mancotal]. July 8, p. 2A.
1980 Gobierno impulsa revolución social. April 19, p. 6A.
1984 November 25, p. 25A.
November 30, p. 43A.
Standard Fruit revela que afronta problema económico. December 25, p. 4A.
1985 Standard cesará a 600 empleados, by Lidette Brenes de Charpentier. February 24, p. 4A.
Standard inició despido de empleados administrativos. February 26, p. 8A.
Gobierno en alerta por agitación social. April 25, p. 9A.
Bananeros anuncian despido de empleados en el Atlántico. June 11, p. 4A.
Standard reactivará producción bananera. August 29, p. 2.
Zona atlántica a la expectativa por el programa de fomento bananero, by Levi Vega M. September 16.
Navarro, Vicente 1984 A critique of the ideological and political positions of the Willy Brandt Report and the WHO Alma Ata Declaration. *Social Science and Medicine* 18(6): 467–74.
New York Times 1942 Hemisphere plan for health set up. March 6, p. 15.
1943 March 16, pp. 21, 38.
Newell, K. (ed.) 1975 *Health by the People*. Geneva: World Health Organization.
1988 Selective primary health care: the counter revolution. *Social Science and Medicine* 26(9): 903–6.
Ortiz Guier, Guillermo 1978 Proyección de las comunidades en el programa de salud rural "Hospital Sin Paredes" en Costa Rica. Paper presented at the 2nd International Congress of the Federación Mundial de Asociaciones de Salud Pública and the Canadian Association of Public Health. Halifax, Canada, May, 1978.
Ortner, Sherry B. 1984 Theory in anthropology since the sixties. *Comparative Studies in Society and History* 26: 126–66.
Packenham, Richard A. 1973 *Liberal America and the Third World*. Princeton: Princeton University Press.
Palmer, C. T. and M. J. Anderson 1986 Assessing the development of community involvement. *World Health Statistics Quarterly* 39: 345–52.
Pan American Health Organization 1973 *Ten-Year Health Plan for the Americas*. Official Document No. 118. Washington, D.C.: Pan American Health Organization.
1978a *Extension of Health Service Coverage Based on the Strategies of Primary Care and Community Participation. Summary of the Situation in the Region of the Americas*. Official Document No. 156. Washington, D.C.: Pan American Health Organization.
1978b *IV Special Meeting of Ministers of Health of the Americas*. Official Document No. 155. Washington, D.C.: Pan American Health Organization.
1984 *Community Participation in Health and Development in the Americas*. Scientific Publication No. 473. Washington, D.C.: Pan American Health Organization.

Pardo A., Marta 1984 Patrones de automedicación. *Cuadernos de Antropología* 3: 73–82.

Parlato, Margaret Burns and Michael N. Favin 1982 *Primary Health Care: Progress and Problems, an Analysis of 52 AID-Assisted Projects*. Washington, D.C.: American Public Health Association.

Paul, Benjamin and William Demarest 1984 Citizen participation overplanned: the case of a health project in the Guatemalan community of San Pedro la Laguna. *Social Science and Medicine* 19(3): 185–92.

Paul, Samuel 1987 *Community Participation in Development Projects: The World Bank Experience*. World Bank Discussion Papers, No. 6. Washington, D.C.: The World Bank.

Pilon, Juliana Geran 1986 *For the World Health Organization, the Moment of Truth*. Backgrounder No. 507. Washington, D.C.: The Heritage Foundation.

Prensa Libre, La 1979a El auge bananero en Costa Rica: Guápiles. Part I. May 22.

1979b El auge bananero en Costa Rica: Guápiles. Part II. May 29.

1985 Rojos se infiltran en comités del sur. March 25, p. 2.

Quimby, Freeman H. 1971 *The Politics of Global Health*. Prepared for the Subcommittee on National Security Policy and Scientific Developments of the Committee on Foreign Affairs. U.S. House of Representatives. Washington, D.C.: U.S. Government Printing Office.

República, La 1965 October 16, p. 4.

1978 Pedida disolución urgente de sindicato STAPPG. September 26, p. 2.

1982 April 17, special supplement.

1984 December 16, p. 3.

1985 Standard quiere abandonar Limón. February 5.

Revista Salud 1944 Volume 8(1,2,3). San José: Ministerio de Salud.

Richardson, Miles and Barbara Bode 1971 Popular medicine in Puntarenas, Costa Rica: urban and societal features. In *Community Culture and National Change*, ed. Richard N. Adams et al. Middle American Research Institute Publication 24, Tulane University.

Rifkin, Susan B. 1985 *Health Planning and Community Participation: Case Studies in South-East Asia*. London: Croom Helm.

Rifkin, Susan B., Frits Muller, and Wolfgang Bichmann 1988 Primary health care: on measuring participation. *Social Science and Medicine* 26(9): 931–40.

Rifkin, Susan B. and G. U. Walt 1986 Why health improves: defining the issues concerning "comprehensive" primary health care and "selective" primary health care. *Social Science and Medicine* 23(6): 559–66.

Robinson, Richard D. 1964 *International Business Policy*. New York: Holt, Rinehart, and Winston.

Roemer, Milton I. 1963 Medical care in Costa Rica. In *Medical Care in Latin America* by Milton I. Roemer, pp. 169–92. Washington, D.C.: Organization of American States.

Rojas Suárez, Juan Francisco 1943 *Costa Rica en la segunda guerra mundial*. San José: Imprenta Nacional.

Rosenberg, Mark B. 1981 Social reform in Costa Rica: social security and the presidency of Rafael Angel Calderon. *Hispanic American Historical Review* 61(2): 278–96.

1983 *Las luchas por el seguro social en Costa Rica*. San José: Editorial Costa Rica.

Rosenfield, Patricia I. 1985 The contribution of social and political factors to good health. In *Good Health at Low Cost. Proceedings of a Rockefeller Foundation Conference, Bellagio, Italy, April 29–May 3, 1985*, ed. Scott B. Halstead, Julia A. Walsh, and Kenneth S. Warren, pp. 173–80. New York: Rockefeller Foundation.

Rosero-Bixby, Luis 1986 Infant mortality in Costa Rica: explaining the recent decline. *Studies in Family Planning* 17(2): 57–65.

Rostow, Walt Whitman 1960 *The Stages of Economic Growth: A Non-Communist Manifesto*. Cambridge: Cambridge University Press.

Sanders, Sol W. 1986 *The Costa Rican Laboratory*. New York: Priority Press Publications/A Twentieth Century Fund Paper.

Schlesinger, Stephen and Stephen Kinzer 1982 *Bitter Fruit*. Garden City, N.Y.: Anchor Books.

Segall, Malcolm 1972 The politics of health in Tanzania. *Development and Change* 4(1): 39–50.

Seligson, Mitchell 1980 *Peasants of Costa Rica and the Development of Agrarian Capitalism*. Madison: University of Wisconsin Press.

Seligson, Mitchell A. and John A. Booth 1976 Political participation in Latin America: an agenda for research. *Latin American Research Review* 11(3): 95–119.

1979 Development, political participation, and the poor in Latin America. In *Political Participation in Latin America*, Volume II: *Politics and the Poor*, ed. Mitchell A. Seligson and John A. Booth, pp. 3–8. New York: Holmes and Meier Publishers.

Seligson, Mitchell A. and Miguel Gómez B. 1989 Ordinary elections in extraordinary times: the political economy of voting in Costa Rica. In *Elections and Democracy in Central America*, ed. John A. Booth and Mitchell A. Seligson, pp. 158–84. Chapel Hill: University of North Carolina Press.

Serra, Jaime and Carlos Brenes 1983 Recuperación crítica de indicadores socioeconómicos: la experiencia del programa de salud comunitaria "Hospital sin paredes." In *Centroamérica: indicadores socioeconómicos para el desarrollo*, by R. Ramalinga Iyer, et al., pp. 269–313. San José: FLACSO.

Shallat, Lezak 1989 AID and the secret parallel state. In *The Costa Rica Reader*, ed. Marc Edelman and Joanne Kenen, pp. 221–7. New York: Grove Weidenfeld.

Sherraden, Margaret Sherrard 1991 Policy impacts of community participation: health services in rural Mexico. *Human Organization* 50(3): 256–63.

Simpson, Sharleen H. 1983 National health system and popular medicine: the case of Costa Rica. In *Third World Medicine and Social Change*, ed. John H. Morgan, pp. 217–28. Lanham, Md.: University Press of America.

1988 Some preliminary considerations on the *sobada*: a traditional treatment for gastrointestinal illness in Costa Rica. *Social Science and Medicine* 27(1): 69–73.

Singer, Merrill 1989 The coming of age of critical medical anthropology. *Social Science and Medicine* 28: 1193–1204.

Solís, Manuel 1989 The fragmentation and disappearance of the Costa Rican left. In *The Costa Rica Reader*, ed. Marc Edelman and Joanne Kenen, pp. 309–13. New York: Grove Weidenfeld.

Solís, Manuel and Francisco Esquivel 1984 *Las perspectivas del reformismo en Costa Rica.* 2nd edition. San José: Departamento Ecuménico de Investigaciones.

Stebbins, Kenyon 1987 Tobacco or health in the Third World? A political-economic perspective with special reference to Mexico. *International Journal of Health Services* 17(3): 521–36.

1990 Transnational tobacco companies and health in underdeveloped countries: recommendations for avoiding a smoking epidemic. *Social Science and Medicine* 30(2): 227–35.

Stewart, Watt 1967 *Keith y Costa Rica.* San José: Editorial de Costa Rica.

Stone, Linda 1989 Cultural crossroads of community participation in development: a case from Nepal. *Human Organization* 48(3): 206–13.

Strouse, Pierre A. D., Jr. 1970 Instability of tropical agriculture: the Atlantic lowlands of Costa Rica. *Economic Geography* 46: 78–97.

Taylor, Carl E. 1979 Implementation of national plans for action on primary health care. *Bulletin of the Pan American Health Organization* 13(1): 1–6.

Tesh, S. 1986 Health education in Cuba: a preface. *International Journal of Health Services* 16(1): 87–104.

Times of Limón 1905 August 12, p. 5.

1913 June 14, p. 1.

Trejos Escalante, Fernando 1963 *Libertad y seguridad.* San José: Asociación Nacional de Fomento Económico.

Tribuna, La 1928 May 31, p. 11.

1936 November 3, p. 1.

Tristan, Mario 1980 Estudios antropológicos de clasificación funcional. *Boletín Informativo del S.I.N.* 6: 24–32.

Turshen, Meredith 1984 *The Political Ecology of Disease in Tanzania.* New Brunswick, N.J.: Rutgers University Press.

Ugalde, Antonio 1985 Ideological dimensions of community participation in Latin American health programs. *Social Science and Medicine* 21(1): 41–53.

UNICEF 1981 Community participation: taking part or taking over? *UNICEF News,* Issue 110/1981/4: 3–4.

1982 Current issues in community participation. *Assignment Children* 59/60: 9–56. Geneva: UNICEF.

1988 Atención primaria de salud y participación comunitaria en los paises de Centro América y Panamá. Unpublished manuscript. San José, Costa Rica: UNICEF.

United Fruit Company, *Medical Department Annual Report*: 1912 [v. 1], 1917, 1921 [v. 10], 1922 [v. 11], 1923 [v. 12], 1925 [v. 14], 1926 [v. 15], 1929 [v. 18]. Boston: United Fruit Company.

United Nations 1955 Principles of community development: social progress through local action. Economic and Social Council, Social Commission, Tenth Session. Document E/CN.5/303, January 31.

1975 *Popular Participation in Decision Making for Development.* Department of Economic and Social Affairs. New York: United Nations.

1981 *Popular Participation as a Strategy for Promoting Community-Level Action and National Development.* Department of International Economic and Social Affairs. New York: United Nations.

1987 *Popular Participation Policies as Methods for Advancing Social Integration.* Department of International Economic and Social Affairs. New York: United Nations.

United Nations Research Institute for Social Development 1983 Popular participation. *Research Notes* No. 6, pp. 33–68. Geneva: United Nations Research Institute for Social Development.

United States Congress 1949 Committee on Foreign Affairs, Institute of Inter-American Affairs. Hearings before a special subcommittee, 81st Congress, 1st Session, on H. 2957. July 5, 6, 11.

1971 International Health Agency Act of 1971. Hearings before the Subcommittee on International Organizations and Movements of the Committee on Foreign Affairs, House of Representatives. 92nd Congress, 1st Session, on H.R. 10042. August 2, 3, 4; October 6, 7, and 12.

1987 *Congressional Appropriations.* Washington, D.C.: U.S. Government Printing Office.

1988 *Congressional Appropriations.* Washington, D.C.: U.S. Government Printing Office.

United States Treaties and Other International Agreements 1951 Volume 2, Part I. Washington, D.C., Department of State.

Valverde Jiménez, Eliecer 1972 Plan de salud rural. *Acta Médica Costarricense* 15(1): 77–90.

Vargas González, William 1977 El programa de salud rural de Costa Rica: un modelo para las poblaciones marginadas. *América Indígena* 37(3): 353–65.

Vega Carballo, José Luis 1981 *La formación del estado nacional en Costa Rica.* San José: Instituto Centroamericana de Administración Pública.

Villalobos, Luis B. 1989 *Salud y sociedad: un enfoque para Centroamérica.* San José: Instituto Centroamericano de Administración Pública.

Villegas, Hugo 1977 Extensión de la cobertura de salud en Costa Rica. *Boletín de la Oficina Sanitaria Panamericana* 83(6): 537–43.

1978 Costa Rica: recursos humanos y participación de la comunidad en los servicios de salud en el medio rural. *Boletín de la Oficina Sanitaria Panamericana* 84(1): 13–22.

Voz del Atlántico 1935 February 2, p. 1.

February 16, p. 1.

Walsh, Julia A. and Kenneth S. Warren 1980 Selective primary health care: an interim strategy for disease control in developing countries. *Social Science and Medicine* 14C: 145–69.

Werner, David n.d. Project Piaxtla: working towards a campesino-run health care network in the mountainous regions of Sinaloa and Durango, Mexico. Palo Alto: The Hesperian Foundation. Microfiche.

1976 Health care and human dignity. *Contact* (Special Series) 3: 91–106.

1983 Health care in Cuba: a model service or a means of social control – or both? In *Practising Health for All*, ed. David Morley, Jon E. Rohde, and Glen Williams, pp. 17–37. Oxford: Oxford University Press.

White, Alastair T. 1982 Why community participation? *Assignment Children* 59/60: 17–34. Geneva: UNICEF.

Whiteford, Michael B. 1985 The social epidemiology of nutritional status among Costa Rican children: a case study. *Human Organization* 44(3): 241–50.

Wilson, Charles Morrow 1942 *Ambassadors in White: The Story of American Tropical Medicine*. New York: Henry Holt and Company.

Wisner, Ben 1988 GOBI versus PHC? Some dangers of selective primary health care. *Social Science and Medicine* 26(9): 963–9.

Wolf, Eric R. 1982 *Europe and the People Without History*. Berkeley: University of California Press.

World Bank 1980 *Health Sector Policy Paper*. Washington, D.C.: World Bank.

World Health Organization 1977 Community involvement in primary health care: a study of the process of community motivation and continued participation. Report for the 1977 UNICEF-WHO Joint Committee on Health Policy.

World Health Organization and UNICEF 1978 *Primary Health Care*. Geneva: World Health Organization.

Index